Come Alive with Illustrations

Come Alive with Illustrations

How to Find, Use, and File Good Stories for Sermons and Speeches

Leslie B. Flynn

BAKER BOOK HOUSE
Grand Rapids, Michigan 49516

Copyright 1987 by
Baker Book House Company

ISBN: 0-8010-3547-3

Printed in the United States of America

To

Robert and **Jean Walker**

They gave me my start in writing for publication
and impressed on me the indispensability of illustrations
and recently told me that I should write this book

Contents

Foreword

Men and women who gather in churches on Sunday resemble those Jews who accosted Jesus on Solomon's porch at the temple: "How long will you keep us in suspense?" they asked. "If you are the Christ, tell us plainly." John liked that word *plainly.* He used it at least nine times in his gospel about Jesus. It means "openly and clearly."

That question was originally used to bait Jesus so that he could be placed under arrest. Yet, the question has often been asked out of a desire to understand. Many congregations offer the plea, "Tell us plainly!"

Sören Kierkegaard commented that if he had asked the noted philosopher Hegel for directions to a street address in Copenhagen, Hegel would have given him a map of Europe. Some preachers resemble that philosopher. They seldom ground their sermons in life. They have a hard time speaking plainly. When we as preachers or teachers are asked for bread, we cannot simply offer people the ingredients. When we are asked for fish, we do not serve hungry men and women abstract lectures on zoology. Theory and theology must be brought down to life.

Illustrations chosen with care and used with thought help us make the message plain. They move us from the map to the house on the corner of Sixth and Main. That explains why effective preachers make illustrations their magnificent obsession. They stalk illustrations and stock them.

You hold in your hands a book that tells you about illustrations and offers you some of the best that Leslie Flynn has captured over the years. Don't put it down. Read it through. Not only will you find illustrations already stalked and stocked, but you will also be led to places where you can hunt them yourself.

Haddon W. Robinson

Preface

Everyone loves a good illustration.

And everyone needs to have interesting illustrations to help make a vital point come alive.

Not just preachers need illustrations but so do

Sunday school teachers

youth advisors

leaders of Christian organizations

writers and journalists

broadcasters

missionaries writing letters to supporters

Christian teachers, professors, and deans

committee chairmen and board members

devotional speakers at church groups

emcees at banquets

Christian Service Brigade and Pioneer Girl leaders

camp counselors

writers of promotional and stewardship letters

gospel team speakers in nursing homes and jail services

every believer who would be a good communicator of the Christian faith and an effective conversationalist

This book describes the benefits of illustrations, explains where to find them, gives cautions in using them, and outlines what to do with them when you find them.

The difference between acceptable and exceptional communication is often a good illustration which clinches an important truth in the listener's mind for years.

Leslie Flynn

Why Use Them?—
Their Value

1

Of Course, You Should Use Illustrations

A company in trouble in both branch factories due to carelessness by assembly-line workers, assigned a senior vice president to visit the two plants and give the employees a pep talk, urging them to pay more attention to detail. An inexperienced public speaker, the vice president approached his first talk with apprehension. He began simply by stating the facts, listing their too-frequent mistakes, and encouraging them to more cautious work. Though the talk was short, they listened poorly and disinterestedly.

In the second plant he decided to begin his talk differently. Immediately after he was introduced, he told a true story:

Men, you probably read the other day about the jet plane that lost altitude on a flight from Miami to the Bahamas, and nearly crashed. An hour out of Florida, it suddenly lost power in one engine, then another shut off, then the third and last. The plane lost four miles in altitude in a few minutes. The pilot prepared the passengers for a crash landing in the ocean. Suddenly he was able to get one of the engines going again, enabling the plane to limp back to Miami. Investigation revealed that a couple of airline mechanics had failed to replace a little rubber covering on the valves of all three engines. Loss of oil caused the engines to fail.

Then the vice president went on to give substantially the same short talk given in the first plant. But this time the workers riveted their eyes on the speaker. A timely illustration had gained their attention.

The president of a Christian organization, buying time for a weekly radio program, began his broadcast each week with a Bible verse and prayer. Without any listener response whatever after two months of this approach, he decided to start with an interesting story from everyday life. To his surprise several letters came in every week. One said, "Sir, you trap me with the way you begin your program. I just have to keep listening."

A new Sunday school teacher was having a difficult time with a class of boys. An experienced teacher took her aside to give some pedagogical suggestions, one of which was to always include a good story or two to illustrate the lesson truth. Discipline improved considerably.

An aspiring writer sent what she thought was a well-written article to a magazine. It was rejected. She sent it to another magazine. Again, it was rejected. Taking a little time to examine articles in various periodicals, she noted the profuse use of anecdotes. So she revised her manuscript, beginning with a fitting illustration and interspersing several apt stories throughout the article. To her delight, it was accepted by a third magazine.

Not only in public speaking and article writing do illustrations make an impact, but also in small, informal "parlor" conversations. Note how often the life of the party seems to be the man or woman who can spin a story well. You can become a more winsome personality, a more interesting individual to be around, a more compelling conversationalist, perhaps a better salesperson, by having the right yarn to tell at the appropriate moment. A radio commentator described a New York City restaurant owner as a colorful character, and a source of many stories. You can win friends and influence people through illustrations.

I once heard a professor in a Christian college suggest that the ideal sermon would have no illustrations. Perhaps he was echoing the philosopher John Locke who opposed the use of illustrations on the ground that they led men astray. (But the misuse of logic has led people astray, which is no reason to forego its proper usage.) Even then as a student I felt for many reasons the professor's statement untenable.

All My Pastors Used Illustrations

I was brought up in a large Canadian church where all my pastors were excellent preachers. In my student years in the Chicago area I often heard Dr. Harry Ironside make a point through a telling anecdote. While in seminary I attended Tenth Presbyterian Church in Philadelphia where Dr. Donald G. Barnhouse was not only a top-notch Bible teacher, but also a master of the use of illustrations. This is one of my favorites:

> Some years ago, enroute to a Bible conference, the late Donald G. Barnhouse was driving into Florida from Alabama one Saturday night. Feeling a tire going flat, he pulled to the side of the road and inwardly groaned at the thought of removing the hundreds of books in the trunk before the spare tire could be reached. Seeing a jeep coming over the hill, he hailed the driver and offered him a dollar to fix the flat. The big, strapping fellow was soon hard at work. When he expressed curiosity about the books, Dr. Barnhouse told him he was a preacher. The man replied, "My wife would be interested. She teaches Sunday school." Then he added, "But I'm not interested in those things."
>
> All the time the man worked, his dog stuck close, licking him every minute. Every now and again the man stopped to pat it. Dr. Barnhouse asked about the dog. The man told how once when corraling cattle, jumping from place to place to miss the quicksand, he slipped, and before he knew it he was in quicksand to the calves of his legs. "I had the presence of mind to throw my body back to spread my weight over a wide area so I wouldn't sink any more, but the position was agony. It was no use to call, for there wasn't a person within a mile. Then I heard a noise in the bush, and there was a dog. The dog sensed something was wrong, came and licked my hands and face. I was able to draw myself upright with my arms around the dog, and the dog pulling away. I got one leg, then the

other, out of the quicksand. Grabbing a dry hummock, I regained solid ground. That dog saved my life, and I'm devoted to it. He eats at my table. Though my wife doesn't like it, he sleeps at the foot of our bed."

Dr. Barnhouse replied, "How strange! A dog has saved your life from quicksand, and you are devoted to it. Yet Christ has done more than the dog, and you are not interested in Christ. You are in a worse plight than quicksand from which Christ came to save you! The dog did not die for you, but Christ did! Yet you thank the dog, but you're not thankful to Christ!"

Preachers of Earlier Generations Used Illustrations

In his *Lectures to My Students*, C. H. Spurgeon devotes five chapters, totaling about one hundred pages, to the theme of illustrations. He points out that preachers from the Reformation era on have employed anecdotes, citing as examples Hugh Latimer, Jeremy Taylor, Thomas Brooks, Thomas Adams, John Flavel, George Whitefield, and D. L. Moody. Here's an example of a Puritan anecdote.

A religious commander being shot in battle, when the wound was searched and the bullet cut out, to some standing by, pitying his pain, he replied, "Though I groan, yet I bless God I do not grumble." God allows his people to groan, though not to grumble!

Perhaps that piece seems a little stilted to us, as does the following, also coming from a Puritan sermon:

You cannot do without the grace of God when you come to die. There was a nobleman that kept a deistical chaplain, and his lady a Christian one; when he was dying, he said to his chaplain, "I liked you very well when I was in health; but it is my lady's chaplain I must have when I am sick."

F. W. Robertson, Phillips Brooks, and Richard Baxter read widely for illustrative purpose. Spurgeon's illustrations enabled him to make an ordinary topic interesting. Thomas Guthrie, master of pictorial preaching and tale telling, claimed that an example will, like a nail, often hang up a thing that otherwise would fall to the ground.

Storytelling Is an Ancient Art

The history of education indicates that illustrations have been used from time immemorial to explain truth. Within the last week this ancient and honorable practice has been exercised by count-less people in a variety of ways, formal and informal: statesmen in the legislature, lawyers in the courtroom, people at parties, teach-ers in the classroom, mother to child during the day, fathers at bedtime, children at play, people at parties, teachers in Sunday school, emcees at banquets, preachers proclaiming divine truth in church. Our love for stories is the result of our creation in the image of God. Ancient Hebrew rabbis went so far as to say, "God made man because he loves stories."

A member of a small church said, "The pastor of that large church across the street is a better storyteller than ours. I think our pastor tells too few stories." This remark might be complimentary or derogatory of the other pastor, depending on his use of illustra-tion. Yet it is true that often the difference between a mediocre speaker and a more capable one may be this. The inferior one says, "Let me say this truth in another way—with different words." Whereas the superior communicator says, "Let me illustrate—with a picture."

Jesus Used Stories

Crowning refutation of the professor's opinion that the ideal sermon would contain no illustration is the example of Jesus, who told stories and told them profusely. His stories have come down through the centuries in the world's best-seller, are read and reread, and are fixed in the minds of millions. Timeless, his stories hit home in every generation, like the parable of the prodigal son. With keen insight into everything around him, he worked illustrations into the very center and circumference of his messages.

The following verses from *The Living Bible* make plain his storytelling propensity:

Mark 4:2 "His usual method of teaching was to tell the people stories."

Matthew 13:34,35 "Jesus constantly used these illustrations when speaking to the crowds. In fact, because the prophets said he would use so many, he never spoke to them without at least one illustration."

Mark 12:1   "Here are some of the story-illustrations Jesus gave to the people at that time."

Matthew 22:1, 2   "Jesus told several other stories to show what the Kingdom of Heaven is like. 'For instance,' he said, 'it can be illustrated by the story of a king who prepared a great wedding dinner for his son.'"

Journalism Requires Illustrations

When I taught Journalism at Nyack (N.Y.) College I always emphasized the need to illustrate articles with anecdotes. To emphasize the point I would have the class examine a *Reader's Digest* inspirational piece, perhaps on the general theme of learning contentment or showing thankfulness. We would invariably discover that over one-half the piece was anecdotal.

Look at any of our magazines today, secular or Christian, and you will discover all of them heavily laced with illustrative material. Anecdotes are the lifeblood of modern journalism.

To make our message come alive, whether writer or speaker, illustrations are indispensable.

Illustrations Subordinate to Message

A woman, asked if she thought there was much spirit in the lecture just delivered, replied, "It was all spirit; there was no body to it at all!"

Every discourse should have body, real meat, sound doctrine, some suitable teaching or timely exhortation for listeners to take to heart. Illustrations must be subordinate to this meaty content. Substance is primary; illustrations are secondary and subsidiary. One homiletician discusses illustrations under the heading of "supportive" material. Illustrations should not obscure teaching nor choke meaning.

If in composing a talk we had to confine ourselves exclusively to either reasoning or illustrating, we would choose reasoning. Naturally we would prefer a house comprised totally of solid walls to a structure made completely of windows. But it does not need to be either or, but can be both. How much more practical, as well as aesthetically pleasing, is a house with both walls and windows.

Though illustrative material is subordinate, it is not trifling. Nothing about communicating God's truth is trivial. Whatever can clarify divine truth cannot be irresponsibly or frivolously fluffed off.

Importance of Illustrations

The fault with many talks is not that they do not contain truth, but that there is little or no illumination of that truth. There is nothing to help describe what is otherwise indescribable. Too often an anecdote may be not only the best but the only way to explain truth to the popular mind. Illustrations can enlighten, prove, paint, arouse, move; in short, appeal to mind, stir emotions, and persuade the will. Who would not be moved to a more discreet use of the tongue by this story?

> In a Pullman car on an overnight train in Texas a baby bawled continuously. A traveling salesman, unable to sleep, yelled out to the man taking care of the infant, "Why don't you take that baby to its mother?" Came the soft reply, "I'd like to, but its mother is in the baggage car in a coffin. We're taking her home for burial!"

Anyone who must write an article every month, or teach Sunday school every week, or make a speech every now and again, or preach two or three different sermons every week, or who wants to make a significant contribution in social conversation, knows the punch of a powerful illustration.

Likewise a listener or reader welcomes words like, "Let me illustrate," "for example," or "for instance," because these transitional words indicate that general truth is about to be pictured in a specific way.

No one can be an effective communicator unless he uses illustrations. An Arab proverb says, "The best speaker is he who turns ears into eyes." The vividness of this proverb should encourage us in the frequent and judicious use of illustrations.

2

Paint a Picture—Prove a Point

A Sunday school teacher wanted to impress on his high school class the importance of worship and rest on Sundays. He recalled this story:

Seven unmarried brothers lived together in a large house. Six went out to work every day but one stayed home. He had the place all lit up when the other six arrived home from work. He also had the house warm, and most importantly, had a delicious, full-course dinner ready for his hungry brothers. One day the six brothers decided that the one that had been staying home should go to work. "It's not fair," they said, "for one to stay home while the others slaved at a job." So they made the seventh brother find work too. But when they all came home the first night, there was no light, nor was there any warmth; and worst of all, there was no hearty dinner awaiting them. And the next night the same thing: darkness, cold, hunger. They soon went back to their former arrangement.

Using his story the next Sunday, the teacher pointed out to the high schoolers, "The day of rest and worship is the day that keeps the other six bright, warm and nourishing. When we desecrate the Lord's Day, we only hurt ourselves."

To *illustrate*, according to the etymology of the word, is to throw luster or light on a topic. English preacher Thomas Fuller said, "Reasons are the pillars of the fabric of a sermon; but similitudes are the windows which give the best lights." The main purpose of windows is to let in light. If a room is dark and shades drawn, you raise a shade so that light enters. When another shade is raised, more light streams in. Similarly, when a didactic approach struggles in its attempt to inform, an illustration will remove the shade from the window of understanding and let light stream in. The command given Noah comes to every communicator of God's Word, "A window shalt thou make to the ark (Gen. 6:16)." Windows may also serve as ornaments. So may illustrations, but they must never be so ornamental that they keep out the light.

Illustrations Help Explain

A little girl, asked about her mother's cooking, replied, "She pours in the abstract, and it comes out concrete." That's bad culinary practice but it's good homiletical procedure. A good communicator takes abstract, abstruse, deep, difficult truth and labors to explain it through use of concrete illustration. John Wesley advised preachers "Though you think with the learned, you must speak with the common people."

We live in a world of pictures. With TV, well-laid-out magazine spreads and enticing space advertising, this generation is visual-minded. To get our concepts across we must employ word pictures. Pictures of faraway scenes give us better understanding than a written description of the scenery. A pictorial drawing of a piece of machinery when accompanying a written manual of instruction will permit us to operate it more easily. Illustrations permit repetition without weariness.

Of all the uses of illustration, its most important is *to explain*. Illustrations assist clear thinking. Contrary to Coleridge who justified his obscure style by claiming it good practice for people to have to dig for ideas, the conscientious teacher, though building up laborious explanations, will through suitable metaphor and story make the sense clear, and bring his hearers out of the dark. An illustration helps truth to be received with less effort and more comprehension.

The length of an illustration is not its test. The real question is: does it let the light in? It may be as short as a word or phrase, like Jesus' description of the witnessing believer as "the light of the world" and "the salt of the earth." Examples from today's life would be: "Self-control is the ability to eat just one salted peanut." And, "Living with worry is like driving your car with the emergency brake on." Or the illustration may be a longer story like the parable of the lost sheep. Or an analogy of some length as when the Lord explained our union with him by using the similitude of the vine and its branches.

Using an Analogy

Analogy takes a doctrinal truth and explains it in terms grounded in life, proceeding from the known to the unknown. By presenting something similar or analogous the matter is made plain. Jesus' parable of the sower so clearly sets forth the four types of response humanity gives to the preaching of his Word. You can almost see birds coming to devour seed which had fallen on a stony path. You can easily visualize seed springing up quickly, but because it has no depth of root, withering away under the blasting of the noonday sun. You can also picture seed springing midst thorns that soon choke its very life. And how gladly you imagine seed springing fruitfully up, even to a hundredfold. Jesus could have said there were four types of hearers: the stony hearted, the shallow listener, the busy-with-the-cares-of-this-world recipient, and the receptive person. But how much more indelibly are these various categories inscribed on our understanding because of Jesus' illustrative approach.

A speaker might say in the course of a talk that too often we get our values mixed up. He could reinforce our need to straighten out our priorities by using the following story:

A gang of little boys decided to have some fun, so one night they climbed through a window into a hardware store, then ran everywhere switching price tags on much of the merchandise. In the morning when the store opened, among other mixed-up prices, bicycles were 29 cents each, TV sets showed 2 cents per pound, nails became $79.95 each, and cork stoppers sold for $6.98.

A speaker didn't want to drone out figures in the millions as to how many in the world have never heard the gospel, or go to bed hungry every night, so made his presentation more graphic by using the following figures:

> If the population of the world could be reduced to a town of 100, 6 would be Americans enjoying 50 percent of the world's total wealth, 33 would never have heard the name of Jesus, another 33 would never have been given the gospel effectively, 68 would go to bed hungry nightly, 75 would be nonwhite, and 3 would be born again.

A commencement speaker who wanted to show that education alone is not enough to enable youth to meet life's problems made his point much more strongly by adding this soliloquy, published a few years ago by the University of Michigan School of Education over the initials of a teacher N.J.W.

> I have taught in high school for ten years. During that time I have given assignments, to, among others, a murderer, an evangelist, a boxer, and a thief. The murderer was a quiet little boy who sat on the front seat and looked at me with pale, blue eyes. The evangelist, easily the most popular boy in the school, had the lead in the junior play. The boxer lounged by the window and let loose at intervals a raucous laugh that startled even the geraniums. And the thief was a gay-hearted lad with a song on his lips.
>
> The murderer awaits death in the state penitentiary; the evangelist has lain a year now in the village churchyard; the boxer lost an eye in a brawl in Hong Kong; and the thief, by standing on tiptoe, can see the windows of my schoolroom from the county jail. All these pupils once sat in my room, and looked at me gravely across worn brown desks. I must have been a great help to those students—I taught them the rhyming scheme of the Elizabethan sonnet and how to diagram complex sentences.

It's almost platitudinous for a preacher to warn people against hoarding wealth on earth, and to urge them to lay up treasure in heaven. This anecdote makes the warning clearer:

> A sailor, shipwrecked on a South Sea island, was seized by the

natives, carried shoulder-high to a rude throne and proclaimed king. He learned that according to custom a king ruled for a year. The idea appealed to the sailor until he began to wonder what had befallen previous kings. He learned that when a king's reign ended, he was banished to a lonely island where he starved. Knowing he had power of kingship for a year, the sailor began issuing orders. Carpenters were to make boats. Farmers were to go ahead to this island and plant crops. Builders were to erect a sturdy home. When his reign finished, he was exiled, not to a barren isle, but to a paradise of plenty.

He clinched the story by quoting the Lord's advice, "Make to yourselves friends of the mammon of unrighteousness; that, when ye fail, they may receive you into everlasting habitations" (Luke 16:9).

Illustrations Help Prove

John Broadus in his classic *Preparation and Delivery of Sermons* claims that illustrations are frequently used to *prove.* He points out that in Romans 6 and 7 Paul introduces three illustrations to show the unreasonableness of supposing that justification by faith will encourage sinning: believers are *dead* to sin and risen to a new life; they have ceased to be *slaves* of sin, but have become servants of righteousness; they have ceased to be *married* to the law, but are joined to a new husband, Christ, to whom they must now bear holy fruit. All three not only explain the believer's position, but also involve an argument from analogy.

Though illustrations assist in argument, we must take care not to infer more than they actually prove. Obviously, argument and illustration are not the same thing. If we get carried away by our subject, and make an illustration assume too much weight, orderly minds will notice our substitution of story for logic and may lose respect for our reasoning powers. Broadus suggests that arguments from analogy are more frequently and safely used in refutation.

The rest of this chapter will show how illustrations may be used to refute the claim of critics that the Bible contains many contradictions. For instance, opponents of the Bible ask where was Jacob's name changed to Israel. They point out that Genesis 32:28 says it was at Peniel whereas Genesis 35:10 puts it at Bethel. We answer by affirming these verses need not be contradictory, but are likely supplementary. The change was probably first announced at Peniel, then later confirmed at Bethel. An example from USA history helps this argument:

> When did Calvin Coolidge take the oath of the presidency? History gives two answers: in Plymouth, Vermont, and in Washington, D.C. How do we explain this seeming contradiction? When President Harding died, Vice president Coolidge was vacationing at his father's home in Plymouth, Vermont. There in the early A.M. hours of August 3, 1923, he took the oath which was administered by his father who was a justice of the peace. Later, the oath was administered a second time in Washington, D.C., by a justice of the Supreme Court. Both accounts are true; there's no contradiction.

Matthew says Jesus healed two blind men, whereas Luke in reporting the same incident mentions a certain blind man (Matt. 20:30; Luke 18:35). If Luke had said only *one* had been healed, we would have a discrepancy on our hands. Though *two* were healed, Luke's interest centered on a particular *one* of the *two*. Mark in recounting the story also focused on the same *one*, giving his name as Bartimaeus (10:46). One Bible-study leader explains this type of discrepancy by this example:

> Suppose while driving down the highway, you spot a policeman giving a ticket to the drivers of *two* cars. Arriving home, you tell your wife you saw *two* men stopped for speeding. Your little boy, who had been with you, has already run into the house and blurted out, "I saw *a* car stopped for speeding." So your wife asks, "Which was it—*two* cars or *one*? The explanation is simple—there were two. Your little lad was impressed with the fact that *a* car had been stopped by a policeman; the number was inconsequential to him. But you gave the total picture.

The Bible seems to possess numerical discrepancies, but so often through the years a new discovery has cleared up another of these disagreements. The following episode shows the need for thorough research of all the facts:

> A history class, studying the French Revolution, was given the assignment of finding out by what vote King Louis XVI was condemned. Nearly half the class reported the vote unanimous, 721–0. Many disagreed, claiming he was condemned by a majority of just

one, 361–360. Still a few others gave the vote as 433–288. Which of the three answers was correct? Further study revealed that three separate votes were taken. The first—was he guilty? No dissenting vote, 721–0. The second—should he get the death penalty? The result, 433–288. The third vote—should the execution be at once or after peace with Austria? The third vote favored immediate death by just a majority of one, 361–360. All three answers were right.

When two biblical events seem to contradict each other, remember that the writers may be writing from different viewpoints.

As two medieval knights approached a large shield standing against the trunk of a tree, one insisted that the shield was made of gold, while the other firmly declared it was made of silver. They argued vehemently, began fighting, and mortally wounded each other. Later a maiden came along, saw the two dead knights, then looking at the shield was amazed, because one side was made of gold, while the other was made of silver. Each knight, approaching from a different direction, had seen only one side. Both were right.

Few people can follow a close argument for any length of time, though some are more trained than others to concentrate. If you indulge in lengthy abstract reasoning, you'll likely leave much of your audience far behind you. Apt illustrations can flash light on what you have said, giving an understanding of your arguments that could not be grasped in any other way.

3

Attention, Please!

A man commented on how to make the most of a convention. "I pick out what seems like a worthwhile workshop and sit near the back of the room. If the first five minutes are dull, I conclude the rest of the hour will also be dull, so I slip out and find my way to my second-choice workshop. However, I find that when a workshop leader begins with an illustration, he will likely keep my interest."

Illustrations Make a Talk Interesting

Probably the best way to grab a person's attention is to begin with an anecdote. I once started a sermon on the need of the members of Christ's body for each other with this incident:

A seminary professor asked one of his married students to occupy his house during vacation as protection against burglars. Aroused in the middle of the night by a strange sound, the student groggily groped for his glasses. He had gone to sleep with one arm in an awkward position, cutting off circulation to that limb. As he reached for the dresser, he encountered his own now cold and clammy hand. Jumping to his feet, he shouted to his wife, "There's a hand under the bed!" She bolted out of bed and began feeling along the wall for the light switch. Suddenly the thought came to him, "Why am I using only one hand?" Even before his wife found the switch, the embarrassing truth dawned on him. The clammy hand was his own!

The story caught their interest.

Not only do illustrations gain a person's interest at the beginning of a discourse, but they recapture it during a talk, particularly if concentration, strained by argument or exposition, has begun to slacken. Spurgeon advised, "We want to win attention at the commencement of the sermon, and to hold it until the close. With this aim, many methods may be tried; but possibly none will succeed better than the introduction of an interesting story." He added that if a worshiper begins to feel drowsy, "another tale will stir him to renewed attention." Spurgeon also suggested that the telling of a story was a way to catch the ear of the careless.

Illustrations make a talk pleasurable. As mentioned earlier, houses are dull affairs without windows. A building without windows would be more like a prison—dark, oppressive, and uninviting. Windows not only let in light but fresh air as well, which can revive an audience doped by the stagnancy of sustained, heavy, colorless explanations. A window should, according to its name, be a wind-door, through which a breath of air may refresh an audience. Similarly, an illustration can convey a breeze of happy thought, blowing over a crowd like an animating zephyr.

Parishioners who have trouble keeping awake during a sermon have been advised to have some sharp peppermints handy—but perhaps the peppermints belong in the sermon itself! In the midst of a message on loneliness (at an appropriate place) a speaker interjected this short piece:

> A man riding in a cab in Times Square was handed this note, "I'd rather you talk to me than tip me. I'm lonely. Your driver."

The reaction on peoples' faces indicated that flagging attention had been reestablished.

Near the end of a talk on the need for us to help each other, a minister told this story:

> A young invalid mother was resting in her bed when her nine-year-old daughter walked in from school. Thinking her mother asleep, she quietly unfolded the blanket at the foot of the bed, and gently tucked it around her mother. The mother stirred, then whispered, "It wasn't too long ago that I was tucking you in. And now you're covering me."
> The little girl bent over her mother, "We take turns."

Interesting anecdotes enliven the message, and prepare people to listen more thoughtfully to what follows.

Illustrations Give Something to the Young

An eccentric carpenter, building a house, suddenly quit. He explained, "Years ago I resolved never to build a house without windows in it low enough for kiddies to see out. The owner won't let me put in windows that low, so I'm stopping."

What a difficult assignment a preacher has every Sunday morning trying to communicate to a few hundred people in all stages of spiritual growth and in all ranges of physical age. Before him are some who have become believers in the last few weeks, as well as others who have been on the Christian path for forty years or more. Also he faces those in their sixties, forties, twenties, and under ten. What can he say to reach all groups? Some pastors include in their morning service an object lesson geared to the children, even inviting the boys and girls to come and sit at the front during its presentation. This object lesson undoubtedly helps, but doesn't make the later sermon more understandable. What does help the formal sermon reach little ones who cannot yet think abstractly is the use of illustrations. This helps everybody, especially children, receive something most every time.

One pastor noted that during the doctrinal and exegetical portions of his homily the children wiggled restlessly. Not too quietly one would push a hymnbook against another who would retaliate by pushing it back. Or a boy would scribble a note on the bulletin, hand it to a girl, and both would end up giggling. But the minute the pastor started a story, the children stopped fidgeting. A smile came over their faces, and their eyes became as big as saucers as they riveted pulpitward. Children like the light that shines through windows.

One Sunday-school teacher said that whenever the pupils in his junior class began to twist and turn, it was a sign he should give them an anecdote. One boy frequently called out, "This is very dull, teacher, Can't you tell us a story?" If we could read the mind of many adults in church, might they not be saying, "Preacher, spin us a yarn?"

No rule says that sermons must be miserably and intolerably dull. To interest children illustrations are indispensable. Adults like them too.

Illustrations Rest the Mind

When you stand for a while, you probably shift from one leg to the other every so often. If ordered to stand on one leg for five minutes, you'd be happy when the time was up, and you could lean on the other leg. How tiring to stand rigidly still in one position for any length of time.

Similarly, a sustained exposition can be wearying, for it taxes one side of the brain. But when an illustration is introduced, monotony is relieved for it permits the hearer to shift from the reasoning side of his brain to the imaginative side.

Because a page of solid, unbroken print can intimidate a potential reader, layout editors make pages more palatable by breaking them up with pictures and marginal spaces. So our minds need the tedium of continuous commentary relieved by illustrations. Illustrations ease the mind, provide respite from concentrated thinking, and renew attention.

A religious broadcaster who had a weekly twenty-minute-radio sermon every Sunday for years would, about five minutes before the end, deliberately and invariably tell a story or say something humorous to lighten the message up. Then he would drive home his final point in those last few minutes, doing it much more effectively because his hearers' minds had been relaxed into a receptive state.

In reviewing several of my sermons I noticed that I sometimes followed this procedure. One message on a serious topic "The Wounds of Christ" includes four points in the outline: the wounds of *Christ* were marks of recognition, marks of suffering, marks of victory, and marks of ownership. Because the material is continuously heavy in stressing the sufferings of Christ, I lighten things up just before the closing appeal. Under the fourth point (marks of ownership), after declaring that because of his sufferings Christ owns our eyes, our ears, and our tongue, so that we cannot look at, listen to, or say what we want, then I interject, "He owns our dispositions too." And then I give a couple of anecdotes:

> A little boy was showing his nextdoor pal around his new house. Pointing to a room in the basement, he said, "This is my father's den." Then he added, "Does your father have a den too?" "No," replied his pal, "My father growls all over the place."

And this one:

> When the well-known Bible teacher, Dr. Ralph Keiper, and his wife were on their honeymoon, the bride decided to try out her new iron (received as a wedding present) on the trousers of her husband's new suit, which had become mussed in travel. When she applied the hot iron, part of the trousers went up in a puff of smoke, leaving a small but gaping hole. The groom rushed in from the next room, "Is everything all right?" Whereupon the bride, not knowing how her husband would react, burst into tears as she tried to relate what had happened. "Honey," he replied, "let's get down on our knees and thank God that my leg wasn't in those trousers!"

The laughter lowers the hearers' level of intensity, resting them for a serious conclusion.

Illustrations Assist the Memory

People often recall some story in the sermon better than the lesson of the sermon. (In fact, when a preacher repeats a story a year later, he is likely to be accused of preaching the same sermon.) But if the story is so fitting that it helps recall the point it illustrates, so much the better.

A young lady heard a sermon "Slightly Soiled—Greatly Reduced in Price." It warned that lowering our moral standards ever so lightly, could easily soil our character. An illustration told of a certain counter in a department store where merchandise was sold at discount. The sign on the counter read: SLIGHTLY SOILED—

GREATLY REDUCED IN PRICE. Months later on a weekend party away from home, the young lady was strongly tempted to an act of immorality. About to yield, she suddenly recalled the illustration of the counter. Not wishing to be "soiled" she resisted.

Perhaps an anecdote, not fully appreciated at the moment, is tucked away in the memory to be recalled months or years later at some dark, needy occasion. At that moment, the shade goes up and light streams in the window, bringing new help and hope.

A college student heard a chapel talk on "The God of the Second Chance," based on the text "The word of the LORD came unto Jonah the second time" (Jonah 3:1). The closing illustration concerned the 1929 New Year's Day Rose Bowl football game in which a University of California player made a serious mistake which ultimately led to his team's defeat.

The misplay happened in the first half. Everyone wondered if the coach would play this player in the second half. In the dressing room at halftime the crestfallen player sat in a corner away from the rest of the team with his face in his hands, crying like a baby. When it came time to go back on the field, the coach announced, "Men, the same team that played the first half will start the second."

The players started out, but the dejected player didn't move, mumbling something about ruining the game, the university, and himself. He whimpered, "I couldn't face the crowd in the stadium to save my life," his cheeks wet with tears. The coach, placing his hands on the player's shoulder, said, "Get up and go out there. The game is only half-over." The opposing team reported that they never saw a man play football as he did the second half.

Years later when he made a bad mistake which cost him his business and nearly his marriage, and he thought about giving up, he recalled the story, especially the line, "The game is only half-over." He recouped his losses, stabilized his marriage, and went on to greater heights.

4

Touch a Tender Spot

In a talk on the danger of judging others without sufficient information, a seminar leader related the following incident:

A woman boarding a streetcar asked the conductor to let her off at a certain corner. He promised to do so, but forgot until the car had passed her street by two blocks. Angrily climbing down, she gave him a violent tongue lashing. He answered not a word. Later, a passenger asked the conductor how he could take such a flow of abuse so quietly.

He replied, "It's true I was to blame for forgetting, but that woman doesn't know that I have a sick wife at home, so sick she needs care day and night. I have a day nurse there while I work, but I've been staying up with her the last two nights. I've worked every day because I need the money to pay for the nurse. So, I haven't had a wink of sleep for two days and nights. That's why my memory isn't working so well. The woman doesn't know that."

The audience, stirred with sympathy for the conductor, and with resentment for the woman, listened responsively as the lecturer remarked, "Often we know so little about our neighbors. Perhaps business isn't good. Or a wife is depressed. Or a husband isn't congenial. If we had more facts, we'd be sorry we judged others so harshly."

Illustrations Arouse Feelings and Emotions

Not only are we creatures who think but who also experience emotion. A story that can play on the heartstrings is well on the way to making its point. The following episode would likely move most Christians to ponder the folly of storing up possessions on earth, while forgetting to lay up treasure in heaven:

> A rich man, confined to bed with terminal illness, enjoyed the company of his little girl who spent many after-school hours in his room, often visibly puzzled over why her daddy was lying there so helplessly. One day his business partners paid him a visit. The little girl somehow sensed an air of finality about their call.
> When they left, she inquired, "Father, are you going away?"
> "Yes, dear, and I'm afraid you won't see me again."
> Then the little girl asked, "Have you got a nice house and lots of friends there?"
> The father was silent for a moment, then turned convulsively toward the wall, muttering, "What a fool I've been! I've built a mansion here. I've made thousands of dollars, but I shall be a pauper there!"

Listeners would be emotionally readied for the punch line, "A man may die, leaving upwards of a million without taking any of it upward."

I was asked to conduct the funeral of a fourteen-year-old boy I had never met. He had committed suicide. As I led the pallbearers and casket out of the funeral home, I saw a dog standing a few feet back of the hearse, watching quietly. Someone whispered, "That's the boy's dog." The dog never let out a bark of any kind, standing at attention, as its master's body was gently placed in the hearse. Somehow the animal had managed to get out of the boy's home, a half-mile away, and find its way with uncanny accuracy to the place where its master was laid out. The emotional reaction to this story indicates that hearers are prepared to evaluate their faithfulness to their heavenly Master.

The pathos in the parable of the prodigal son melts hearts, readily turning them to the thought of God's eagerness to welcome a returning sinner. Many skillful speakers employ illustrations freely for the purpose of tenderizing hearts. This is a lawful practice providing the speaker is not telling the story just to awaken and toy with a listener's passing emotion, but rather to soften the soil of the human heart so that the seeds of divine truth may be more easily planted therein.

The late Dr. P. W. Philpott, founder of the church in which I was raised in Hamilton, Canada, often related a touching personal experience somewhat as follows:

I was awakened at 3 A.M. one morning by a stranger pounding at my door who said, "I've come to ask you to go with me to pray with a dying girl." He took me into a bad district and into a house of evil reputation, where I found a poor girl yet in her teens. It was evident she was soon to meet her Maker. I turned the shade of the lamp on her bedside table to see if I could recognize her. She said, "I don't think you know me, but I know you, and I knew you would come and pray with me, for I'm going to die. The girls here don't believe I'm going to die, but I know I am."

I wondered how I could best bring her to Christ when she solved the problem by asking if there wasn't a story in the Bible about a sheep that had strayed very far from the fold, and of the Shepherd who had gone after it. "Can you find the story in the Bible?" she asked.

I read her the story, then turned to the verse which tells of the Shepherd giving his life for the sheep. As I knelt to pray by the dying girl, the other girls knelt too, sobbing by their companion's bed. What an audience! When I looked up at the end of my prayer, I shall never forget the expression on her face.

"Oh!" she cried, "it's wonderful! The Good Shepherd has found me and he's holding me close to his heart." She kept repeating it. Thinking the poor girl might rally, I went home. When I returned at dawn, I met the funeral director entering the house. One of the girls came out to meet me. Her first words were, "We wish you had been here when Mary passed away. She was so happy. She kept saying, 'The Shepherd has found me, and he's holding me close to his heart.'"

A few years later, in another city, a young woman came up to me after a service, and smilingly asked, "Don't you recognize me?" When I couldn't say for sure, she said, "I think you do. I'm that girl that told you of Mary's passing that morning, and how happy she was. But there was something else I wanted to tell you. Once or twice I've started to write you but I didn't have the courage to finish the letter."

"Well," I asked, "what is it you wanted to tell me?"

"Just this," she replied, "that morning when the Good Shepherd brought Mary in on one shoulder, I came in on the other!'

It's pretty hard not to be stirred emotionally by a story like that.

Illustrations Help Persuade

Illustrations not only help in enlightening the mind, aid in arousing the emotions, but also assist in moving the will. People are rarely motivated to goals by dull material. In fact, according to considerable research evidence, we are more influenced by anecdotes than by data. However, the fact that minds are swayed as much by vivid stories as by dry facts can work against, as well as for truth. A gruesome report of some driver in a burning car, trapped there because he wore his seat belt, should not be used by any speaker to argue against the use of seat belts, when the facts overwhelmingly show that wearing them saves far more lives than they cost. A Christian communicator loses integrity and credibility if he uses any illustration to promote an untrue thesis.

In any speech to persuade one of the steps in the outline formula is called *visualization.* In trying to convince a person to buy a new car, a salesman will get the prospect to picture himself behind the wheel of a lovely new model, cruising down the highway in a supersmooth ride. Illustrations often provide visualization in which a Christian hearer identifies with the good character in a story, and determines to be like him, as in the following incident reported in the Moody Bible Institute student newspaper some years ago.

An official of a large hospital in Atlanta, Georgia, watching the lives of professing Christians day by day, concluded, "They don't live what they preach. And if they can't, I can't either."

Someone mentioned to him the godly life of Dr. Will H. Houghton, pastor of Atlanta's Baptist Tabernacle, who later became president of Moody Bible Institute. The hospital official, wanting to see if this preacher's life was true to his profession, hired a private detective to follow Dr. Houghton everywhere for several days. At the end of the period the detective declared, "He lives it—no flaw there."

These words were inescapable evidence. A little later in an hour of great despair, when he almost took his life, the hospital official recalled the detective's verdict, and accepted Christ. With a new outlook on life he spent his spare hours laboring for the Master. His daughter enrolled in Moody Bible Institute, and gave this account to the student newspaper. The article ended with the daughter's question, "Suppose Dr. Houghton had *not* lived a consistent Christian life—one that would bear close scrutiny?"

Would not most believers, on hearing this story, ask themselves, "What if a private eye were to follow me around for a week, would my life ring true?" And wouldn't most of us resolve, "Lord, help me so live that anyone watching me will say, 'He lives it—no flaw there.'"

Well-placed anecdotes about stewardship can stimulate faithfulness in giving.

A young man promised God a tithe of his income. His first week's pay was ten dollars, so he gave one dollar. Promoted several times, he later earned one hundred dollars a week, then two hundred, then five hundred dollars. One day he asked his pastor, "How can I get released from my promise to God to tithe? You see—it's like this. When I made that promise I had to give only a dollar a week, but now my tithe amounts to fifty dollars a week, and I just can't afford to give away that much.

His old pastor replied, "I'm afraid I cannot get you released from your promise. But there is something we can do. Let's kneel right down and ask the Lord to shrink your income to the point where you'll again only have to give one dollar a week."

Evangelists often use stories at the close of their sermons to help people respond to the invitation. One evangelist, emphasizing there are only two destinations in afterlife, related this bit of history:

When news of the tragic sinking of the *Titanic* reached England, the scene outside the steamship office was indescribable. Relatives of those on the ill-fated vessel crowded the street. All traffic stopped. On either side of the main entrance a large board had been hammered up in place. Above one board was printed in large letters: KNOWN TO BE SAVED. Above the other was also printed in equally large letters: KNOWN TO BE LOST. Every now and again a man would emerge from the office, carrying a large piece of cardboard on which was written the name of a passenger. A deathlike stillness would sweep over the crowd, as it watched breathlessly to see in which direction he would turn. Would he pin the name on the side of the saved, or on the side of the lost? The crowd realized there were but two classes among those who had traveled on the *Titanic*. Everyone would end up in one category or the other: the saved or the lost.

How easy for the evangelist to draw the net, "So it is with the journey across the sea of life. At the end all of us will be saved or lost. There is no neutral qualification. Is your name in the Book of Life?"

Likewise, persuasion to dedication of our life to the Lord, and to the giving of our best to the Master, can be urged through a Scripture-supporting anecdote like this:

> Queen Mary of England used to visit Balmoral Castle in Scotland every summer, often walking unescorted for miles around the countryside, where she was well known. One afternoon, venturing far from the castle, she was caught in a sudden storm, so stopped at a nearby door to ask to borrow an umbrella. Not recognizing the queen, the lady of the house, reluctant to lend her brand-new umbrella to a stranger, recalled her cast-off umbrella with broken ribs and several holes. With a half-apology she handed it to the queen.
>
> The next day the lady answered a knock at her door. There stood a man in gold braid who held a long envelope. He bowed, "The queen sends her thanks for the loan of your umbrella."
>
> For a moment the woman was stunned, then burst into tears. As the messenger turned away, he could hear her muttering over and over, "Had I known it was for the queen, I'd have given her my best!"

A good communicator will not just speak words that are true. He will so speak that his hearers will be motivated to rise up and become doers of the Word.

If we illustrate the truth clearly, our audiences will more likely act on it. Of course, we shall be looking to the Holy Spirit for his divine leading and action in all of this. Without him, our illustrations can do nothing.

Where Do You Find Them?—
Their Sources

5

You Find Them Everywhere

A brilliant conversationalist was asked, "Where do you get your illustrations?" He answered, "Oh, everywhere!"

If we have eyes to see and ears to hear, illustrations will reach out to us from every direction—from experience, observation, listening, reading, science, history, art, and literature.

Your Experience

Jane Foxwell, when a missionary in the Orient, began a missionary letter with a personal experience involving her husband, Phil:

Do you believe that marriages made in the will of God will result in empty stomachs? The students of our Japan Christian seminary and Bible College were informed that seeking God's guidance in the matter of marriage would guarantee stomachs that would always be empty! Speaking at our seminary chapel just before summer vacation, Phil meant to say "kofuku" but said instead "kufuku." Now *kofuku* means happiness but *kufuku* means an empty stomach. Unconscious of the error made, Phil couldn't understand why the students laughed at the assertion that to marry in the will of God would result in unending empty stomachs!

Far better than resurrecting some old musty story from a book of illustrations is to reach into our own lives and draw from some personal history. Often I have related something from trips abroad to drive home some practical point, such as visits to the *S.S. Arizona* Memorial at Pearl Harbor, the ruins of Babylon, the amphitheatre at Ephesus, the burning ghats of Calcutta, a leprosy colony in India, the Taj Mahal, Dachau Concentration Camp, Paul's Mamertine prison, and the catacomb paintings.

Visitors to the Holy Land can refer to the Mount of Olives, Bethany, the upper room, Gethsemane, the pavement where Jesus stood before Pilate, and Golgotha. Many times at funeral services I have mentioned my visit to the garden tomb to emphasize the comforting truth of Christ's power over death. My wife has used her experience of crawling through Hezekiah's Tunnel in speaking to women's groups.

To illustrate the point that many believers may be unaware of the wealth that the Holy Spirit has given them in the form of spiritual gifts, I sometimes tell this story.

On a trip around the world my wife and I arrived in Switzerland for a three-day stay. Checking into our hotel in late afternoon, we decided to eat dinner in the hotel dining room. The meal was excellent but expensive. When I asked the waiter to put the meal on our hotel bill, he smiled. To save money we ate most meals elsewhere, but never had as fine food as the first evening. Checking our bill at the end of our stay, I noticed they had not charged for that fine dinner. We learned to our chagrin that reservations, paid in advance by our church, had included not only room but meals as well. We could have eaten every meal for all three days in the hotel dining room at no extra cost.

Many believers go through life without using the resources of their spiritual gifts. Stories about ourselves sit better when they show us to be human or dumb, instead of making us brilliant.

Years ago, when a fire broke out in Moody Bible Institute's original wooden building at 4 A.M. one winter night, I joined the dozens of students who evacuated this men's dormitory, most of us with only the clothes we could quickly slip into. However, a few fellows managed to grab an extra item or two. One carried his violin, another his Bible, and still another (a student pastor), his two sermons for the coming Sunday. What each of us took, if anything, revealed what we considered of value.

A salesman, asked to speak at a Rotary Club, and wishing to get in a brief testimony, told how becoming a citizen of the USA was like becoming a citizen in God's kingdom. His entire talk became an illustration, as he made these comparisons:

> Citizenship cost me so little, it was a virtual gift. Becoming a Christian was absolutely free.
>
> I had to follow the procedures and regulations of the U.S. Immigration and Naturalization Department. To get into God's kingdom I had to come through his Son who is the only way.
>
> When I became a citizen my lifestyle changed. I wanted to stop telling jokes that made fun of the USA. I observed certain holidays. Likewise, when I became a member of God's kingdom, I had to forget a lot of unclean jokes and observe the Lord's Day.
>
> Finally, on becoming a U.S. citizen I swore allegiance to a new flag, giving up loyalty to my former country. Similarly, on becoming a citizen of God's commonwealth, I promised to serve my new Lord and Master.

His personal history not only caught the hearers' imagination, but also made the gospel more understandable.

Interest picks up immediately when a speaker relates a personal experience with which the hearer can identify. A deacon, conversing with a fellow believer at work who couldn't understand why God was permitting him to go through some hard times, recounted this from early memory:

> When I was six years old the doctor gave me a shot for some childhood disease, given all children in that era. He promised it wouldn't hurt but it did. The next day my arm was quite sore, so I asked my father why. He couldn't explain to a child's satisfaction the scientific cause of my pain nor how this shot could prevent serious illness. Then he added, "Son, I know you don't understand your pain, but you do know that I love you, and this shot was something you had to have in order to protect you."

The suffering worker identified with the deacon's boyhood experience, because without explanation for his present pain, he knew he had to trust in his Father's love.

Your Observation

The aspiring communicator must be a close observer of life. An inexhaustible store of illustrations abounds everywhere, even in the common things of life.

Jesus' stories came from hens and chicks, lilies, seeds, swine, pearls, red sky, yellow grain, vineyards, widows, rich men, kings, servants, wars, feasts, judges, prisoners, merchants, fishermen, farmers, unemployed workmen, two sons of opposing dispositions, patched garments, lost coins, shepherd and sheep, returning prodigal, unexpected guests, sowing, watering, harvesting, storing in barns, building houses, leavening bread, talents, debtors, creditors, tax collectors, dogs eating crumbs under the table, weddings, and guests refusing invitations or coming without proper wedding garments.

One day when you were trying to back out of a parking space into a line of endless traffic, suddenly a driver stopped to let you out. You thought, *What a kind driver!* As you drove away, you saw him pull into the space you just vacated. Immediately you suspected his act stemmed from self-interest rather than from altruism. You made a mental observation, and later a written note, with the comment, "Actions aren't always what they seem to be. Seeming good deeds may spring from selfish motives. It's what's inside that God sees."

Observing children can prove profitable. Jesus commended, not childishness, but childlikeness. Setting a child in the midst of his disciples, he told them they should become like that little one. In fact, he warned, unless adults humbled themselves like a child, they would not inherit the kingdom of God.

Note how children are not afraid to ask questions. And how adults often refrain lest they reveal their ignorance. Children, who make no pretense of false knowledge, blurt out uninhibited and unembarrassed their "Why this?" and "Why that?"

Observe how children forgive so quickly. Psychologists tell us that for marital health mates should clear up all arguments within twenty-four hours. Children seem to do this naturally. How unlike adults whose hurt vanity makes them hold grudges to the third and fourth generation.

Watch youngsters at a picnic. They grab extra sandwiches, and boast of drinking a dozen glasses of punch. But fifteen years later, those same children, after imbibing the niceties of polite but pretentious society, when offered another helping, reply, "No, thanks, couldn't eat another thing." Adult sham can take a few lessons from youthful straightforwardness.

The quality which probably sums up childlikeness best is *humility.* You have to be humble to ask questions, forgive easily, and be open and honest. I observed childlike humility in actions some years back.

> While attending seminary in Philadelphia, I worked several hours a week behind a meat counter to help pay the bills. Because it was wartime and meat was scarce, the counter was crowded. While women waited their turn, I saw many of them gaze at themselves in the wide mirror at the back of the counter. Now and again I would look at a woman in the mirror, then back directly at her, to let her know I had seen her admiring herself in the mirror. Without exception, every woman turned quickly away, avoiding my eyes as if to say, "I wasn't looking at myself! Not me! I'm not vain!"
>
> But more than once, when I caught a little girl admiring herself, she would not avoid me, but look back at me and smile, as if to say, "You caught me! I admit—I was looking at myself!"

Your Hearing

A while back I heard Dr. J. Edwin Orr tell a story in a college chapel service to illustrate the power of imagination.

> On a fishing trip Pat and Pete stayed overnight at a hotel. Pat woke, screaming, "I'm suffocating! Open the window!"
>
> Pete, in the other bed, slowly emerged from deep sleep. Again Pat pleaded, "Quick, open the window! I'm suffocating!"
>
> Groggily stumbling to the window, Pete moaned, "I can't get it open! It's stuck!"
>
> "Break it," Pat begged, "I need air!"
>
> So Pete shattered the glass with his fist. With relief Pat sighed, "I can breathe now," then fell asleep. In the morning they discovered Pete had broken the dresser mirror. Imagination, though mistaken, had exerted its power.

How often in daily conversation with neighbors, fellow-workers or church friends, we hear an incident that will stand us in good stead when we need to make a point in communicating with others. While picking up my newspaper in a local store, I heard a neighbor relate this tale, which I have often used to highlight spiritual truth. My neighbor tells it in his own words:

> My wife and I were out for dinner one night with several others in a friend's home. The husbands sat around, chatting while our wives were finishing up in the kitchen. One man of high moral character, who never told an off-color story, related a dirty joke that brought an uproarious response, as well as looks of amazement from some who knew his usually high standards. When the ladies returned to the living room the host announced, "I've a surprise for you. I bought a tape recorder last week, and I've had it on the whole time you were out. I thought you might like to hear what the men were talking about while you were finishing up."
>
> The man who had told the off-color story began to turn red with anticipated embarrassment. The recording reproduced the conversations, word for word, every tone, every inflection. As it neared the joke, the man began to squirm in his chair. Perspiration stood out on his forehead. He looked as if he wished the floor would open up and swallow him. Then his voice came forth. The first part of the story sounded out just as he had related it. It was about to reach the line that gave the story its off-color punch, when suddenly the doorbell rang, and several exclaimed loudly, "There's someone at the door!" This noise blotted out his voice so that the words were not heard. The man gave a sigh of relief, relaxed in his chair, and wiped the perspiration from his forehead as a smile played across his lips.

The story makes a strong reminder of our accountability someday for every idle word, and also of the wonderful possibility of obliteration of our idle words.

Illustrations abound around. As you walk the street, drive the highway, or move among people, something said or happening will surely catch your attention as a possible illustration of some truth. Develop this kind of mind-set. Raise your antenna to draw out valuable material.

Keep your eyes and ears open!

6

Make Your Reading Count

A high school teacher wished to get across to her classes the Christian viewpoint of life. Knowing the limitations imposed by the separation of church and state, she found the introduction of current events both an acceptable and effective way to inject biblical truth. From the daily newspaper she brought this story to class:

> Thirteen-year-old Andrew Flosdorf of Fonda, NY, doing well in the National Spelling Bee, eliminated himself when he told judges he had misspelled "echolalia." The judges had not caught his mistake. Shrugged Flosdorf, "I didn't want to feel like a slime."

This news item led to a heated discussion on honesty.

Reading in General

Newspapers provide current illustrations. If a preacher uses this source to excess, critics will rightly claim, "He gets his text from

the Bible but his sermon from the newspaper." However, overuse
by some should not repel us from a judicious reference to recent
events that will make a discourse more pertinent.

Even the comics can help make a point. Dr. Bruce Shelley, professor of Church History at Denver Conservative Baptist Seminary,
is known for his frequent use of "Peanuts" cartoons, like this:

> Lucy once demanded that Linus change TV channels, threatening
> him with her fist if he didn't.
>
> "What makes you think you can walk right in here and take
> over?" asks Linus.
>
> "These five fingers," says Lucy. "Individually they're nothing but
> when I curl them together like this into a single unit, they form a
> weapon that is terrible to behold."
>
> "Which channel do you want?" asks Linus.
>
> Turning away, he looks at his fingers and says, "Why can't you
> guys get organized like that?"

Shelley makes the point that mobilizing for effective action is
always a problem, especially in the matter of church growth.

The well-crafted feature articles in the *Wall Street Journal* have
been a fruitful source of illustrative material for the opening section of my weekly radio broadcast. This first section always contains some current incident to capture attention for the later
presentation of biblical truth. Here is the substance of a story that
caught interest:

> The Procrastinators Club of America, located in Philadelphia,
> composed of about eighty advertising and professional men, enjoys
> putting things off, and putting people on. Organized in 1957, proba-
> bly a couple of years after the idea was born, the club has had the
> same officers ever since. They never got around to having elections.
> The members have no Fourth of July celebration in the summer, but
> have observed it on a cold, wintry day in February. Once they cele-
> brated Christmas the following June.
>
> A while back they picketed the city hall with an anti-war demon-
> stration—they were protesting the War of 1812. Once they chartered
> a bus which bore the sign: EXCURSION TO NEW YORK WORLD'S FAIR.
> It arrived forty minutes behind schedule, and more than a year after
> the fair had closed.
>
> However, they do not carry their procrastination into everyday
> affairs, but feel the idea has some practical applications.

The story led ideally into a discussion of the dangers of procrastination in spiritual matters.

Magazines like *Reader's Digest* are filled with usable anecdotes, like this one that shows how another's superiority may arouse ill will in us, leading to envy:

> A mother of four was talking about her neighbor who had eight children. "She's amazing! Her house is always neat as a pin; she's a wonderful cook and does her own sewing. Her children are polite and well-behaved. She is active in P.T.A. and helps with the Brownies and is a den mother for the Cub Scouts. She is pretty and has loads of personality. She makes me sick!"[1]

Books yield appropriate stories. Dr. Clarence Roddy, seminary professor, told his classes that when he was in the pastorate he used to read in one area a year, and derive all his illustrations from that field. For example, his area one year was Alaska Arctic expeditions.

A man in public relations, who wrote promotional letters to raise money for Christian organizations, came across this story in his reading and incorporated it into one of his stewardship pieces:

> A woman who lived in Philadelphia was commonly called the Duck Lady because of her severe nervous disorder which resulted in her making a quacking sound almost constantly. Though an attempt had been made to institutionalize her, she was well enough to be on the streets, wandering for years among the crowds in downtown Philadelphia, quacking in her uncontrolled way. Mocked and ridiculed, she was a dirty and sad sight.
>
> One day a Christian woman waiting for the light to change at a corner, sensed the Duck Lady by her side. She was quacking wildly. At first the Christian woman wanted to turn away and hurry off. But she knew that God loved that woman, so unlovely and disturbed, so she turned to her, "How are you feeling today? I see you every now and again and I worry about you. Is there any way I can help?"
>
> Amazingly, the woman stopped her quacking, turned to the Christian woman and said, "I'm not feeling well, and it is so very thoughtful of you to think of me in my suffering. God bless you for being so kind."
>
> The light changed. People began to move across the street. The Duck Lady continued on her way, again quacking loudly. But for a brief span kindness had broken through, temporarily giving her a respite of peace.

Science

Since the same God who created the world also inspired the Bible, it's not surprising that nature teems with analogies of moral truth. Several of Jesus' parables were drawn from nature. One medieval preacher was fond of illustrating from the characteristics of plants, another from the habits of animals.

A camp counselor, giving the devotional at a summer corn roast, used the ant as the basis of his message. He pointed out two facts: that the ant is industrious, and that it is provident, storing up food in the summer for the cold winter ahead (Prov. 6:6–8). Another night, after a swim party, he referred to the moon, by itself a cold, dead mass of volcanic craters, but which, when reflecting the light of the sun, becomes an object of beauty and a source of light to a darkened world. The lesson is self-evident.

An astronomer, speaking at a Rotary Club, used the following analogy to make vivid the smallness of man contrasted to the vastness of the universe:

Imagine a perfectly smooth glass pavement on which the finest speck can be seen. Then shrink our sun from 865,000 miles in diameter to only 2 feet, and place this gilt ball on the pavement to represent the sun.

Step off 82 paces of about 2 feet each, and to proportionately represent the first planet, Mercury, put down a mustard seed.

Take 60 steps more, each about 2 feet, and for Venus, put down an ordinary shot the size of a BB.

Mark 78 steps more, and for our earth, put down a pea.

Step off 108 paces from there, and for Mars, put down a pinhead.

Sprinkle some fine dust for the asteroids, then take 788 steps more, and for Jupiter, put down an orange.

Take 934 steps, and for Saturn, put down a golf ball.

Mark 2,086 steps more, and for Uranus, put down a marble.

Step off 2,322 steps more, and for Neptune put down a cherry. This will take us 2½ miles, and doesn't include Pluto.

If we swing completely around, we have a smooth glass surface 5 miles in diameter, representing our solar system, just a tiny fraction of the heavens. On this surface, 5 miles across, we have only a mustard seed, BB, pea, pinhead, dust, orange, golf ball, marble, and a cherry. And we should have to go 6,720 miles, not feet, on the same scale to represent the nearest star.

History

Because a person lived three thousand years ago does not mean he must be uninteresting to a twentieth-century audience. If relative to the present scene and narrated in a lively manner, an historical character or event has its place in talks today.

A committee chairman sensed a prima-donna mentality in some of the committee members. To encourage them to pull together, and not seek individual credit for the project assigned them, he opened the meeting with prayer and this story:

> Phidias, fifth century B.C. sculptor, carved a statue of a god, then chiseled his name in small letters in the corner. The elders claimed that the statue could not be worshiped as a god, nor be considered sacred, as long as it bore the sculptor's name. It was even suggested that Phidias should be stoned to death because he had so desecrated the statue. How dare he put his own name on the image of a god?

Some years ago the *Saturday Evening Post* carried an unusual article titled, "Battle by Bible," relating an incident in which the Bible supplied a precise plan of battle to the British in the Near East under General Allenby in 1918.

> The British, out to capture Jericho, knew they must first eliminate a Turkish garrison at the village of Michmash. A frontal attack was decided on, despite possible heavy casualties. On the eve of the attack, the British Chief of Staff outlined to his officers the plan for taking Michmash by direct assault. One of the officers, Major Petrie, thought the name of the village had a familiar ring. Trying to sleep, the word *Michmash* kept running through his mind. Suddenly he remembered—it was in the Bible. He found the reference in 1 Samuel 13 and 14. Then he rushed to the quarters of the commanding officer, roused him from sleep and announced his find.
>
> It was the account of how Jonathan had taken Michmash from the Philistines nearly thirty centuries before. Various landmarks were mentioned, two sharp rocks which indicated a pass, and a plot of ground overlooking the town. On a hunch the commander sent scouts out to look for the landmarks. They returned to report them all there.
>
> That night Major Petrie and his commander pored over the biblical passage, then completely changed the plan of attack. Just before

daybreak a small force set out for the plot of ground above Michmash. At dawn they emerged from hiding, with loud cries. The Turks poured from their huts, saw the men on the strategic ledge behind them. Confused and terrorized, they were easily subdued. Michmash was taken with amazingly few casualties, opening the door for a great British victory.

This unusual historical illustration joins the increasing mass of evidence for the historicity of the Bible.

With the celebration of the anniversary of Martin Luther's 500th birthday, anecdotes from his life were and still are timely.

In a small Bible-study group someone began to attack another denomination, which, though quite evangelical, held minor differences of doctrine. Another member countered with this story which led the group to unanimously support a proposed city-wide evangelistic crusade involving all evangelical groups:

> When the English and French were at war in colonial Canada, Admiral Phipps, in charge of the British Fleet, was ordered to anchor outside Quebec, a city on the Saint Lawrence River. He was to wait the coming of British infantry and then join the land forces on attack. Arriving early, Admiral Phipps, an ardent nonconformist, was annoyed by the statues of the saints that adorned the roof and towers of the Catholic cathedral. So he spent his time shooting at them with the ships' guns. How many he hit we don't know, but history recorded that when the infantry arrived and the signal was given for attack, the admiral found himself out of ammunition. He had used it for shooting at the saints.

New information on well-known historical characters enhances a talk. While a seminary student in Philadelphia, I met a nearby Episcopalian rector who was a grandson of Lincoln's Washington minister, Dr. Phineas Gurley. He showed me a collection of memorabilia that indicated his grandfather's close relationship with the famous president. That day I learned some not too widely known facts which I later included at appropriate places in articles and talks such as this account:

> During the critical stages of the Civil War Lincoln used to slip into the pastor's study from an outside door, and sit there during Thursday-evening-prayer meetings, listening in the dark through a slightly open door. Also Lincoln used to often send for Dr. Gurley in

the middle of the night to come to the White House to pray. Lincoln had made all arrangements to join New York Avenue Presbyterian Church, and but for his assassination the day before would have made public confession of his faith on Easter 1865.

Citing several episodes when God punished the wilderness wandering Israelites, Paul added that "these things happened to them as examples and were written down as warnings for us . . ." (1 Cor. 10:11, NIV). Thus, the recounting of historical happenings for hortatory purposes has biblical precedent.

The scientifically minded and history buffs have ready access to valuable illustrative wealth. So do literature enthusiasts and art lovers.

1. Reprinted with permission from the May 1961 Reader's Digest. Copyright © 1961 by the Reader's Digest Assn., Inc.

7

Literature and Art

A mother, concerned over the envious spirit of her high school daughter toward her schoolmate who had been chosen over her as high-school festival queen, told her this story she had heard in literature class many years before:

A statue was erected to a Grecian champion for his exploits in the public games. But another Greek, a rival of the honored athlete, so burned with the fever of jealousy that he vowed he would destroy that statue. Every night he sneaked out in the dark and chipped away at its base to weaken it and make it topple. He finally succeeded. But when it fell, it toppled on him. He died, a victim of his own envy.

Literature, ancient and modern, prose and poetry, offers a huge store of illustrative material. Striking figures of speech, proverbs, epigrams, and plays may be quoted. Appropriate allusions to literary works and characters reinforce a point with interest and impact.

Poetry

If not used to excess, poetry can bring an idea into focus with more beauty and power than the usual prose. Poetry also pleases through rhythm, cadence, and verse. The emptiness of fame finds heightened expression in Gray's *Elegy in a Country Churchyard*, in the line "The paths of glory lead but to the grave."

In Tennyson's *Enoch Arden* an incident illustrates the folly of blindly putting our finger on some verse in the Bible for guidance in finding God's will. Because Enoch had been long gone on a sea voyage, his wife, Annie, wondered if he had been shipwrecked and drowned, in which case she would be free to marry her would-be suitor. Unable to sleep one night, she prayed for a sign,

> Started from bed, and struck herself a light,
> Then desperately seized the holy Book,
> Suddenly set it wide to find a sign,
> Suddenly put her finger on the text,
> "Under the palm-tree." That was nothing to her;
> No meaning there: she closed the Book and slept:
> When lo! Her Enoch sitting on a height,
> Under a palm-tree, over him the Sun:
> "He is gone," she thought, "he is happy, he is singing
> Hosanna in the highest: yonder shines
> The Sun of Righteousness, and these be palms
> Whereof the happy people strowing cried
> 'Hosanna in the Highest!' . . ."

Awakening, she concluded Enoch was in heaven so consented to marriage. But tragically, Enoch, who was not dead, came back to see together his wife and her new husband. All this despite Annie's so-called guidance from the Bible.

Hymns

These come under the category of poetry. At the end of a devotional on the sufferings of Christ on the cross, how fitting to quote the hymn "When I Survey the Wondrous Cross," or this stanza from another familiar hymn,

> I gave My life for thee,
> My precious blood I shed,

That thou might'st ransomed be,
And quickened from the dead;
I gave, I gave My life for thee,
What hast thou given for Me?

Plays

These often have lines that throw light on spiritual truth. These two quotes from Macbeth have often been recited to reinforce their respective truths of sin's reality and life's brevity:

Will all great Neptune's ocean wash this blood
Clean from my hand? No, this my hand will rather
The multitudinous seas incarnadine,
Making the green one red.

And:

. . . Out, out, brief candle!
Life's but a walking shadow, a poor player,
That struts and frets his hour upon the stage
And then is heard no more; it is a tale
Told by an idiot, full of sound and fury,
Signifying nothing.

A prison worker, whose church team visited the county jail every Sunday afternoon, used this episode from Thornton Wilder's tender play, *Our Town*, to show that no one anywhere is forgotten by God:

A brother and sister are chatting on a summer evening. The sister mentions a letter their friend, Jane Crofut, received from her previous minister when she was sick. The address on the envelope went like this:
"Jane Crofut; The Crofut Farm; Grover Corners; Sutton County; New Hampshire, the United States of America."
When the brother asks what's so funny about that address, the sister adds:
"But listen, it's not finished: the United States of America; the Continent of North America; Western Hemisphere; the Earth; the Solar System; the Universe; the Mind of God. . . ."

Other Sources

Mythology mentions Janus, a Roman god identified with doors, gates, and all beginnings, and represented by two faces, looking in opposite directions. The month January is named after this god. How fitting for a New Year's devotional when we need to both look back and forward.

Autobiographies provide illustrative ammunition. In his *Confessions*, Augustine records his conversion, how in the garden at Milan, in the midst of great moral conflict, he was strangely attracted by a voice, "Take and read." He went to his copy of Romans which he had recently put down. He wrote:

> I read in silence the first place on which my eyes fell,
> "Not in revelling and drunkenness, not in chambering and wantonness, not in strife and envying; but put ye on the Lord Jesus Christ, and make no provision for the flesh and its lusts." I neither cared, nor needed to read further. At the close of the sentence, as if a ray of certainty were poured into my heart, the clouds of hesitation fled at once.

Philosophy, fiction, essays are among other areas of literature which make good fishing grounds for anecdotal matter. C. S. Lewis and Madeleine L'Engle are but two of many modern sources.

Art

A Sunday-school teacher warned his class of high-school boys, soon to leave for college, the military, or employment elsewhere, that without the restraining power of Christ they could so easily wander from his path. He said, "Without his strength you don't know where you'll be two years from now." Then to reinforce his warning he told a story revolving around Leonardo da Vinci's masterpiece *The Last Supper*, depicting Christ surrounded by his disciples at the upper room table:

> The artist worked on this painting from 1496 to 1498. Wishing to paint Christ first, da Vinci sent an assistant out into the streets of Rome to find a model. A kind-faced, innocent, choir-singing lad was selected. Nearly two years later when he wanted a model for betrayer Judas, the painter found his subject in a human derelict in the slums.

Arriving at the studio, the derelict looked at the painting, then pointing to the central figure exclaimed, "It is I! I was the model for the Christ!"

The largest piece of statuary in Glendale's (California) Forest Lawn is called *The Mystery of Life*. Nearly nine feet tall and fifteen feet wide, it contains eighteen life-sized figures. Portraying a wide range of ages and interests, and each expressing a different but typical view of the meaning of life, together they form a significant allegory that has inspired many an illustration. Here's the usual interpretation of the eighteen figures:

> The boy is amazed at the miracle that has taken place in his hand—one moment an egg, the next a living chick. He looks questioningly at his grandmother who admits she does not know the answer to the mystery of life. Two young lovers think they have found the answer in their embrace. A young girl is lost in reverie with no concern for serious questions. A scientist is troubled because all his learning has not solved the mystery. A mother finds the answer in her baby at her breast. A happy family of four are unperturbed as they watch the mating of birds. A learned philosopher admits he does not have the solution. A monk and nun are sure they have discovered it in their religion. An atheist grins foolishly at the sage who sits in contemplation of truth that he thinks he glimpses in the stream of life.

The answer to the mystery of life is symbolically found in a stream of water which has its source at the "Christus" statue in a court some distance away. This stream, which rises at the feet of Christ, then falls in a bright cascade, disappears into the ground to reappear some distance away in the midst of the *Mystery of Life* group. Christ is the answer to the meaning of life.

Films such as *Chariots of Fire, E.T.,* and *Ghandi* also contain illustrative values.

The Bible

Doctors learn to put the principles of medicine into practice through actual cases. Similarly, the Lord wants us to translate belief into behavior so has given us not only a history book but a case-history book as well. The Bible is not only a theology text, but also a casebook in which are examples of almost every type of moral behavior. Thus the Bible from start to finish provides an excellent source of illustration.

Since biblical material is already familiar to so many, hearers are able to identify immediately with the participants in the story. If the Bible is not familiar to the hearer, its use will increase his knowledge of Scripture. Since the Bible is an inspired book, the Holy Spirit will make the message "profitable for doctrine, for reproof, for correction, for instruction in righteousness." As mentioned earlier, many Old Testament incidents were recorded for the admonition of later generations. Despite the cultural gap of several centuries, sufficient commonality exists with the people of our century to make Bible lessons meaningful to us today.

". . . whatsoever a man soweth, that shall he also reap" (Gal. 6:7) is a biblical truth. If we sow potatoes, we reap potatoes. The Bible is rich in examples:

Jacob deceived his father; later when he was a father, he was deceived by his sons. Jacob deceived his father in connection with a favorite son (Esau); Jacob, in turn, was deceived about a favorite son (Joseph). Jacob used a goat skin to fool his father; a goat's blood was sprinkled on his son's coat of many colors to deceive Jacob (Gen. 27, 37).

The children of Israel (sons of Jacob) sold Joseph into slavery in Egypt. Several years later the children of Israel became slaves in Egypt (Gen. 37; Exod. 1).

Pharaoh ordered male babies born to Jewish mothers drowned (Ex. 1:22). Later Pharaoh and his army were drowned in the Red Sea, pursuing a people whose sons they had decreed should be drowned (Exod. 14:27, 28; Ps. 136:15).

Adoni-bezek cut off the thumbs and big toes of seventy conquered kings. When he was captured, his thumbs and big toes were dismembered (Judg. 1:5–7).

Wicked Haman had gallows built on which to hang Mordecai. Haman was hanged on his own gallows (Esther 7:10).

David destroyed another's home through lust, only to have his own family torn apart through similar passion by his sons (2 Sam. 11:13).

Ahab caused Naboth to be slain. Then dogs came to lick his blood. When Ahab died in Samaria, dogs licked his blood (1 Kings 21:19; 22:37, 38).

Those who concocted the plot that ultimately threw Daniel into the lions' den were themselves thrown in and devoured (Dan. 6:24).

The command to "Flee youthful lusts" (2 Tim. 2:22), is graphically portrayed in Joseph's flight from Mrs. Potiphar's seductive advances (Gen. 39:12).

We are told to "be strong in the Lord" (Eph. 6:10). Daniel's courage as a teenager in a strange land in refusing to obey a king's command and ultimately winning the king's favor exemplifies the command to be strong, and encourages hearers to "Dare to be a Daniel and dare to stand alone."

When a Christian brother is overtaken in a fault, spiritual believers are to restore the erring one (Gal. 6:1). The story of Jonah shows God's willingness to restore a disobedient servant. When Jonah tried to escape God's commission by traveling in the other direction and as far away from Nineveh as possible, wouldn't the Lord have had the right to say to Jonah, "You have disobeyed me. I disbar you from future service. I put you on the shelf"? Yet we read, "the word of the Lord came unto Jonah the second time (Jonah 3:1). He was given a renewed commission to go to Nineveh and preach God's bidding. He illustrates the gracious truth that our Lord is the God of the second chance.

The Bible is a treasure house of examples,
And it's impossible to plagiarize the Bible.

But are there other sources of illustration? Is it permissible to make up our own illustrations?

8

Suppose . . .

A young woman shared her faith with another officeworker. Her friend accepted all the facts of the gospel, but
somehow didn't understand the necessity of committing herself to
the Savior. Suddenly the young believer recalled a hypothetical
illustration often used by Dr. Vernon Grounds of Denver Seminary.
It goes something like this:

> Suppose I am in New York City, will be busy there until evening,
> but I wish to reach Chicago by midnight. I phone my travel agency
> and learn that the last plane to reach Chicago before midnight leaves
> LaGuardia at 10:00 P.M. To check the information I secure a time-
> table, verify the 10:00 P.M. departure and make a reservation. I buy a
> ticket. In plenty of time I take a limousine to the airport, check in,
> and get my boarding pass. To make sure I'm at the right gate area, I
> ask a passenger or two if this is the 10:00 P.M. flight to Chicago. I am
> told that it is. I mentally review the situation. The travel agency, the
> timetable, the airline clerk, the passengers, all assure me this is the

10:00 P.M. flight to Chicago. Without doubt this is the right plane, and I have a seat guaranteed. Suddenly the airline clerk announces the flight is ready to board. Passengers begin moving through the doorway to the plane. I stand there nodding my head in sincere assent—this is the 10:00 P.M. flight to Chicago. I keep nodding my head in genuine agreement while the gate is shut and the plane begins to move toward the takeoff area. I even watch it accelerate down the runway and zoom off into the night without me.

Without taking action, I missed the plane. If the officeworker doesn't claim Jesus as her Savior, she will not gain salvation.

It's legitimate to invent an illustration from imagination, providing the story is not far-fetched, is more or less true to life, and not palmed off as truth.

James likely made up a hypothetical case to get across his prohibition of snobbery (2:1–9). Hearing of actual instances where the poor were treated with contempt, and the wealthy with ostentatious respect, he *supposes* a situation in which a stranger enters a church service with a gold ring on his finger, and wearing an expensive robe. His appearance causes a sensation. He is offered a place of honor. Then the door opens again, and in steps another stranger, without jewelry, wearing only shabby clothes. He is shunted off into a corner.

An adult Sunday-school class was studying the attributes of God when they came to the fact of his eternity. How could God take in past, present and future all at once? They were enlightened when one of the class members gave this hypothetical example:

> When you watch a parade go by, you stand in one spot and take in the start, the middle and the end, in sequence. First are the marching bands, then the firemen, then old cars, business floats, and so on. It takes over an hour to go by, as you see it in progression. But suppose there's a high building in your city that gives a view of the whole area. By going to its observation tower, you are able to see the entire parade in one sweep of your eyes. All at once you see its beginning, middle, and end. So God, because of eternity, sees past, present, and future as one. Because he is the great *I Am*, a thousand years are as one day; and a day as a thousand years.

Literary Types

Figures of speech are forms of illustrations. Here are some literary types.

Parables. A parable, a form of the hypothetical category, is imaginary, fictitious, not true, yet a true-to-life story that enshrines a spiritual truth. It seems to be the Savior's favorite pedagogical device.

Because a parable teaches by induction and indirection, it has the advantage of breaking through our guard before we realize we are a part of the story and become defensive. Whereas a frontal approach would have been premature, a parable often disarms resistance.

For example, when David continued in unrepentance after his double sin of adultery and murder, it took a parable to convict him of his iniquity. The prophet Nathan told him the story of a rich man, who, though owning a vast flock of sheep, took a poor man's only lamb to feed a stranger. When David's anger was kindled against the wealthy man, Nathan made his point, "Thou art the man!" Then David saw his own sin, mirrored for him in the parable (2 Sam. 12:1-12). As a rich king, David had taken a soldier's only wife, and then engineered the soldier's death.

To motivate his fellow workers to greater concern for the lost, the chairman of a city-wide evangelistic crusade, began a committee meeting with this parable:

> In a dangerous area where boats frequently capsized on rocks in bad weather, a harbor town was known for its fine rescue team. Whenever the alarm sounded, a team of men rowed quickly to the scene, risking their lives to rescue sailors from heaving waves.
>
> After a few years the townsfolk collected money to build a rescue station near the shore. With their equipment stored there, rescue work was easier. Special training was also offered all who wanted to become rescuers. The operation became most efficient, saving hundreds from a watery grave.
>
> But as time elapsed, comforts and conveniences were added to the building—cupboards, food, lounge, dining room, thick carpets, and reclining chairs. The building became a club where townspeople loved to eat, play games, and socialize. Though the alarm still sounded to signal a wreck, only a handful responded, for others didn't wish to leave their creature comforts.

The chairman concluded, "Our churches are too often afflicted with a country-club mentality, undermining our purpose and paralyzing our outreach.

Visual Speaking

Visual speaking assists effective communication. By using color-ful verbs and picturesque nouns, and by speaking in particulars instead of generalities, we create images in the hearers' minds. Examples: "Ants swarmed over the picnic area." And, "The chimes and bells of the town clocks were discussing midnight."

Simile. This is a figure of speech comparing two unlike things, introduced by *like* or *as.* For example, "As Moses lifted up the serpent in the wilderness, even so must the Son of man be lifted up (John 3:14).

Metaphor. This is an implied simile. In this figure of speech a word or phrase literally denoting one kind of object or idea is used in place of another to suggest a likeness, as in, "The ship plows the sea." Someone counted over fifty metaphors in the Sermon on the Mount, such as, "Ye are the salt of the earth," and "Ye are the light of the world." Henry Jowett, preacher of an earlier generation, once saw the track of a bleeding hare across the snow. He spoke meta-phorically, "Whenever I think on Paul's missionary journeys, priva-tions, beatings, and stonings, I seem to see the track of a bleeding hare across the snow."

Analogy. This is a resemblance between things otherwise un-like. Jesus used the fact of physical birth to teach about spiritual birth. Both lead to new life. Other analogies are evident: both involve seed, require a prenatal period, and are followed by gradual growth.

A youth pastor used an analogy to show the irrationality of teaching sex from a neutral viewpoint. He had in mind the teach-ing of methods to escape pregnancy to youth who insisted on in-dulging in premarital sex. "Do we say to youth," analogized the youth pastor, "if you insist on pickpocketing, we want to teach you the ways to act so as not to get caught"? Why do we assume picking pockets is wrong and premarital sex neutral?

Allegory. This is an extended, imaginary narrative that carries a second meaning along with its primary story. Vices and virtues are personalized as in *Pilgrim's Progress,* best-known allegory so rich in

theological and psychological insights, in which we have Obsti-
nate, Talkative, Greatheart, and Pliable, among others. Abstract
ideas are incarnated, like Slough of Despond, Delectable Mountains, and Celestial City.

A speaker on a nursing-home team wanted to remind the pa-
tients of the promises of God in his Word. So he told how in
Pilgrim's Progress both Christian and Hope, after imprisonment for
several days in Doubting Castle by Giant Despair, suddenly
thought:

> . . . What a fool . . . am I, thus to lie in a stinking *Dungeon*, when
> I may as well walk at liberty. I have a Key in my bosom called
> *Promise*, that will, I am persuaded, open any Lock in *Doubting*
> Castle. Then said *Hopeful*, That's good news, good brother, pluck it
> out of thy bosom and try.
>
> Then *Christian* pulled it out of his bosom, and began to try at the
> Dungeon door, whose bolt . . . flew open with ease, and *Christian*
> and *Hopeful* both came out. Then he went to the outward door that
> leads into the Castle-yard, and with his Key opened that door
> also. . . . Then they went on, and came to the King's High-way again,
> and so were safe because they were out of his jurisdiction.

Fable. This is a nonfactual story in which truth is imparted by
having animals, trees, and birds speak and act like people. *Aesop's
Fables* is a very instructive book.

Asked to write a short article for the church-youth newspaper on
the theme of boastfulness, a high schooler began thus:

> An ant climbed on an elephant's back and asked for a ride over a
> bridge. After they had crossed, the ant exclaimed, "My, didn't we
> shake that bridge!"

Part way through the article he used another fable:

> Two ducks and a frog had to leave their home pond when it began
> to dry up. The ducks knew they could easily fly to another location,
> but wishing to transport frog friend, they decided to fly with a stick
> between their two bills with the frog hanging on to the stick with
> his mouth. A farmer, looking up at the flying trio, remarked, "Isn't
> that a clever idea! I wonder who thought of it?" The frog said, "I
> did."

The high schooler added, "Boastfulness, like pride, goeth before a fall."

A church board, concerned that the congregation was becoming legalistic by emphasizing negatives and majoring in the minors, paraphrased James Thurber's "The Bear Who Let It Alone," and enclosed it in a Sunday bulletin:

> In the woods lived a brown bear who could take it or leave it alone. He would go into a bar where they sold a fermented drink made of honey and have two glasses. Then he began to drink more and more, until he would stagger home at night, kick over the umbrella stand, knock down the living-room lamps, and ram his elbows through the windows. Then, collapsing on the floor, he would lie there until he fell asleep. His wife and children were terrified.
>
> Then the bear saw the error of his ways and reformed. Later he became a teetotaler and frequent temperance lecturer. Whenever anyone came to his house he would tell them about the awful effects of drink, and boast how strong he had become since no longer touching the stuff. To demonstrate, he would stand on his head, turn cartwheels on the living-room floor, kicking over the umbrella stand, knocking down the lamps, and ramming his elbows through the windows. Then lying down on the floor, tired by his healthy exercise, he would go to sleep. His wife and children were much distressed.

The board added this comment, "You might as well fall flat on your face as lean over too far backward. The bear should have gone home and loved his wife and children in kindness because he had been made into a lamb!

Proverbs. These are valuable means of stating truth succinctly and forcibly. Epigrams and maxims with their pointed, pithy statements have power to impress the popular mind. Admittedly, they sometimes make an imperfect generalization, but on the other hand they often linger long to leave a terse reminder of truth and duty. What communication would not be enhanced by statements like these:

A man wrapped up in himself makes a mighty small package.

He who is forced to swallow his pride soon gets fed up with himself.

You have to be little to belittle.

A long tongue means a short life.

If we don't come apart and rest awhile, we'll come apart.

Psychology

Psychology is big today, providing lots of illustrative fodder.

A few years ago the parable of the good Samaritan was reenacted, not on the road from Jerusalem to Jericho, but on a street in Princeton, New Jersey. Two psychologists recruited forty students from Princeton Seminary for an experiment. Half of the seminarians were asked to prepare a talk on the parable of the good Samaritan, while the other half were given a different subject. Then one by one, at fifteen-minute intervals, they were told to go to another building to record their talk. Each found on his way, lying in a doorway in the alley, a young man coughing and groaning and in possible pain. The "victim" had been planted there by the psychologists to see if the seminarians would play the role of the good Samaritan or pass him by. Especially, would those who were on their way to record a talk on the good Samaritan stop? Of the forty students, a total of sixteen stopped. Twenty-four did not swerve from their path. What determined whether a man stopped or passed by? It was not whether or not he had prepared a talk on the good Samaritan. The psychologists had introduced another factor. They told some of the boys they would be early for their recording; some, that they had just enough time; and others, that they were already running late, hinting that they should rush. Whether or not a seminarian helped varied more or less directly with the amount of time he had. Those in the "low" hurry group had the highest percentage of those who stopped to help. Those in the "high" hurry group had the smallest percentage. Willingness to help seemed to depend on whether or not one was in a hurry. This experiment could be filed under THE GOOD SAMARITAN, TIME, or PRIORITIES.

Illustrations are everywhere. Be alert to seize them.

But are there some cautions for using them?

What Are the Cautions?—
Their Dangers

9

Some Cautions

Make Sure the Illustration Fits

Back in England some years ago when the window tax was still in effect, many people living in country homes closed several of their excess, taxable windows by plastering them up, and then painted the plaster to look like panes. To outsiders they still looked like windows, but let no sunlight in.

Illustrations which do not illumine the topic are like those sham windows, or like windows with the blinds drawn. *Illustrate* is a verb requiring an object. Technically, there is no such thing as a good illustration, but there is a good illustration of a particular truth. Proverbs says, "A rebel will misapply an illustration so that its point will no more be felt than a thorn in the hand of a drunkard" (26:9 TLB). Though this misapplication refers to the hearer, unfitting illustrations are equally inappropriate for the communicator.

If an illustration is apt, it's not necessary to announce your intent to illustrate. Though there's nothing inherently wrong in saying, "Let me give you an illustration," it's preferable to swing right into a story unheralded. Never should we begin, "I heard this story the other day, which might or might not possibly illustrate this point. I'd like to pass it on to you, so you can judge if it illustrates or not."

An illustration should need no explanation. A story that needs explaining requires omitting. If you cannot put it clearly to others, likely it's not clear to you.

Don't labor the explanation or application. Sometimes, no comment is necessary. If one is helpful, say it once and briefly. To labor the moral of a story is superfluous. A substitute teacher told several stories to her elementary class, always concluding with, "Now, here's the moral," then proceeded to moralize for several minutes. When the regular teacher returned to class, the students told her, "We like you better than that substitute teacher because you have no morals!"

Some Additional Don'ts

Mixed metaphors make for muddled illustrations. One speaker made this confusing statement, "I smell a rat; I see it floating in the air; I'll nip it in the bud." A seminary student once expressed the wish "that every student might be enabled to sound the gospel trumpet with such clear and certain sound that the blind might see." (He should have said, "that the deaf might hear"!)

Don't tell a story just for the sake of including it in the sermon. Too often a preacher hears a good story during the week which he feels must somehow be included in Sunday morning's message. Usually his attempt leaves much to be desired, like the pastor who at the end of his sermon on the need for soul winning added this exhortation, "We need to get on the ball and win souls." This pseudoslang postscript paved the way for the story he was itching to spring on his unsuspecting flock. He then told of five ants on a golf course, standing near a tee. A learner teed off the ball and took four wild swipes at it, missing the ball completely, though coming dangerously near the ants. Excitedly, one ant said to the others, "If we want to get out of here alive, we'd better get on the ball!" The extraneous story weakened the message.

Nor should a communicator build a talk around an illustration. A lady, scheduled to give a devotional talk at the next women's missionary meeting, heard a wonderful story and decided to arch her message around the illustration. But sensing that the tail should not wag the dog, but the dog the tail, she waited on the Lord to lay his message on her heart, then sought for a fitting illustration. We don't build a mansion to display a stained-glass window, nor do we look for a text to accompany a good anecdote. Illustrations should serve, not shape, the truth.

Seek Variety

If you use illustrations over any substantial length of time, you'll need to draw from various sources. Earlier chapters suggested literature, history, science, psychology, art, newspapers, magazines, and experience. If your audience is composed mainly of scholars, you may want to draw much material from the academic world, using variety, of course. If your hearers are more blue-collar, you may wish to keep your scholarly references to a minimum.

One pastor, who tailored his illustrations to his congregation, commented, "If I have a sailor in my audience, I may select a story from the sea. If a watchmaker is present week by week, I'll use a story from horology. If a teacher is out there, I'll try to find some incident from the field of education."

Just as houses often have different types of windows, so sermons need various forms of illumination. A fanciful suggestion has a regular window typifying the usual, regular-size illustration. The tiny aperture is like the simile or metaphor. The picture window represents the longer, major story. The fancy window makes you think of poetry, while the skylight symbolizes the biblical illustration.

Don't ride a hobbyhorse by always referring to your Holy Land trip, or to your special interest, whether astronomy, poetry, geology, or your own family. A denominational publishing house, in accepting a book manuscript of mine a few years ago, said I had too many references to a well-known nondenominational Bible institute, and asked me to delete a few of them. Unconsciously, I had overloaded the manuscript in this direction.

Don't Use Every Illustration that Occurs to You

As verbosity of speech can tire, so overabundance of illustrations can be wearing. We should not tell any story that comes to mind, but need to make judicious selection, searching, discarding, looking again, removing, then striving to locate the right one. Too many stories makes us entertainers. This fault sometimes happens in addressing children. A mere succession of stories may amuse but fail to instruct.

Windows are not houses. Too many windows and it wouldn't be a house—perhaps a glass house. If a room has plenty of light, and you put in another window, the result may be too much light—and glare.

Too many illustrations weaken a talk. Illustrations are not substitutes for thoughts. Don't let preoccupation with illustrations keep you from analytical thinking and reasoned exposition. The secondary should never squeeze out the substantial. Too many stories may clutter the truth. Flowers are lovely on the dining table, but not so many they leave no room for nourishing food.

How many illustrations should there be in a thirty-minute talk? Perhaps no hard-and-fast rule can be given, but the answer relates to the number of points covered, and the clarity of the material. If a particular point is quite clear, an illustration is a waste of time, perhaps intellectually insulting. Yet since what may be obvious to one may be obscure to another, the quick listener should be patient, realizing that the illustration is for the purpose of giving the slower member time to catch up with the argument.

Where should the illustrations be located? A good distribution would be: in the introduction, at each major point, so that each main proposition may be seen as well as heard, and at the conclusion.

No better way exists to awaken interest at the start of a talk than the use of a story. But remember that the introduction is only the porch, and therefore should be much shorter than the building.

You can use your judgment as to how much light is needed on each major point. Since you spend some time on a major point, a longer story is permissible. At minor points and at transitions, use short, specific instances of a few sentences or a short paragraph. Just as a landing halfway to the second floor needs a window, so minor transitions need little incidents to let in light, so as not to draw attention away from the main point.

Often the most effective way to end a talk is with a story. Many of the great pulpiteers of the past have done so.

At times it may be effective to run a series of short incidents together. One speaker, trying to drive home the absurdity of not practicing what we preach, threw out these examples one after another:

What would you think of an English teacher who said, "Don't say 'ain't.' It ain't right"?

What would you think of a composition teacher who said, "Don't end a sentence with a preposition. 'With' is a bad word to end a sentence with"?

What would you think of a father who, whipping his little boy for swearing, let the whip slip, and he swore too?

What would you think of a salesman for a pen company, who, having lauded the virtues of his pens and made a sale, signed the invoice with a pencil?

Perhaps in such a context a short series in staccato fashion is justifiable. But usually when we are tempted to tack on another sizable illustration, we should resist.

Don't Let the Illustration Overshadow Your Point

A good illustration doesn't call attention to itself but throws light on the truth to be highlighted. Carefully avoid diverting reflection by something strange or too long. The right story strengthens the talk. However, if the incident is weak, the clout is feathery. If the story is too big or bizarre, impact is decreased. A Spanish artist, painting the *Last Supper*, put on the table some silver cups so beautiful they were the first items to attract admiring glances. Noting this, the artist with a few strokes of his brush erased them so that nothing would detract from the face of Jesus.

I learned this lesson the hard way. On vacation from seminary I was speaking to the youth group of my home church. As I came to the climax, I was dramatically picturing the fate of those who had refused the invitation to enter Noah's ark. Graphically I described the falling torrents that rose higher and higher, forcing people to seek the mountains, and emphasizing that these people not many days before had laughed at Noah. Suddenly I exclaimed, "Now their giggles changed to gurgles!" My audience broke into titters. The whole serious train of thought was dissipated.

One preacher took into the pulpit a little box from which he lifted, at the start of his sermon, a small pair of scales. Then turning over the pages of the Bible with great deliberation, he held up the balances and announced his text, "Thou art weighed in the balances, and art found wanting." The effort was more puerile than powerful.

It's possible to turn attention away by giving too long a story. A few times I have concluded a message on "What Is Faith?" with an extended narration of Blondin's feats of tightroping over Niagara Falls back in the mid-nineteenth century. You can see an audience react with amazement to his increasingly difficult antics, turning somersaults, cooking an entire meal on his coal stove on the top and serving it to the Maid-of-the-Mist passengers, crossing with feet chained together, blindfolded, on stilts. But the climactic episode was carrying his manager, Harry Colcord, across on his shoulders. When near the middle, Blondin suddenly stumbled, his balancing pole thrashing the air like a hummingbird's wings. Harry Colcord tells the story:

> I was faint with terror, but responsive to orders. He told me to make myself a dead weight. Trying to regain his equilibrium, Blondin dashed twenty feet to the first guy rope, trusting to his impetus to keep him erect. But the moment he stepped on the rope, it broke, jerking the cable violently sideways. We discovered later that some murderous gambler had deliberately frayed it, thus hoping to win some money. Blondin managed to sprint another twenty feet to the next guy rope. There to my horror, he shouted to me to get off quick. Just think of the situation—getting off a man's back, feeling with your feet for a vibrating rope, and holding to his slippery tights, and then repeating it seven times. By and by, we toiled up the American side. Excited men had tears streaming down their cheeks. A band was trying to play, but the wrought-up musicians could make only discordant notes. Cheers rose louder than Niagara. Everybody went into a frenzy. The journey, which was an age to me, occupied forty-five minutes.

The point of the story, of course, is the faith of Harry Colcord in trusting himself to Blondin to carry him over. I would then tell the anecdote (who can prove it?) of the little boy Blondin approached one day with the question, "Do you think I could carry you over on my back?" The boy who had seen most of Blondin's great feats answered immediately, "Sure, you could." When Blondin replied, "Hop on, then, and I'll take you over," the little boy did exactly what most of us would have done. He disappeared in the crowd as fast as he could. The boy's faith was deficient, for he wasn't willing to commit himself to Blondin.

However, I question my own use of the story. In the first place, it takes over eight minutes to relate in full. And in the second place, it grabs an audience's interest so strongly that the point of the story seems to pale into insignificance.

The best illustrations are those which are not so much meant to be seen, as to be seen through.

10

Keep Them Fresh

Speaking on the indestructability of the Bible, a Christian Service Brigade ranger thought he would conclude the story-time period with a poem about a blacksmith's shop, which ends:

> And so, thought I,
> The anvil of God's word
> For ages skeptic blows have beat upon,
> And though the sound of falling blows is heard,
> The anvil is untouched, the hammers gone.

It suddenly dawned on the ranger that probably most of the boys in his battalion had never seen a blacksmith's shop nor an anvil. Realizing that the imagery, though forceful and accurate, would be lost on them, he wisely omitted the poem.

Beware of Stale Stories

Illustrations pack more wallop if contemporary, relevant, and fresh. Admittedly, some top-notch stories seem timeless, coming from history, art, literature, and the Bible. On the other hand, many become musty and stale (perhaps some in this book!). How often have you heard this one, used to instill confidence in the sovereignty of the heavenly Father even in dark days:

> A ship was passing slowly through dense fog. Most passengers seemed apprehensive as they stood on deck, straining their eyes to see what was ahead, hoping they wouldn't collide with another boat, or run aground on shoals. But one little boy seemed unperturbed. Asked why he was so calm, he replied, with great assurance, "The pilot of the ship up on the bridge is my father!"

A pastor untruthfully adapted a story from an earlier source:

> When I was walking down the main street of our business section the other day, I met one of my adherents who was intoxicated.
> "Don't you know me, preacher?" the inebriated man said. "I'm one of your converts!"

Not only is it wrong to palm off fiction as fact, but this anecdote has been attributed to many preachers through the years including William Biederwolf, Spurgeon, and Moody. Worn, threadbare stories belong in the ragbag. A story may sound interesting the first time we hear it. The second time we may still like it, but not as much. The third time we couldn't care less if we never heard it again. Next time we can tell from the very first sentence it's the same old story!

Be Current

We should seek to be up-to-date. The National Religious Broadcasters opened their 1983 convention in the nation's capital the evening the Washington Redskins won the Super Bowl. That night pandemonium broke loose in the streets of Washington. Groups of young people ran excitedly through the lobby of the convention hotel. The following Wednesday, the last day of the NRB convention, thousands of the team's fans braved a pouring rain to welcome the champion players in a victory parade. One of the broadcasters, speaking in his home pulpit the following Sunday on the need for enthusiastic dedication in the Lord's work, alluded to the wild fanaticism of the Washington zealots.

A men's breakfast speaker, fresh from a visit to Disney World's new Epcot Centre in Florida, referred to the exhibit "Imagination." Citing some of the interesting items, he reminded the men of the power of imagination and of the need to get victory in the mind.

A college dean of women, often approached by senior women for counsel on their forthcoming marriage, noticed an AP newspaper article which she immediately clipped out. In essence, it told of a lady psychologist in California who conducted workshops to help women having extramarital affairs not to feel guilty. The dean, a Christian, used this up-to-date item as a jumping off spot to counteract such a philosophy.

Most publishers advise would-be writers to use current anecdotes in material they submit.

Literally, an anecdote is an unpublished item. But the word has come to mean a short narrative of an interesting, amusing, or biographical incident. Many do not appear in any history book or other source, so are unverifiable. The following is anecdotal:

> When the *Titanic* was going down, people were grabbing their jewels and heading for the lifeboats. One lady went back to her stateroom, saw her diamonds, but left them while she took three oranges instead.

Care must be exercised so as to tell anecdotes without exaggeration or embellishment, and with the admission of possible nonfactuality.

Get Your Facts Straight

A well-circulated story concerns the favorite hymn, "O Love That Wilt Not Let Me Go." The story goes:

> A young man, George Matheson, fell in love with a girl. But when he began to go blind, she broke the engagement. Then it was that he wrote the hymn of God's unfailing love.

The facts are: he became blind at fifteen, wrote the hymn at forty out of a difficult experience, different from the alleged tale above.

Be sure of your facts. One night a speaker, referring to a book, casually mentioned that its author had died recently. Whereupon someone exclaimed from his seat, "Oh, my, you mean that he died over the weekend? I heard him lecture last week!" The speaker was quite embarrassed.

A California preacher, criticizing the book *"I'm OK—You're OK,"* proceeded to tell his audience that the author had committed suicide about two years ago. The author sued the preacher on the basis that he was okay—not dead. Though the preacher told the court his source was a tape from another preacher who, in turn, said he got it from still another preacher's recording, who got it from a friend he had bumped into at the Atlanta airport, the court awarded the author $150,000 in damages.

One speaker followed this principle—if he had the slightest suspicion about the truth of a story, he would not touch it with a ten-foot pole. On the other hand, another speaker, using a dubious incident, would preface it, "I cannot vouch for the veracity of this story."

How easy for stories to grow up without factual foundation, then gain credence through constant repetition. Who hasn't heard the popular explanation of Jesus' statement, "It is easier for a camel to go through the eye of a needle, than for a rich man to enter into the kingdom of God?" Purportedly, so goes the explanation, one of the gates in Jerusalem was known as the "Needle's Eye," which camels could go through only by kneeling, and with great difficulty. This interpretation makes the point that a camel could have gone through the "Needle's Eye."

The trouble with this explanation is that it is simply not true. There never was such a gate in Jerusalem at any time in its history. The earliest mention of that explanation is found in the eleventh century in a commentary by a Greek churchman, Theophylact, who had the same difficulty with the text that we do. The truth is that it is impossible for any camel to go through the eye of a needle. This is exactly the point Jesus was making—and with hyperbole— it is impossible for anyone who trusts in riches to enter the kingdom. Since it would take a miracle for this to happen, Jesus follows with "All things are possible with God."

In earlier generations the preacher was the best informed person in the locality. Today a good percentage of most congregations are college-bred and well informed. Facing such educated audiences, speakers better have their facts straight.

When we talk about matters in which people are well versed, we must know whereof we speak. Speakers should not be guilty of inaccuracies in their illustrations. If you have a sailor in the crowd, don't get starboard and port sides confused. I once gave a scientific formula incorrectly. I was thankful when a scientist put me straight the minute the meeting finished.

Another time in an illustration I referred to Teddy Roosevelt's sudden falling in love with Anne Hathaway. A lady made a beeline in my direction after the benediction to rightly inform me that Anne Hathaway was Shakespeare's wife. It was *Alice* Hathaway Lee whom Roosevelt married. Knowledgeable people who hear a speaker make a factual error in an illustration will wonder, "If that speaker doesn't have his facts straight about earthly items, can I trust him when he talks of eternal matters?"

It often takes only a phone call or letter to check a story. I recall a report I heard for many years which said that the famous *Chicago Tribune* cartoonist, Vaughn Shoemaker, had a cartoon all ready for the day when the rapture would occur, depicting the sudden catching up of believers at the coming of Christ. After using the story myself a few times, I decided to write Shoemaker about its accuracy. He wrote back a gracious letter, informing me that no such cartoon had ever been drawn, and that he would appreciate anything I could do to squelch this rumor. Naturally, I dropped this story from my repertoire.

Someone once mentioned to me that Harry Emerson Fosdick, noted liberal pastor of Riverside Church, had been a student at Moody Bible Institute for a short time. I thought this would make a good illustration of the possibility of someone receiving evangelical training, and then departing from it. So I wrote Dr. George Sweeting, president of Moody Bible Institute, who kindly replied that a search of the Institute's records indicated Fosdick had never been a Moody student.

Some years ago several churches cooperated in a town-wide evangelistic crusade led by a man who said he was an Indian, an Indian chief, and the last living chief of the Sioux. He made other claims including being a graduate of National Bible Institute, a singer at the Metropolitan Opera, the recipient of an honorary doctor's degree from Friends College in Kansas, a broadcaster over

all major radio networks, and a U.S intelligence agent in both
theaters of World War II. This evangelist spoke at many of our
leading Bible conferences and churches. As I interviewed him for
an article for a Christian magazine, I noted that many of his experi-
ences would make good sermonic illustrations.

But a preacher friend with a more jaundiced view suggested I
check some of his claims. The results were surprising. Friends
College had never heard of him, nor had the Metropolitan Opera,
nor the radio networks. National Bible Institute said that he had
been a student there but had been expelled. The Indian Bureau in
Washington had been investigating him for over ten years. When I
sent him a copy of all these letters, he replied that if he had known
I was going to investigate his claims he would have given me all his
aliases. Then I noticed he had penned "Matt. 28:17" by his signature. Turning to the verse, I saw that he was calling me a skeptic.
It read, "And when they saw Him [the risen Christ], they wor-
shipped him; but some doubted."

I then submitted all my correspondence to the editor, Robert
Walker of *Christian Life,* for whom I was writing the article. He
asked the chief to visit the editorial offices on his next trip to that
area. He came and insisted all his claims were true. A few weeks
later, however he returned to the office and broke down in tears,
admitting most of his statements were false. The editor insisted he
refrain in the future from making such claims on threat of ex-
posure. There went not only my article but also all the excellent
illustrations contained in the story. (But I do have an excellent
story to illustrate the need to check out facts!)

Don't Reveal Confidences

Just as doctors, psychiatrists, psychologists, and counselors do
not divulge secrets told them in confidence, so no Christian leader
or layperson should relate private conversations held with fellow
believers, either recently or distantly. Especially should pastors not
betray confidences, because that will make members hesitate to
come for help for fear they'll hear their story in next Sunday's
sermon.

On the other hand, a conversation can be so generalized that no
one can say, "I know who he's talking about!" With sufficient
safeguards a counselor can sift from private conversations a

healthy amount of usable, anonymous material. For example, a pastor can say, "From time to time people come to me, lacking in assurance of their salvation." Adequately disguised, the event will not lead people to try to guess who.

Too Much "I"

Not only should we avoid telling tales out of school, but we should also beware lest we come across as bragging. We do this by making ourself the hero who has every prayer answered gloriously, who wins every prospect to Christ, who never has a failure, who never worries nor suffers depression. Coming across as Superman lessens our credulity. Nor should we be guilty of namedropping, such as "Last week I was talking with Astronaut James Irwin, the eighth man to walk on the moon. Later I was chatting with Chuck Colson, former presidential hatchetman who now has a wonderful prison ministry." It's wise to periodically make ourself the fall guy or dumb-dumb in a story.

Watch out for stories that call more attention to the speaker than to his subject.

And what about humor? Are there some safeguards in that area?

11

It's Not Funny, My Friend

A deacon was studying passengers as they came off a plane, trying to pick out the visiting preacher he was to entertain, but whom he had never seen. Selecting a likely looking fellow, he asked, "Pardon me, but are you a minister?"

"No," came the curt reply, "it's my indigestion that makes me look like this!"

People are prone to associate the sunny, smiling face with the shallow, superficial disposition, and to link up the sad countenance with deep piety. Laughter is considered a satanic instrument and melancholy a divine characteristic. Humor need not be surreptitiously sneaked in the backdoor of the Christian life, but has its legitimate place even in illustrations used in church meetings.

Gift of God

God created man to enjoy humor. Of all creatures in the world only man can laugh. Moreover, God has given man an environment with a touch of the comical. Who isn't amused by the long neck of the giraffe, the built-in baby buggy of the kangaroo, the vacuum-cleaner mouth of the anteater, the delicate legs of the flamingo, the antics of the monkey, the squeaky phrases of the parrot, the revolving head of the praying mantis, or the wild chuck-wallas which when frightened actually inflate themselves like balloons to scare their enemies? Lincoln reportedly said, "God must have meant us to laugh, else he wouldn't have made so many mules, parrots, monkeys, apes, and human beings."

Moreover, the Bible contains lots of humor. Dr. A. T. Pierson in *Knowing the Scriptures*, has a chapter "The Humorous Element in Scripture," claiming that almost every type of humor was used by prophets, apostles, and even by our Lord himself to expose error and reflect truth. Jesus told of a man with a tree trunk protruding from his eye who was criticizing another man for the little sliver in his eye. He also spoke of straining out a tiny insect from your beverage, then proceeding to drink from your cup into which a camel has stepped, swallowing the camel, humps and all. He also spoke of a fellow trying to patch his trousers with the wrong kind of material, which meant that when a little pressure was later exerted, the patch would rip away, leaving him embarrassingly exposed.

A Christian musician doesn't give up the use of the note *C*. Nor does the Christian poet refrain from using the letter *M*. Nor does the Christian mathematician stop employing the number 5. Why should a Christian communicator surrender the faculty of humor?

A Teaching Device

Humor can be a teaching device, clarifying, illustrating, objectifying.

> A farmer whose barns were full of corn used to pray that the poor be supplied, but when anyone in need asked for corn he said he had none to spare. One day after hearing his father pray for the needy, his little son said, "Father, I wish I had your corn."
> "What would you do with it?" asked the father.
> The child replied, "I would answer your prayer."

Humor wrapped in the barb of an anecdote not only makes truth plainer but more palatable. Erasmus pointed out that the greatest minds of classical antiquity wrote humorously on topics because they knew that readers would reap more advantages from such treatment. Humor is like the sugarcoating of a healthful pill. Many a truth is spoken in jest. Someone said, "In proper place nonsense may be sense." One communicator said, "When I get people laughing with a well-placed joke, I pour a dose of truth into their mouths."

A speaker at a senior citizens' club gained rapport with his audience when he began, "There are many advantages to growing old." Pausing three seconds, he added, "Right now I can't think of any."

Relieving Tension

At an organization's annual banquet which began at 6:30 P.M., due to a lengthy program beyond his control, the emcee was unable to introduce the guest speaker until 10:10 P.M. This is how the speaker began:

> I'm reminded of Sir Winston Churchill who at a banquet was given the floor for his speech very late in the evening. He said, "I have been asked to give a short address. Here it is: 'Number 10 Downing Street,' and I'm going there right now!"

Though the hour was late, the laughter that greeted the story seemed to put everyone at ease.

A humorous story at a well-chosen spot can recapture attention that so easily flags after brief concentration on a subject. Also, if a topic is deeply emotional, interjection of a humorous anecdote can untie emotional knots and give relief from sustained tension. In the old-fashioned melodrama the overwrought feelings of the spectators were relaxed by the entrance of the comic man. Ready for tears, the audience burst into the respite of laughter. Lincoln once said, "If I didn't laugh with the strain on me night and day, I should go mad." In our hectic age few prescriptions are as inexpensive and as potent as the wonder drug of laughter. Your flashes of wit, whether from podium, in classroom or in private conversation, may make life more bearable for others who labor under great anxiety.

The chairman of a church board at the end of a difficult meeting in which some sharp disagreement and acrimonious debate had occurred, called for a vote on a matter then on the floor, which was noncontroversial. After a unanimous affirmative vote was taken, he remarked, "That vote is very much like the human face, 'The ayes [eyes] are above the nos [nose].'" The laughter at this pun sent the men out in good humor.

The chairman of a stewardship committee found humor a way to make the subject of money less unpleasant to an audience. He began his five-minute financial report to the church one Sunday morning, "The most sensitive nerve in the human body is the one that leads to the pocketbook." When he wrote his annual stewardship letter to the congregation, he included this anecdote concerning a man who needed convincing in the matter of tithing:

> I had a horrible dream. The Lord took my regular Sunday offering and multiplied it by ten; and that became my weekly income. In no time I lost my color TV—had to give up my new car—couldn't make my house payment. After all, what can a fellow do on ten dollars a week?

Humor should be limited to proper times and topics. It should always be clean, never suggestive, and used with caution.

Don't Be Unkind

Humor should be mild, never injurious. Pleasantries are all right; "meaneries" all wrong. Kindness, an element of genuine humor, keeps communicators from capitalizing on others' handicaps, appearances, names, or misfortunes. Mercy, not malice, must manipulate the scalpel of laughter. Racial jokes have long since gone out of style.

Make yourself, not others, the butt of your jokes. Said a preacher, "I've been called *Neverend* instead of *Reverend*. He added, "My sermons aren't long; they just seem that way!"

Keep in mind these don'ts:

1. *Don't announce humor in advance.*

Don't inform your audience that you are about to tell a humorous story. Let *them* decide if it's funny. They may ask in bewilderment, "What was so funny about that?"

2. *Don't overdo it.*

If humor comes naturally, do not stifle it, for all of God's faculties have been given for his service. Though it has its place in the pulpit, humor can be overdone. The spirit of a service can evaporate if a speaker mistakes himself for a clown in a circus operating on a "laugh-a-minute or your-money-back" offer. Levity, where gravity should prevail, is wrong.

3. *Don't use humor just to be funny.*

If you make people laugh just to court favor, entertain, show your power over an audience, or display your cleverness, it is out of place, even bordering on the sacrilegious.

Humor should be purposeful not pointless. One speaker confessed that more than once he has confused people by telling them something funny in the midst of a serious point, and getting them off track. A serious illustration would have been much wiser. If it's not your nature to be humorous, use humor sparingly.

4. *Don't be coarse, vulgar or sacrilegious.*

Humor must be reverent. Serious truths should not be joked about, such as hell, the Spirit, or "Peter at the pearly gates." By doing so, we dull the solemn edge of these truths for those who hear our flippant treatment.

We now turn back from the area of humorous stories to stories in general.

Beware Lest Illustrations Become Overdrawn or Rambling

A lady giving devotions at her missionary society began:

> Now let me tell you a story about a boat. Now you all know what a boat is. It is what we sail on when we want to cross a lake.

Or a man teaching his class of junior boys:

I met my neighbor on the street this week. He lives two doors from me, and likes to jog. I've gotten to know him quite well. He likes to read C.S. Lewis as I do. But his daughters like sports better than reading. They play on the high school team. They have a younger brother who plays Little League baseball. Their grandmother passed away last week suddenly. She hadn't had a sick day in years. Well, anyhow, I met my neighbor on the street this week.

We should not waste time getting into a story, but dive right in, and when finished, climb right out. There is no need to over-explain, comment, apologize, or editorialize. After a terse start, we should proceed in a concise manner, eliminating excessive words. Instead of saying, "He tendered his resignation," say, "He resigned." Instead of "He spoke in most disparaging terms about agnostic beliefs," say, "He denounced agnosticism." We should choose words that are fresh, forceful, and colorful.

A good story has a beginning that arouses interest; does not dawdle but moves with action, omitting irrelevant parts; has crisis or conflict, then reaches a climax and resolution. If the incident is not to the point, no one will get it. Jesus' parables are masterpieces of the short-story form. With few and unwasted words, simple style, and down-to-earth setting, his stories move with vitality and speed, and so are apt to the point he is making.

Since many illustrations are in public domain, it may not be necessary to give credit. But where credit is due, it should be introduced as inconspicuously as possible to avoid distraction. Even scholarly articles place credits at the bottom of the page or at the end of the book, so that the flow of thought will not be interrupted. In my radio messages I do not give my sources unless necessary, but the written copy, offered to the public, often credits the sources. Even when you do not include credits in your talk, it is wise to have the documentation in your own notes. In other words, when you come across an illustration, make a note on it of its source, like "*Psychology Today*, June 1983, p. 24."

Learn the Illustration Thoroughly

When a speaker was introduced at a banquet as a businessman who had made twenty-five thousand dollars in potatoes in Maine, he replied, "That is only approximately correct. It was not in Maine; it was in Texas. It was not in potatoes; it was in oil. It was not twenty-five thousand dollars, it was two-hundred and fifty thousand. I didn't make it; I lost it. And it wasn't me; it was my brother."

It's not enough to select the right illustration; you need to deliver it well. This requires mastering it thoroughly, entering into it feelingly, and reciting it aloud several times until you can repeat it without hesitation. If you can mimic the dialogue, or use brogue or accent, so much in your favor as a storyteller. If it's a short poem, it's best to memorize it. If very lengthy, read it over several times to familiarize yourself with it.

Who likes to hear a speaker say:

On Thursday; no, it was Wednesday; or was it Friday; well, it must have been one of the days late in the week.

Or:

A college senior whose name was Jean; I mean Joan; perhaps it was June; was working in Washington last February; no, it was Orlando in March.

Who likes to hear a speaker muff a story:

A man who had to emcee church banquets now and again heard a joke in the form of a riddle, "Why is a man's head like a typewriter?" Answer: "Because it's UNDERWOOD."

Presiding at the next church dinner, he said, "I've got a riddle for you," then repeated, "Why is a man's head like a typewriter?" After he paused, he gave this answer, "Because it's REMINGTON." He couldn't understand why no one laughed.

When a speaker hems and haws in giving his illustrations, his audience will likely tread on his heels. An audience stumbles when they think more quickly than the speaker, so, master your stories well.

When you have gathered valuable illustrations from a wide variety of sources, planning to use them wisely, what do you do with them?

What to Do with Them?— Their Filing

12

How to Handle Them
When You Find Them

A Christian businessman, who began to receive some invitations to speak at church affairs around the city, thought it time to do something about the illustrations he gathered from here and there. One day he heard a story about a factory worker that he thought would fit somewhere in a talk he was scheduled to give to a nearby youth group. So on a piece of scrap paper he wrote down the words *factory story*, and stuck it just inside the cover of his Bible. When it came time to finalize the youth message, he remembered the slip of paper inside his Bible, but despite his mental effort, he could not remember the incident designated by the "factory story."

The businessman was to be commended for writing down something for future use, even though he failed to capitalize on his two-word jotting. But what *should* he do with illustrations both to conserve them, and make them retrievable on demand?

Always Be Collecting

On vacation one July morning I wondered what the weather would be like for a scheduled swim later in the afternoon. Turning on the TV I heard three local weather reports within the space of three minutes over ABC, NBC, and CBS affiliates. One said, "Showers today." The second, "Cloudy." And the third, "Sunny, hot, and humid." Which of the three turned out to be correct? All three! The day began sunny, hot, and humid. Then it turned cloudy. Then showers fell. Then the sun came out again for a hot, humid late afternoon. How could I use this? I incorporated it a few Sundays later in a sermon on the omniscience of God to illustrate that only he knows the future.

We should develop the "illustration" mentality, or the "window" mind. Always be on the outlook for illustrative stuff. Just as you keep making deposits in your savings account, so keep storing up anecdotes in your message files. Keep your anecdotal antennae up, ever ready to pull in potential material. Though encyclopedias of illustrations exist that contain many splendid stories, it's more gratifying to garner your own. Many communicators make it a point to get four or five every day.

Jot It Down

Record it immediately. And write it in sufficient detail else you'll have another useless "factory story" on your hands. Unless we jot down enough of the facts, we'll likely not have the foggiest idea what those two or three key words mean, even a few hours later, much less three months after. Illustrations are fleeting, so our overtaxed memories will require full notation, lest these nuggets slip away.

For over thirty years I have carried a small notebook in my jacket inside pocket, plus pen. I am rarely without it during waking hours. The minute an illustration comes to mind, out comes the notebook and down goes the scribbling. Recently I heard someone say, "The man who seeks revenge should dig two graves." Immediately I jotted this proverb down, knowing that soon I would be speaking on resentment.

For many years I've kept a pad and flashlight pen on my headboard. Some keep a small recorder by their bedside as well, and also use it all day in place of a notebook.

In the context of this book, illustrations come in a wide range of types, including such items as quotes and statistics. Hence, we'll always need immediately available some means to capture valuable items.

File It

What do you do with illustrations once you've jotted them down? You must put them somewhere. Unless you have a photographic mind, you'll need a system. Some people throw them in a box, but as the illustrations pile up, how would you ever locate what you wanted? Some paste them in a book, but unless they are cataloged and indexed, you would have to look all through the notebook every time you needed one. Someone suggested that a book with illustrations haphazardly pasted in is no better than a bin!

Some communicators use envelopes into which they file illustrations, writing the topic on the outside. Some recommend the use of a computer to store their anecdotal material. Some use the Dewey Decimal System, used by libraries in cataloging, whereas others utilize some of the excellent filing systems available on the market. The system you use isn't as important as the fact that you use *some* system. Use the one that suits your personality and work methods. You need one that is simple, compact, and enables you to file with the least consumption of time and difficulty of retrievability.

We must beware of too complicated a system that keeps us from more important matters. A supersalesman sold an incredibly efficient filing system to a business concern. The salesman stopped by six months later to ask, "How is the system working?"

"Beyond our wildest dream," came the answer.

"And how's business?" the salesman asked.

Came the answer, "Oh, we had to give up our business in order to run the filing system!"

We must make sure we are masters over our filing system, and not our systems master over us.

Three Major Files

I have three major file drawers: SEASONAL, TEXTUAL and TOPICAL.

Seasonal. Here I have folders for all the main holidays and religious seasons of the year. I keep these in chronological order: New Year's, Lincoln, Washington, Saint Patrick, Passion of Christ (including Lent and the events leading up to the cross), Easter, Mother's Day, Memorial Day, Children's Day, Father's Day, Independence Day, Labor Day, Reformation Sunday, Thanksgiving, Universal Bible Sunday, and Christmas.

In an earlier chapter I referred to some interesting material on Lincoln. Those illustrations I filed under LINCOLN.

In my reading I came across this story, told by G. K. Chesterton:

> A young Oxford tutor who had adopted the pessimism of Schopenhauer, frequently complained in his lectures of his dreary house and the silly duck pond that was his main view from his second-floor rooming-house window. Also, in his teaching, he remarked on the meaninglessness of existence, concluding that the only sane course of action for intelligent people would be to get out of this world completely. A strongly built student, given to the practical, decided the time had come to put the tutor's thesis to the test. So one evening he knocked on his tutor's door, pointed a revolver at him, declaring he had come to put the tutor out of his empty existence. The tutor, absolutely terrified, suddenly losing his philosophy, and begging for his life, climbed out his window onto a flagpole, hoping to attract some passerby. The student, sitting on the windowsill and brandishing his revolver, made the tutor, perched precariously on the flagpole, recant his pessimism. He forced him to give thanks for his dreary life, the stars, and even the silly duck pond. In full surrender the weary tutor climbed back to freedom, hopefully to do less complaining than before.

I filed this incident in my THANKSGIVING folder, and used it later in a Thanksgiving meditation.

Textual. The second of my major file sections is the textual or biblical drawer. I have a folder for every small Old Testament book, and several folders for the longer books. Only for Genesis do I have a folder for every chapter.

For the New Testament I have a folder for every chapter from Acts to Revelation. Any illustration that alluded to the story of the Philippian jail would be filed under Acts 16.

I handle the four gospels differently. For Matthew, Mark, Luke, and John I follow Robertson's *Harmony of the Gospels* with his chronological breakdown into 184 sections. This enables me to file in one place all material on any event recorded in more than one gospel. For example, if I didn't use this system, where would I file anecdotes dealing with the feeding of the five thousand that occurs in all four gospels? Robertson's *Harmony* places all four accounts in section #72, so this is where I drop it. Instead of filing in and retrieving from four different locations, all the illustrations relative to the five thousand are in one place.

Topical. My third major section is the topical drawer. Material is filed alphabetically by subject matter. Under *A* are several topics like Abortion, Alcohol, Ambition, Angels, Anger, Anxiety, and so forth. Altogether I have about three hundred topics. Years ago when I began, I made folders as I found illustrations for a particular topic. Then as I progressively accumulated more illustrations through the years, the number of folders grew proportionately. New ones were added as needed. The Abortion folder has been there only the last few years. This gradual approach to building up your files according to interest and need may be better than setting up in advance a whole series of folders for 300 topics.

You Have To Make a Judgment

When I come across an illustration in a book that I wish to keep, I figure out where it should be filed. If it best fits just one category, whether seasonal, textual, or topical, I ask my secretary to Xerox a copy of that page or pages. Then I file it in the proper folder. If I think the anecdote fits two of the categories, I ask for two copies. If it seems to fit all three categories, I ask for three copies. As I understand it, copyright laws permit copying for personal, private use.

Coming across the following story, I knew I wanted to file it, but where?

An elderly mother was bedridden with her final illnesses. Her three married children, two sons and a daughter, were called to her bedside. Conscious but weak, the mother smiled weakly at their presence. One of the sons bent over, "You've been a good mother." With a sigh the mother whispered, "Do you mean that?" "Of course

you have," all three children joined in. The mother's voice came
again, very faintly. "I didn't know. You never said it before, and I
didn't know."

Thinking how sad that a mother could live out her life before
hearing a word of appreciation from her children, I decided to file
this story in the seasonal section under "Thanksgiving." I decided
also to place it in the textual section under Ephesians 6 where in
verse 2 it speaks of children honoring parents.

If one wished to do a lot of cross-filing, the above story could
also be placed in the season section under MOTHER'S DAY and
CHILDREN'S DAY. It could also go in the topical drawer under
DECALOGUE—TEN COMMANDMENTS. You have to make the judgment as to where you want to put it.

I follow the same procedure with items from newspapers and
magazines. I do not keep my magazines to pile up on some shelf,
but read them within days of arrival, then dispose of them after
clipping out what I wish. The clippings I file as described above. If I
wish to file the story in more than one place, I have the clipping
copied in the desired number.

For example, an article in *Psychology Today* (December 1983) is
headed, "Soft Words Speak Louder with Kids." In essence, it says
that according to experiments, children respond to commands
from adults made in a soft voice without much hesitation. I filed
this in the textual section under Proverbs. It fits "A soft answer
turneth away wrath . . ." (15:1).

Often my future sermon planning will determine where an anecdote is filed. When anticipating an expository series on Colossians a year ago, I read through Colossians several times to get
familiar with the topics handled. Some were: the preeminence of
Christ, thanksgiving, prayer, fruitfulness, reconciliation, anger,
malice, covetousness, kindness, meekness, long-suffering, satura-
tion with the word of God, singing psalms, hymns, and spiritual
songs, forgiveness, wives, husbands, children, parents, servants,
master, to name many. In my reading the next few months, whenever I came across any illustration that related to any of those
subjects, I filed it under the textual section, in the proper Colossians folder, whether chapter 1, 2, 3, or 4.

If I plan to devote an entire series to some particular topic like
worship, the gifts of the Spirit, envy, money, time, the tongue, I will

start months ahead reaching up my illustration antenna to detect stories that I would have otherwise missed, had not my mind been conditioned in that direction.

Start Now

Someone said, "The only way to get a good illustration for a talk or article is to begin ten years ago." If we have not been gathering illustrations before, we should begin now. And we should be constantly and everlastingly at it. If we can accumulate an abundant store of illustrations, then out of quantity we can select quality.

A master preacher of an earlier generation, Dr. W. B. Riley, said that the "gathering of material constitutes your accumulated fortune. It is exactly as the laying aside of money for the day of need. The savings account comes in handy when there is a crisis, or an unusual call. You will be surprised, as you go on in your ministry, to find how often you will draw on these past years, and how richly they will supply you with incident and illustration, born of experience and observation" (*Pastoral Problems*, Revell, 1936, p. 38, 39).

Illustrations stored for ready withdrawal, will make us richer communicators of the Word.

Appendix

Still More Illustrations—
A Categorical Listing

In addition to the illustrations in the first section of this book, this Appendix contains many more stories and anecdotes, listed alphabetically under various categories.

The categories are quite often general, so the reader may have to discover the particular aspect of the category to which the illustration applies, which in most cases will not be difficult.

Also the reader may find that the illustration just as aptly fits some other area of truth, and may wish to classify it under some different but related topic.

This collection of illustrations, some of which go back in time and history, is a partial listing, not an exhaustive one. It is intended to arouse interest in the discipline and practice of finding, classifying, and using illustrations.

Even though the original source of most of these stories cannot be traced and credited, gratitude is nevertheless expressed to all the unknown original authors.

Adversity

⦿ An apple farmer in Michigan, pruning his orchard, made a big pile of branches away from all his buildings. One morning he noted a bird with its beak full of materials, starting to make a nest in that heap of prunings. Returning that way at

113

sundown, he reached into the pile and tore the nest apart. The bird flew around, chirping wildly, as if to say, "You cruel man!"

The next day the farmer saw the bird again trying to build a nest at another place but in the same pile. Again that night he destroyed all the labor the bird had expended. The bird's wild flutterings and chirpings seemed to say, "How terrible you are to destroy my nest!"

The third day the farmer noticed that the bird was building in a rose bush quite a distance from the pile of prunings. Smiling, he let the bird alone. The nest was finished, and eggs were laid, but before the birds could leave the nest, all the branches in that pile where the bird had twice tried to build had been burned. The farmer who planned to burn that pile knew that if the bird were allowed to build there, the nest and its little fledglings would have been destroyed. Kindness motivated the farmer to tear the two earlier nests apart.

o When Winston Churchill lost the election of 1946 in Britain, his wife said to him, "It might be a blessing in disguise."

He replied, "If it's a blessing, it's well disguised."

o The president of a Christian college was seated in his office when a brokenhearted father, who had recently lost his only son in a tragic accident, pushed open the door, and in anguish asked, "Where was God when my son's life was snuffed out?"

The president, in a moment of inspiration, replied, "Right where he was when he gave up his own Son."

Alcohol

o William Jennings Bryan, on a visit to Japan, attended a banquet in honor of a Japanese admiral. To drink a toast the guests lifted their champagne glasses, but the American raised a glass of water. As guests gasped, someone grabbed the statesman's arm and whispered that such a toast was considered an insult. Equal to the situation, the American replied, turning to the admiral, "You have won victories on the water, so I drink your health in water. Whenever you win on champagne, I shall drink your health in champagne."

o In 1841 a thirty-three-year-old Englishman was walking to a temperance meeting some fifteen miles away. He read a newspaper account of plans to open a railroad line in the same direction and reasoned that perhaps the railroad could be enticed to give reduced fares for groups of people who planned to travel together to the same destination. The outcome was a special round-trip fare for the normal one-way rate. The man's name was Thomas Cook who, virtually uncontested, remained the only travel agency of any size for the next fifty years. Though Cook began as a temperance leader, not a travel agent, cynics might have assumed that the prosperity of his business would have weakened his primary interest—temperance. But during his half-century in business, almost all of his earnings went to combat intemperance.

Anger

o A Sunday-school teacher asked the meaning of "righteous indignation." Little Jeremy replied, "Being mad without swearing."

● An oil executive was irritated by his wife at the breakfast table in their New Jersey home. When he arrived at his New York office he laid down the law to workers there. One of the office staff passed on his exasperation in a cable to a ship's captain in a Japanese harbor. He in turn passed it on to some of his sailors, who on shore later that afternoon acted with ill will toward the Japanese they met. In five hours the lost temper at the breakfast table had gone half-way around the world.

Antisemitism

o During the persecution of the Jews in Nazi Germany some Jews began going to church on Sundays. The Nazis sent orders to ask them to leave. So in the middle of a service a pastor asked the folks to bow their heads, and all who had Jewish fathers to leave. There was some rustling. Then he asked all who had Jewish mothers to leave. There was more noise. When the congregation looked up, the form on the cross was gone.

Assurance

✗● When the Golden Gate bridge was constructed, it was then the longest, highest, widest, costliest bridge in the world. Because of the danger, work proceeded behind schedule. Then someone hit on a brilliant idea. Why not build a net under the construction area? Then, if any workman fell, he would not tumble to his death, but would land in the net and thus be saved. So a giant safety net of stout cord was made and swung under the construction work, the first time in history of major construction that such a net had been used. This safety net reportedly cost around one hundred thousand dollars. Because the workmen knew that if they did slip, they would not fall to their death, the work then proceeded at a much faster rate.

o When Dr. J. Wilbur Chapman was a student for the ministry at Lake Forest University, Illinois, he heard the famous evangelist D. L. Moody speak. Charmed by Moody's simple presentation, Chapman followed him from one service to another. Finally one day he told Moody that he didn't have assurance of salvation. Though he was studying for the ministry, one day he was sure he would be in heaven, then the next day was in despair for he did not know for sure if he were saved.

Moody pointed him to the verse, "He that believeth on the Son shall not come into condemnation" (see John 5:24). Moody asked, "Do you believe on the Son?"

"Yes," replied the young student.

"Will you come into condemnation?"

"That's what I don't know for sure. That's why I've come to see you," answered the young man.

Then D. L. Moody said in his firm way of dealing with people, "See here, young man, whom are you doubting?"

In a flash it dawned on young Chapman that he was doubting none other than the Lord Jesus Christ, whose word is truth and cannot be broken. That was the beginning of better days for young Chapman. He never doubted his salvation from that day on, and became an evangelist known the world over.

o A newcomer to Alaska came to a wide river that he wished to cross. Stepping gingerly on the ice, he thought he heard the ice cracking. To distribute his weight over a wider ice surface he gently lowered himself on his knees and began painfully to inch his way across the river on all fours. After twenty minutes of painful crawling, just a hundred yards from the other shore, he heard the hum of a motor. Then he caught sight of a jeep coming across the river from the opposite shore. In a few moments it had sped past him to the shore from which he had started. The timid traveler leaped to his feet and walked the rest of the way with normal gait.

Atheism

● An atheist wrote on a blackboard, "God is nowhere." A little later when he returned to the room, a little child with one stroke of a brush made it read, "God is now here."

o A quarrelsome atheist was filling the train compartment with his profane language. "God! God!" he shouted. "There isn't any such being as a God!"

"That's curious," observed a quiet man in the compartment. "I happen to know Him." After a pause he added, to the atheist, "More curious still, you happen to hate him!"

o A God-fearing astronomer once made a small planetarium, then invited an atheist friend to see it. The little machine represented the various planets of the solar system in their orbits. The atheist who had made a study of astronomy in his leisure was delighted over the precision with which the planets and their satellites were represented. After the first look at the mechanism, he exclaimed, "Who made it?"

The God-fearing astronomer dryly replied, "Oh, it made itself. I had bits of metal here in my laboratory, pieces of leather there on the shelf, other odd parts of apparatus on the floor. The wind blew through the window one afternoon. At the same time there was considerable vibration in the building because of passing cars. Gradually these pieces arranged themselves in their present form."

The atheist was amused by the answer. "What nonsense," he exclaimed. "Suppose the parts did come together by accident. Their correspondence to the planets in their orbits must have been worked out by some competent mathematician, someone with intelligence, someone who could think."

"Oh, well," said the God-fearing astronomer. "There was a kind of blind purpose in it all. The various parts seemed to want to come together without realizing what they were doing. The wind was blowing very hard that day and that helped it along."

Blind purpose seemed a very laughable suggestion to the visitor. Finally, a little impatient, he turned to the astronomer, "I really should like to know who is the author of this device. Please answer my question intelligently."

The astronomer then made his point with the atheist. "If this little miniature solar system could not come to be by itself by chance, how could the universe, after which it is patterned, which runs like clockwork with never a split-second deviation, ever come into existence without an intelligent maker?"

Avarice

O A man was promised that he could have for his own all the land that he could circle around from sunrise to sunset. He began slowly enough at sunrise, thankful for his strong legs. Then the lure of the black soil stirred him into a faster pace, so that he could encircle more land. The farther he went, the faster he went. He burned with fever. Echoing in his mind was one word: *more*. Late in the day the sun was setting in the west. His legs began to weaken. Throwing off his shirt and shoes, and with heart beating like a triphammer, he forced himself to the utmost. Just as the sun fell beyond the horizon, he flung himself forward with his fingertips touching the goal, and dropped there—dead. They took a shovel and gave him his land: a strip of soil six by two.

● The owner of a factory overheard a conversation between two of his employees. "If only I had a hundred dollars, I would be completely happy," said one young woman. The owner recognized her voice behind the door. Knowing she was a conscientious and reliable worker, he decided that she should be completely satisfied. So the next day he handed her an envelope with a hundred dollars in it. She was surprised and thanked him cordially.

A little while later the owner overheard her speaking to her friend. She said, "I wish now that I had said two hundred dollars."

O James, a good man who had never harmed anyone, was the chauffeur for a fine Christian businessman. Many times the employer tried to tell James that he needed the Savior, but whenever he did so, the standard reply was, "I keep the Ten Commandments. What more do I need?"

One day the employer said to James, "If you can keep God's law for half an hour, I'll give you that Buick of mine—the one you like to drive around when you don't have to use the Cadillac."

"Oh, thank you, sir," James said excitedly. "That's so good of you. I do like that Buick. I can easily keep the Ten Commandments for half an hour, for I always keep them."

His employer told him to go up to the rumpus room over the garage and lock the door to keep out noise and to lessen temptation. The half-hour soon passed. Down came James, saying, "I certainly want to thank you for the Buick."

But his employer asked, "What did you do while you were up in the rumpus room?"

"Oh, I was just thinking."

"And what were you thinking?" asked the businessman.

"Why to tell the truth, sir," said the chauffeur, "I was just thinking that since you're so good as to give me the Buick, maybe you'd let me have that set of extra new tires in the garage, because the tires are not good on that Buick."

"Oh, James," replied the employer, "I'm sorry to say that I cannot give you even the Buick. The law says, 'Thou shalt not covet!' and you were coveting while up in that rumpus room. You haven't kept the Ten Commandments even half an hour, much less all your life!"

Bible

● One man said, "One morning I spoke to eighty students in a class in a state university. I was informed that it would be better if I did not mention the Bible in the university. That same afternoon I was invited to speak to eight hundred men in the state prison, and the warden asked me to give them Bible truths."

● A women's Bible class was having a weekday meeting in a member's home. The gathering met on the day when the cleaning woman came, but that day she was ill and sent a friend in her place. As the devotions were about to begin, the leader said to the hostess, "I came away without my Bible today. Could I borrow yours?"

The hostess hurried to get her Bible but couldn't find it. She knew where it was, for she had used it the day before. But it wasn't anywhere to be found. She searched everywhere. The noise of opening and shutting drawers reached the women. "What will they think of me?" wondered the embarrassed hostess. In panic she ran down to the kitchen where the cleaning woman was at work. "Did you see anything of my Bible?" she asked breathlessly.

"Praise the Lord," exclaimed the cleaning woman.

"What do you mean?"

"Praise the Lord," she continued. "The first thing I do when I start working for someone is to hide their Bible."

"But why?"

"Just to see how long it takes the people there to miss it. Yours is in the linen closet."

O A few months before Pearl Harbor the Gideons were able to place fifty thousand copies of the New Testament on all ships in the Pacific fleet. After the disastrous attack many of the bodies were found in the posture of reading their Testaments. Many had signed their names on a blank line on the last page signifying their acceptance of Jesus Christ as their Savior.

A nurse whose son was in the navy came to Honolulu to work in one of the hospitals. She hadn't heard from her son for two years. When the attack came she offered her services to the navy, and was assigned the unpleasant duty of assisting in the identification of the dead at the morgue. One by one she uncovered the boys to secure their serial numbers so word could be sent to the nearest of kin.

After a while she uncovered a body only to look into the face of her own son.

She fainted and was carried to her quarters. Later her son's personal effects were brought to her. Among these was a small, white New Testament, watersoaked and unreadable. But she noticed her son had signed his name on the last page. This mother never went to church, never read the Bible. But she asked the chaplain for a Testament like the one her son had. She read it from cover to cover, learned that she was a sinner but that God so loved her he gave his son to die on the cross to be her Savior. She noted on the last page a blank space where she could sign her name if she would receive Christ as her Savior. Seeing the signature in her son's water-soaked Testament, she realized he had accepted Christ before he died. Taking her son's Testament she signed her name under the name of her son.

● A preacher entered a Sunday-school class while the lesson was in progress and asked the children some questions. "Now, who broke down the walls of Jericho?" he asked. A boy answered, "Not me, sir."

The preacher turned to the teacher and asked, "Is this the usual standard in this class?" The teacher answered, "This boy is honest, and I believe him. I really don't think he did it."

Leaving the room in disgust, the preacher sought out the deacon in charge of the teaching and explained what had happened. The deacon said, "I have known both the teacher and the boy for some time, and neither of them would do such a thing."

By this time the preacher was heartsick and reported it to the elders. They said, "We see no point in being disturbed. Let's pay the bill for the damage to the walls and charge it to maintenance."

● When a boy went off to college, his father said, "Don't ever let them take away your faith."

Back home after two years of college the son was asked, "Do you still believe the Bible? I hope you didn't let them weaken your faith in the Bible. You still believe Jonah was swallowed by a fish?"

"Oh, now, Father," said John, "you don't mean to say that you still believe that story about Jonah?"

The father threw up his hands, horror-stricken. "Oh, son, you've forsaken your father's faith!"

"Father, is Jonah still in your Bible? Have you read about him lately? Father, get your Bible and show me where you find anything about Jonah."

With considerable indignation the father took down his Bible and began to turn over the leaves excitedly, but could not find Jonah.

"Now, father, I may have played a mean trick, but two years ago when I went to college, I took your Bible and carefully cut out the pages of Jonah, and you have never missed it."

The father's face revealed an inward struggle. Then he quietly said, "I see it. I'm as bad as the unbelievers. There has been no Jonah in my Bible for two years."

O A girl picked up a book of poems. They were dry as dust. They meant nothing to her. One day she was introduced to a man. She began to become quite interested in him. She learned he was a poet. Furthermore, that he had written a book of poems, the same book she had looked at. Now when she picked up the book of poems, she found them very interesting. The difference—she knew the author.

Blood of Jesus

● For many years in the marketplace of Rotterdam, Holland, stood an old corner house known as "the house of a thousand terrors." In the sixteenth century King Philip II of Spain ruled over Holland. In his hatred of the Dutch, he tortured, maimed, imprisoned, and exiled thousands. When the people rose up in defiance, he sent a Spanish army under the Duke of Alva to put down the rebellion.

The city of Rotterdam held out valiantly for some while, then finally fell before the Spanish army. The victors went from house to house, ferreting out the citizens, then slaying them wholesale in their houses. In one house a group of men, women and children huddled together, a thousand terrors gripping their hearts as the Spanish soldiers approached.

Suddenly a young man had an idea. Taking a young goat belonging to the premises, he killed it, then with a broom swept its blood under the door of the house. Then they waited breathlessly, as footsteps approached. Soon the Spaniards were battering at the door. Then they heard one of them say, "Look at the blood running under the door. Come away, men, the work here is already done!"

A little later the army withdrew, allowing a band of thankful people to emerge, safe and sound. They lived because a goat had died.

● Many days ago in Detroit, Michigan, the well-known evangelist, Dr. Charles Finney, preached on the text "The blood of Jesus Christ, God's Son, cleanseth us from all sin" (see 1 John 1:7). After the service a stranger asked Dr. Finney to walk home with him. Advised against it by church officials who knew the man, Dr. Finney went with the man.

Ushering the preacher into the rear of a building, the stranger locked the door, put the key in his pocket, and said, "Don't be afraid. I'm not going to hurt you. I just want to ask a few questions. Do you believe what you preached tonight?"

Dr. Finney said, "I most certainly do."

The man continued, "We're in the back of a saloon. I'm sole proprietor. Mothers come in here, lay their babies on the counter, and beg me not to sell liquor to their husbands. I turn a deaf ear to their cry. We see to it when a man leaves here he's well under the influence. More than one night a man leaving here has been killed by the express at the tracks. Dr. Finney, tell me, can God forgive a man like me?"

Dr. Finney replied, "I have but one authority, the Word of God which says, 'The blood of Jesus Christ, God's Son, cleanseth us from all sin.'"

"But that's not all," added the man. "In another room we run a gambling hall. If a man doesn't spend all his money on liquor, we bring him back here and with marked cards see to it that he's fleeced out of his last dollar. We send him home penniless to a hungry family. Dr. Finney, I'm sole owner. Tell me honestly, can God forgive a man with a heart like that?"

Again Dr. Finney replied, "I have but one authority, the Word of God which says, 'The blood of Jesus Christ, God's Son, cleanseth us from all sin.'"

The man spoke again. "That's not all. Across the street is my home where live my wife and little daughter. Neither one has had a kind word from me for five years. Their bodies bear marks of my brutal attacks. Dr. Finney, do you think God could forgive a man with a heart like that?"

Dr. Finney's head lowered. His eyes filled with tears as he said, "My friend, you have painted one of the darkest pictures I have ever gazed on, but I still have one authority which says, 'The blood of Jesus Christ cleanseth us from all sin.'"

The man opened the door, ushered the preacher into the night, then never left that room till daybreak—not before ripping up decks of cards and pouring the contents of bottles down the sink. Across the road at home he sat in his living room. His little girl called, "Daddy, Mother says breakfast is ready." When he answered his little girl kindly, she ran back to her mother, "Daddy spoke kind to me! Something is the matter!" The mother followed her little girl to the living room. The man beckoned them both. Taking one on each knee, he explained to their amazement that they had a new husband and daddy. He ended, "I'm done with that business across the street!" The man later became a member, then an official in a leading Detroit church. When asked to tell how his life was changed, he would reply, "The blood of Jesus Christ, God's Son, cleanseth us from all sin."

Boasting

O At Waterloo, Napoleon was the strongest in every way. He had the most men, the most guns, and the best, and he knew how to use them, and his officers were all "men of renown." And as the tide of battle ebbed and flowed over the bloody field, he was so sure of victory that he actually sent three messages to Paris saying that he had won the victory.

O One afternoon the German author, Goethe, and the composer Beethoven, took a walk together. Everywhere they went men and women saluted them, pointed them out and bowed. Goethe exclaimed, "Isn't it maddening! I simply can't escape this homage."

Beethoven replied, "Don't be too much distressed by it; it is just possible that some of it may be for me."

Christ

O Emperor Theodosius, in the fourth century, denied the deity of Christ. When his son was sixteen, he decided to make him his partner in the government of the empire. Among the great men who assembled to congratulate the new wearer of the imperial purple was Bishop Amphilocus, a believer in the deity of Christ. He made a handsome address to the emperor and was about to leave when the emperor exclaimed, "What! Do you take no notice of my son?"

Then the bishop went up to the son, put his hands upon his head, and said, "The Lord bless thee, my son."

The emperor, roused to fury by this slight, exclaimed, "What! Is this all the respect you pay to a prince that I have made of equal dignity with myself?"

The bishop replied, "Sir, you do so highly resent my apparent neglect of your son, because I do not give him equal honors with yourself. Then what must the Eternal God think of you when you degrade his co-equal and co-eternal Son to the level of one of his creatures?"

O A little boy was taken by his mother to an art gallery where he saw for the first time the picture Holman Hunt's "Light of the World." As the little fellow looked at it there was something he could not understand. He saw that the face of the One standing at the door, asking admittance was the face of a loving, patient person. He noted the nail-pierced hand, the thorn-crowned brow. He knew that if admitted he would do no harm, only good. After several moments of silence he looked into his mother's face and asked, "Mother, why don't they let him in?"

● A little girl kept bothering her father. To keep her quiet the father gave his little girl a new jigsaw puzzle—a map of the world. He scattered the pieces on the floor. Part of Brazil fell beside Italy. A piece of Alaska lay atop Zaire. The father thought to himself, "That'll keep her occupied for a long time." To his amazement she had the puzzle together in almost nothing flat. "How did you do it?" he asked.

"Oh, it was simple," she answered. "On the other side of the mixed-up world was the face of Jesus. I put his face together and the world came out right."

● At the close of a service a stranger accosted the preacher. "I don't like your preaching. I don't care for the cross. I think it would be far better to preach Jesus, the teacher and example."

"Would you be willing to follow him if I preach Christ as the example?" the preacher asked.

When the stranger assured the preacher that his wish was to follow in Christ's steps, the preacher suggested, "Then, let us take the first step. It says of Jesus that he 'did no sin.' Can you take this step?"

The stranger looked confused. "No," he admitted, "I do sin. I acknowledge it."

"Well, then," replied the preacher, "your first need of Christ is not as an example but as a Savior."

A man sinking in quicksand and hearing a man on shore say, "Walk like me. Follow my example and all will be well," would be helpless to follow the pattern advised. He needs first to be rescued. Then he can walk like the example on shore.

O A French philosopher said he intended to found a new religion that would force Christianity to fade out of the picture.

A Christian quietly answered, "All you need to do is to live a perfect life, be crucified, rise again the third day from the dead, and get the world to believe that you are still alive. Then your religion will have some chance of success."

Christ-likeness

● A brilliant preacher aimed his lectures at a learned infidel who attended. When the lectures were over, the infidel became a Christian. "Which one of my lectures brought conviction to you?" asked the gratified preacher.

With a chilling smile the convert answered, "My dear sir, it was not through your lectures that I was converted. I slept through most of them. Why, it was an old woman, who used to hobble up the steps of your church, limping and leaning on her crutches, and between every thump of the crutch on the stone steps exclaimed, 'My blessed Jesus. My blessed Jesus.' As I looked at the poor disabled woman and saw the genuine content and peace on her face, and found out she lived a consistent life in the face of poverty and loneliness, I saw a living book to which I could not reply. So I wanted the Christ whom she professed."

● A well-to-do family was scheduled to entertain a famous preacher who was coming for a series of meetings in their town. The mistress sent the maid downtown to buy the finest cut of meat, adding, "I want the best for the minister."

In the butcher shop the maid sneered, "Some saint is coming to our town to speak, and my mistress is entertaining him. I must have the finest cut of meat. You would think that the Lord himself is coming."

A few days later the maid returned to the butcher shop for more meat. She seemed subdued. The butcher asked how she was getting along with the saintly visitor.

Meekly the maid replied, "A few days ago I said you would think that the Lord himself was coming. I want you to know that I think I have seen the Lord this week!"

Christmas

O Two missionaries, captured by bandits and shut up in a filthy hole without fire, were miserably cold. To make things worse, the guard ordered them not to talk, not even to make signs to each other. Christmas came. One of the missionaries, shivering and silent, sat on the floor. His face suddenly lit up, for he thought of a way to communicate with his comrade. Idly toying with bits of hay around him he spelled out a word on the hard-packed mud. With a glance he drew his friend's attention to it. Immediately the friend's face brightened with triumphant joy. For the straws on the mud spelled out *Emmanuel!* What if they were captives of the bandits? What if in peril of death? What if their prison was dirty and frigid? Inwardly they exulted, *God is with us everywhere and at all times!*

O A family in Philadelphia found out that a temporary guest was to have a birthday during his stay. Delighted, they planned for over a week to celebrate it. They cooked large quantities of goodies. They arranged lovely decorations. They bought little gifts for him and each other. The entire house was in confusion for days before the birthday. Finally the day came. Guests arrived. Gifts were exchanged.

A little child asked, "Mother, where is the man whose birthday it is?"
They found him in an upstairs bedroom. They had forgotten to invite him.

O In his book *When Iron Gates Yield*, a British missionary to Tibet, a captive of
the Chinese Communists for three years, tells of an experience one December
twenty-fourth. After a long, tiring day crossing a famous mountain pass and
stumbling down the other side mid heavy wind, his captors brought him to a
small group of houses about 4:30 that afternoon. A Tibetan landlord had swept
out an upstairs room for the missionary-prisoner, who had rarely seen cleaner
accommodations in a Central Asian country. After a meal, when it was already
dark, he was ordered to go downstairs to give hay to the horses. He clambered
down the notched tree trunk to the lower floor which was given over in the usual
custom to stabling. It was pitch-black. The missionary described his feelings,
"My boots squished in the manure and straw on the floor and the fetid smell of
the animals was nauseating. I felt my way amongst the mules and horses, expecting to be kicked any moment.

What a place, I thought. Then as I continued to grope my way in the darkness
towards the gray it suddenly flashed into my mind. *What's today?* I thought for a
moment. In the traveling, the days had become a little muddled in my mind.
Then it came to me. *It's Christmas Eve.* I stood suddenly still in that oriental
manger. To think that my Savior was born in a place like this. To think that he
came all the way from heaven to some wretched, eastern stable, and what is more,
to think that he came for *me*. How men beautify the cross and the crib, as if to
hide the fact that at birth we resigned him to the stench of beasts and at death
exposed him to the shame of rogues. God forgive us. I returned to the warm, clean
room, which I enjoyed even as a prisoner, bowed to thankfulness and worship.

O Some years ago a Christmas card pictured a world into which Christ had not
come. A clergyman fell asleep in his study on Christmas morn. In his dream he
found himself looking through his home, but no little stockings hung by the
chimney. No Christmas wreaths nor holly decorated the house. He walked out on
the street, but nowhere could he see a church with its spire pointing to heaven.
Returning to his library, he wanted to read a book on the Christian faith, but
every book about the Savior had disappeared. His doorbell rang. A messenger
asked him to visit a dying woman. He hurried to her home. Sitting down beside
the lady, he said, "I have something here that will comfort you." He opened his
Bible to look for a familiar New Testament verse, but the Bible ended at Malachi.
He could only bow his head and weep with her in bitter despair.

Two days later he stood beside this woman's coffin to conduct the funeral
service. But there was no message of consolation. As the service concluded by the
grave, there was no word of a glorious resurrection, no open heaven, but only
"ashes to ashes, dust to dust," and one long farewell. Realizing that Christ had
not come, the clergyman in his dreams burst into sobbing. Suddenly he woke
with a start. He heard the choir rehearsing in his church next door. A shout of
praise poured from his lips as he listened to the message of the carol "O come, all
ye faithful, come let us adore him."

o Excitedly dressing early one Christmas morning, a little girl was singing "Happy birthday to you." Below in the kitchen making breakfast her mother immediately thought, "Dear little thing is all confused. She's gotten Christmas mixed with someone's birthday." But as she listened more closely she heard her daughter sing, "Happy birthday, dear Jesus, happy birthday to you."

o A few days before Christmas two women stood looking into a department-store window at a large display of the manger scene with clay figures of the baby Jesus, his mother, Joseph, the shepherds, the wise men, and the animals. Disgustedly, one said, "Look at that. The church trying to horn in on Christmas."

o A lady who served on many civic committees, asked to select carols suitable for a community Christmas-tree lighting, sought the help of her pastor. When she scanned the list he had selected, she exclaimed in dismay, "But they're all so theological!"

Church Attendance

o A man had been looking for a good church to attend, and he happened into a small one in which the congregation was reading with the minister. They were repeating:

"We have left undone those things which we ought to have done and we have done those things which we ought not to have done."

The man dropped into a seat and sighed with relief, "I've found my crowd at last."

● Every Sunday morning without fail an elderly man could be seen walking to church. Everyone in the block knew he was deaf, unable to hear a word of the congregational hymns, the choir music, or the sermon. A cynical neighbor wrote him a note, "Why do you spend your Sundays in church when you can't hear a word?"

He answered, "I want my neighbors to know which side I'm on!"

● An elderly grandmother had to go to work in spite of arthritis and advancing years. She worked as charwoman in a big city hotel, on the job at the stroke of six every morning. Said a guest to her one day, "So you wash this floor six mornings a week?" Then he added, "Well, at least on Sunday morning you can sleep in. I hope you get plenty of rest that day."

The grandmother looked at him with a smile. "No, that's the morning I get up early, too, to take my grandchildren to church.

The stranger paused, "Wouldn't it help you to keep going if you slept in that one morning a week?"

The elderly lady leaned back on her knees, her red hands in the pail of water beside her, "Oh, it's going to church on Sundays that keeps me going the other six days of the week!"

Conscience

O A Hindu once said to a British official in India, "Our conscience tells us it is right to burn our widows on the funeral pyres of their husbands."

"Yes," replied the officer, "and our conscience tells us it is right to hang you if you do."

O For several years a county commissioner in North Carolina offered his self-kicking machine to anyone who felt he should not have done something and wanted to kick himself for doing it. The commissioner's machine was erected on Highway 70, called North Carolina's Broadway. Thousands have used the machine. Some even formed the "Self-Kicking Club" with members scattered in every state and even some foreign countries. In three years of use a new belt was needed and three pair of shoes. To work it you just stood in front of it and worked a gadget that made the shoes revolve and kick you.

O Perhaps the most unusual letter in all of the White House collection of letters is one which came from a teenager to President Cleveland, written in 1895. It said, "To His Majesty President Cleveland! Dear President: I am in a dreadful state of mind, and I thought I would write and tell you all. About two years ago— I used two postage stamps that had been used before on a letter, perhaps more than two stamps, but I can only remember doing it twice. I did not realize what I had done until lately. My mind is constantly on that subject. I think of it night and day. Now, dear President, will you please forgive me, and I will promise you I will never do it again. Enclosed find cost of three stamps, and please forgive me, for I was then but thirteen years old, for I am heartily sorry for what I have done. From one of your subjects."

Conversion

● When Benjamin Disraeli married the widow of his close friend, he did not love her. He married her for her money and social position. But in the aura of tenderness that she provided for him during the thirty-three years of their married lives, Disraeli in time became charmed by her and devoted to her.

On the other hand, around the same time, Teddy Roosevelt, a student at Harvard met Alice Hathaway Lee, the woman who became his wife. Here's what Roosevelt wrote, "I first saw her on October 18, 1878, and loved her as soon as I saw her sweet, fair, young face. We spent years of happiness such as rarely comes to man or woman." Disraeli fell in love slowly, but to Roosevelt the experience was sudden. Like falling in love, conversion may happen suddenly or over a period of time.

Convictions

● Ben-Gurion once stayed in the same hotel in Haifa with another Zionist leader. All night long they argued whether the windows should be closed or open.

Ben-Gurion wanted them open, his roommate, closed. So they argued back and forth all night. In the morning when the sun rose Ben-Gurion's roommate said, "Look what idiots we have been, fighting all night whether the windows should be open or closed. They do not even have window panes anyway."

"I knew it all along," said Ben-Gurion, "but it was just the principle of the thing."

● Mrs. John Welch, daughter of John Knox, partook of her father's spirit. Her husband was imprisoned for his faith, and was severely stricken with tuberculosis, when she made her way before King James to plead for his release.

"I will send him home with you," said the king, "if you will persuade him to submit to the bishops."

Holding out her apron, she said, "Please, your majesty, I'd rather carry his head home there, than tempt him to sin against his conscience."

O Eric Liddel, a young Scottish ministerial student, the best sprinter in the British Empire, was favored to win the 100-meter race in the Olympic Games in Paris, July 1924. But a few weeks before the Olympics he learned that the preliminary 100-meter races were scheduled for a Sunday afternoon. He considered Sunday sports wrong. For the few weeks before the Games he excused himself after evening dinner from the usual bull sessions with classmates, returning home hours later exhausted. A few weeks later the whole world knew his secret. He had spent those evening hours practicing for another event that was scheduled for a weekday and which required a different type of speed and endurance. On the closing day of the Olympics he stood on the winners' platform and received the Gold Medal as 400-meter champion. Liddel, who became a missionary, died as a prisoner in a concentration camp in the Far East during World War II. His story was told in the film *Chariots of Fire*.

Counting the Cost

● Out in Kansas is a large and picturesque home. A local citizen named Stone had started to build a mansion for himself. Halfway through, he ran out of money. The downstairs was magnificent: carved staircases, massive fireplaces, expensive paneling. But the upstairs was finished in the cheapest pine. Around the area the building had a nickname: "Stone's Folly."

Courtesy

O After a concert given by a famous pianist a woman approached the musician for his autograph. "I'm sorry," he said, "but I can't give it to you. You see—my hands are tired from playing."

She replied, "My hands are tired too—from clapping."

Cross

● A plane, just three hundred miles out of San Francisco bound for Hawaii, developed engine trouble. The pilot turned back. In less than an hour the plane was over San Francisco, but a dense fog had settled over the bay area. Turning to his co-pilot, he said, "There's a mountain east of the city on top of which is a cemetery distinguished by a huge cross. If I can find the arms of that cross, I can bring my ship safely to the airport." He did spot the cross rising high above the fog, and brought his plane safely down the runway.

⊕ A man who visited an indoor swimming pool regularly always dipped his toe in the water before taking a beautiful dive from the highest diving board. Asked why an expert swimmer should resort to the novice habit of sticking his toe into the water before diving in, he told the story of one night, when unable to sleep, he went to the pool of a large college where he was swimming instructor, hoping the exercise would induce sleep.

"I did not put on the lights in the pool," he continued," for I knew every inch of the place, plus the roof was made of glass. As I stood poised on the diving board, the moonlight threw the shadow of my extended arms on the opposite wall, making a perfect sign of the cross. Though not a Christian, I began repeating the words of a hymn I had learned as a boy: 'He died that we might be forgiven . . . that we might go at last to heaven, saved by his precious blood.'

"I cannot tell you how long I stood poised on the diving board. But without diving, I came down from the board and walked to the edge of the pool, and climbed down the steps to the bottom. To my amazement I discovered there was no water in the pool. That evening the caretaker had drained the pool dry. Then I realized that had I jumped, I would have plunged to my death.

"The cross on the wall saved me that night. I was so thankful to God for his mercy that I knelt on the cold bricks on the bottom and asked the Christ of the cross to save my soul. That night I experienced a two-fold deliverance. That is why I always put my toe into the water before diving."

○ On an upper bookshelf of his study a California pastor kept a little wooden cross, which had been presented to him by the members of his Bible class. One evening in March 1933 the Long Beach earthquake struck. While the earth was still shaking, the pastor made his way through the debris in the street to see what damage had been done in his study. When he arrived, he found hundreds of books piled high on the floor, as well as the floor lamp, desk set, and other articles. He pushed his way through to view the chaos. On the one side of the room the books were stacked high. Squarely on top of them all was a book with its title printed *The World in Convulsion*. And behold, standing firmly on this book, absolutely upright, and with nothing to lean against, was that little wooden cross. The earth was still trembling, and had been every few minutes since the main tremor, but there stood that cross. No wonder that pastor began to sing,

> In the cross of Christ, I glory,
> Tow'ring o'er the wrecks of time . . .

Crucifixion of Self

● A young man went to an old preacher and asked, "How can I get victory over pride and criticism?"

The preacher said to him, "Go to the grave of Brother Jones who recently passed away and as you stand by the grave say all the nice things you can about him. Flatter him greatly."

He did as the old preacher advised. When he returned the old preacher asked, "What did he say?"

The answer, "Nothing. He is dead."

The old preacher then told the young fellow to go out to the grave and criticize Brother Jones. "Say many mean things to him."

When he came back the old preacher asked, "What did he say?"

The young preacher said, "Nothing. He's dead!"

Reckoning ourselves dead with Christ, we will be unmoved by flattery or criticism.

● Dr. R. A. Torrey, founder of Montrose Bible Conference and first dean for both Moody and Biola schools, walked into a service at which Dr. A. B. Simpson, founder of the Christian and Missionary Alliance, was preaching. Dr. Simpson, occupied with his sermon, noticed Dr. Torrey but forgot to introduce him and have him pray, so later he wired Dr. Torrey his apologies. Dr. Torrey wired back, "Dead—didn't even notice it."

Day at a Time

O An invalid who had to spend all her time in a twisted condition in bed was once asked, "How long must you lie like that?"

Her answer, "Just one day at a time."

Death

O When his health began to fail, an Easterner decided to go west to the wide-open spaces. In a small town in Arizona, he approached an old man sitting on the steps of the local store. "Say," he asked, "what is the death rate around here?"

"Same as it is back east, brother," replied the old fellow, "one to a person."

O Dr. Donald Grey Barnhouse was driving with his children to his wife's funeral service. Coming to a stoplight, they found themselves behind a huge truck. The sun was shining in such a position that it cast the truck's shadow across the snow-covered field beside it. As the shadow loomed large, Dr. Barnhouse said, "Look, children, at that truck, and look at its shadow. If you had to be run over, which would you rather be run over by? By the truck or by its shadow?"

His youngest child spoke up. "The shadow. It couldn't hurt anybody."

"That's right," continued Barnhouse. "Death is a truck, but the shadow is all that ever touches the Christian. The truck ran over the Lord Jesus. Only the shadow passed over mother."

O A boy living in northern Idaho could never forget a timber buyer by the name of Benham who stopped for a week in the boy's home. An outspoken atheist, Mr. Benham could recite with persuasiveness the main arguments of Robert G. Ingersoll. He frankly stated that he had spent most of his money and years proving

God did not exist. He held, and he held it irrevocably, that there was no afterlife, neither heaven nor hell.

Twenty years later the boy, now grown into successful manhood, was attending a business convention in St. Paul, Minnesota, when his attention was drawn to a familiar-looking, gray-haired gentleman in the lobby. It was Mr. Benham. Though two decades had passed, he remembered the young man and invited him to lunch. Immediately it was evident the atheist had lost his poise. He acted like a man awaiting a death sentence.

Now seventy-one years old, the old man explained that he was an incurable anemic and had less than a year to live. He then launched into an unforgettable story about an old woman who lay at death's door in a local hospital where he had gone for a checkup. While there he had been conscripted by a nurse sent out by the dying woman to get three witnesses to a deathbed will that she could not sign due to a paralyzed arm. Entering the woman's room, he was struck by the utter serenity of this patient who had been bedridden for several years and who was now facing the end with a smiling countenance. The nurse rapidly wrote the whispered instructions of the stricken woman for the disposal of her property. When the three witnesses had signed the paper, she smiled, thanked them, and said, "And now I am ready to leave this pain-wracked body to meet my Maker, my husband, my father, my mother, and all my friends who had gone before me. Won't that be wonderful?"

As Mr. Benham reached this point, tears started down his pale, wrinkled cheeks. "Look at me," he said in a hoarse whisper. "I've lain awake many nights since I learned my days were numbered, staring at the ceiling with nothing to look forward to except that my life would end in a handful of ashes. That's the difference between me, an atheist, and the woman I have described. She, believing, faces her final days with a smile. Here am I, a nonbeliever, with every moment a nightmare, facing nothing but a cold tomb." He hesitated a few moments, then added, "I would shove my hands into a bed of red hot coals if by so doing I could secure a belief in a Supreme Being and an afterlife."

O According to an old legend, a man made an agreement with Death. The man said he would be willing to go when Death called, provided Death would agree to send a messenger well in advance to warn him. Death nodded agreement. Months and years passed. Then, one bitter evening, Death suddenly appeared and tapped him on the shoulder. In frightful despair the man cried, "It is you. You are here too soon. You haven't kept your part of the bargain."

Death leaned over and whispered, "I have more than kept my part. I have sent you, not just one, but many messengers. Look in the mirror, and you will see all of them." The man looked, gazing long and deep, for the last time. Death continued, "Look at your hair. Once it was black, but now it is thinned white. See the way you turn your head to hear my voice! You cannot hear as well as once you did. And how closely you peer into the glass to behold yourself, for your eyes have lost their clearness. How lined is your face. And your form is so bent. These have been my messengers, but you have been too busy with things to pay attention. I have more than kept my part of the bargain. Now you must keep yours. The time has come for you to leave."

○ A young minister was called to the bedside of an elderly woman who was approaching the end of life. He tried to comfort her and muttered something about how sorry he was that she had to die, when she interrupted. "God bless you, young man, there's nothing to be afraid about. I'm just going to cross over Jordan in a few hours, and my Father owns the land on both sides of the river."

Deathbed Repentance

○ Two men, who had been friends, became enemies over some minor disagreement. One was sick and dying. The other came to visit him, feeling it was his duty. The dying man apologized, "I'm sorry for all the unkind things I've said."
    The other accepted his apology.
    Then added the dying man, "That's just in case I die."

○ An old rabbi used to say to his congregation, "Repent the day before you die."
    But someone said to him, "Rabbi, we do not know the day on which we shall die. How then shall we repent the day before?"
    The Rabbi replied, "Then repent today."

Dedication

○ When the film *With Stanley in Africa* was being filmed some years ago in Hollywood, the director said, "We're having trouble with this picture. It's not hard to build up scenes of jungle life, or to create an African atmosphere. But here's our problem—how are we going to get across to the public the power that sent David Livingstone out to Africa and kept him there?"

● A mother was teaching her child to pray. When he got to the part, "I surrender everything to Thee, everything I own," he abruptly broke off and whispered to himself, "except my baby rabbit."

● Three men were playing cards for stakes on a commuter's train. Needing a fourth player, they asked a fellow sitting nearby if he would join them. Politely he declined. After trying several others without success, they again approached the same fellow. When again he graciously refused, they asked why he wouldn't play. He replied, "I have no hands."
    "What are those things dangling by your side?"
    "Those are hands," he admitted. "But," he added, "not my hands. Two years ago I gave myself to Christ. He owns me now. These hands belong to him. And he doesn't wish them to gamble."

● Three man walked by a building, one at a time. The first man said, "That's my house." The second man, "That's my house." The third man, "That's my house."
    All spoke the truth—the first man built it, the second man bought it, and the third man rented it. So, the triune God owns every believer on the same three counts. The Father created us. The Son bought us. The Spirit indwells us.

Denominations

● A story is told of a vision John Wesley had in which he was taken to the gate of heaven where he asked, "Have you any Presbyterians here?"

"No, none," responded the angel.

Wesley was amazed. "Well, have you any Baptists?" he asked.

"None," answered the angel quickly.

Wesley grew pale. He could scarcely muster up courage to ask his next question.

"Well, then," continued the founder of Methodism, "how many Methodists have you here?"

"Not one," replied the angel. And Wesley's heart was filled with dismay. "We are unacquainted with earthly distinctions and denominations up here," explained the angel.

"Well, then, whom have you here?" cried Wesley.

"Just a company of people who love the Lord," answered the angel quietly.

Wesley was then conducted to the regions of despair. "Have you any Presbyterians here?" he asked.

"Yes, lots of them," responded the keeper at the gate.

Wesley was mystified.

"Have you any Baptists here?" was his next question.

"Yes," came the reply.

In fear and trembling, Wesley put his third question. "Have you any Methodists here?" he asked, almost in a whisper.

"Oh, yes, many of them," quickly responded the gatekeeper. Wesley was stunned. No Methodists, Presbyterians, Baptists in heaven, and lots of them in hell. What did it mean? Remembering what was said by the angel at the gate of heaven, Wesley mustered his courage and asked, "Do you have any people here who love the Lord?"

"Oh, no, no!" roared the gatekeeper. "Not one. Nobody here loves the Lord."

Disappointment

● The lone survivor of a shipwreck, marooned on a lonely island, managed to build a hut in which he placed all he had saved from the wreck. He prayed for rescue and anxiously scanned the horizon every day to signal any passing ship.

One day on returning from a hunt for food he was horror-stricken to find his hut in flames. All his possessions had gone up in smoke!

The next day a ship arrived. "We saw your smoke signal yesterday," the captain explained.

● When the battle of Waterloo was being fought, all England waited for the result of the struggle. Then signals flashed from hill to hill by semaphore. The message was "Wellington defeated . . ." At that moment folks waiting at one spot saw sudden fog descend. Their hearts fell. News of the disaster spread like wildfire to London, spreading almost unbearable gloom. Then just as suddenly, the fog lifted and the rest of the message was flashed. The completed sentence read, "Wellington defeated the enemy."

Discipline of Children

● The governess of an eight-year-old girl in Evanston, Illinois, tells how the little girl's parents, both psychology majors, brought her up. They followed a rule of never commanding her or punishing her, but always trying to reason with her. One snowy morning they asked her to wear her snowpants. She refused. They reasoned with her—the snow is deep—you'll get damp legs—you'll catch cold and get sick. The girl, unimpressed by reason, refused. But somehow she gave in and put on her snowpants. But once outside, standing in full view of her parents who were watching from the living-room window, she pulled off her snowpants, threw them in the snow, and went on to school. The parents went out in the snow to retrieve the garment and agreed that they must not mention the episode to their daughter on her return from school.

That evening at the dinner table the father asked his eight-year-old to please pass the salt. She refused.

He reasoned with her. "My food will taste better with salt. You want your daddy to enjoy his meat and potatoes, don't you?"

The little girl still refused to pass the salt.

For five full minutes he reasoned, cajoled, and coaxed. Then finally he got up from his chair, walked around the table and picked up the salt and walked back to his place.

Commented the governess, "If that had happened when I was a girl, my father would have gotten up from the table too—but not to get the salt."

Discouragement

○ A man gave out tracts for years on a certain corner. Because there were no results he gave it up. Five months later he saw a man giving out tracts on the same corner. Striking up a conversation he learned that the man had been led to Christ through a tract given out there six months before.

"Many a time I've come back to thank the man, but I never could find him. I concluded he must have died and gone to his reward, so I decided to take his place on the corner."

Disposition

● A minister, unable to find one cuff link when dressing for his pastoral calls, stormed around the house in a rage. When he found the missing cuff link and left the house, his wife was in tears. Home two hours later he rehearsed his calls to his wife. First was an old man who though paralyzed from a stroke was cheerful and patient. Next, a young man dying of an incurable disease who displayed no rebellion. His third and final visit had been to an elderly woman confined to a small room who radiantly looked forward to heaven. Concluded the pastor, "How wonderful is God's grace! There's nothing too hard for it!"

"It is wonderful," his wife replied, "but there is one thing it doesn't seem to have the power to accomplish."

"What's that?"

"It doesn't seem to have the power to control a minister when he's lost his cuff link!"

O Someone asked if a certain man was a Christian. Came the answer, "I don't know. I haven't asked his wife."

O Jonathan Edwards, third president of Princeton, had a daughter with an ungovernable temper, but this was not known to the outside world. A worthy young man fell in love with this daughter and sought her hand in marriage.

"You can't have her," was the abrupt answer of Jonathan Edwards.

"But I love her," said the young man.

"You can't have her."

"Why?"

"Because she is not worthy of you!"

"But, she is a Christian, is she not?"

"Yes, she is a Christian but the grace of God can live with some people with whom no one else could ever live."

Doers

● A small boy asked his twelve-year-old sister, just as the sermon concluded, "Now, is it all done?"

"No," she whispered back, "It's just all said. Now we must go out and do it."

● Two men in a railroad coach were passing through the slum area on the outskirts of a great city. One of them pulled down the shade.

"Why did you do that?"

The other replied, "Because I hate to see that dehumanizing place. I know it is wrong, but there is nothing I can do to help it.

Came the reply, "There's one thing you can do. Stop pulling down the shade."

Emptiness of Material Things

● Leading lady of the theater, Helen Hayes, related how years ago, on the *Sante Fe Chief*, she crossed the continent with a beautiful woman she knew slightly. This woman was in the final stages of TB and was going back to her home in England to die. She had been a successful performer with the usual string of admirers and had amassed a lovely collection of jewelry.

When the train was well under way, she sent a message to Helen Hayes to come to her compartment. Conversation was impossible since even the effort to whisper left her spent. But it was not conversation she wished. Very soon she indicated by a nod to her maid that she was ready for what probably was a daily ritual. The maid placed a large, leather jewel case beside her mistress, unlocked, and opened it. For the next hour and a half Helen Hayes was required to take each piece from the drawers, hold it up to the light, and turn it this way and that while the lady feverishly studied first the jewel, and then Helen Hayes' face for a reaction.

Inside Miss Hayes really wanted to cry. All that life had given this woman to hold on to was this box of hard, bright objects. And with the lights out—in the dark—when one needs comfort most, she couldn't even see her treasures.

Envy

O When the widely acclaimed Bible teacher, F. B. Meyer, first began his visits to America from England to preach at Northfield Bible Conference in New England at the invitation of D. L. Moody, he was greatly admired by crowds who hung on his ministry. Then came the day his fellow countryman, Dr. G. Campbell Morgan, was invited to Northfield. His excellent expositions attracted throngs away from Meyer. Not many knew it but Meyer confessed there came the temptation to jealousy. But then he said, "The only way I can conquer my feeling is to pray for him daily, which I do."

Later, when Meyer pastored in London, he heard that Morgan was coming to London to pastor a church. He strode the floor, greatly perturbed, convinced Morgan would draw all his congregation from him. After much praying he won the victory, crying out, "Lord, fill Campbell Morgan's church so full that it can't hold any more, and then send the overflow to me!"

Everyone Needed

● Called up by compulsory military service in Argentina, a fellow without arms appeared at army headquarters. He said, "What good would I be in the army? I have no arms."

They put him in the army anyway. He appeared at basic training and said to the commanding officer, "What can I do? I have no arms."

The officer said, "See that fellow up there on the hill pumping water? Go tell him when the pail is filled. He's blind."

● A doctor in a small French village was about to retire. He had cared for the villagers day and night, despite the inability of the people to pay him much. In appreciation, it was proposed that each family bring a pitcher of wine from their own cellars and pour it into a large barrel placed on the village square. All day long people were seen pouring their offering into the barrel. In the evening the barrel of wine was taken to the doctor's residence. With the people gone the doctor was left alone with the memory of their love. Drawing a cup of wine, he sat by the fire to enjoy it. The first sip was a shock. It tasted like water. Thinking there must be a mistake, he sampled more. The barrel was filled with water. Everyone in the village reasoned, "My little pitcher of wine won't be missed. I have so little for myself. The others will take care of it. The little water I substitute won't be noticed."

Example

● When Billy Graham went to a southern city for meetings, the governor of the state assigned a state trooper to drive him around for three weeks. The trooper delegated to show Graham the courtesies of the governor's office was so impressed that he went forward during the campaign, accepted Christ, dedicated his life, and later joined Graham's team as personal secretary.

⊙ Four clergymen were discussing the merits of the various translations of the Bible. One admired the King James Version for its beautiful language. A second, the Revised Standard Version for its accuracy. The third, the Williams for its up-to-date vocabulary. The fourth was silent, then finally announced that he liked his mother's best of all.

Amazed, the others said, "We didn't know your mother translated the Bible."

"Oh, yes," came the reply, "she translated it into life, and it was the most convincing translation I ever saw."

○ George W. Truett, well-known Southern Baptist preacher, was conducting a revival in a certain city. Night after night two fine looking young men came into the service and sat near the front. They were such attentive listeners that Dr. Truett became greatly interested in them. The pastor told him they were the two most promising lawyers in the area. Though they were not members of any church, they were clean, moral fellows. One morning Dr. Truett went to the office of these young men. They were delighted at the visit.

"Gentlemen," said Dr. Truett, "I want to ask you a personal question. You seem to be intelligent men. Why are you not Christians?"

One of them answered, "Doctor, you will think us foolish, but we will tell you why. We graduated in the same class at college, and finished our course in law together. We decided to go into a partnership. We looked over this state to find a model after whom we could pattern our lives and profession. We chose Judge White for our model. He is a man above reproach, one of the most honorable lawyers in the state. We learned that he was not a member of any church and made no profession of religion. We are not unbelievers, but we are living up to our resolution to model our lives after the judge."

"Gentlemen, I'm glad to have met you, and will look for you at the service tonight," said Dr. Truett as he left. The preacher found out where the prominent judge had his chambers.

"My name is Truett, and I've come here to ask you a question in ethics. I want to know if it is right for any man to occupy a position in his community that stands in the way of another's welfare."

"Why, certainly not," the judge replied.

"That's what you are doing," said the preacher.

"Me, how?" asked the stunned judge.

Dr. Truett related the conversation with the young lawyers. The judge walked to the window, looked out on the passing traffic, then turning around looked straight into the eye of the preacher. "I will come out to hear you preach tonight."

That night as Dr. Truett sat in the pulpit looking out upon the crowd he saw the prominent judge take a seat near the front. A minute later the two young lawyers came down the aisle and found a seat just behind the judge. Dr. Truett preached on influence. When he gave an invitation for people to come forward and accept Christ, the influential judge came down the aisle, and just behind him followed the two young lawyers. That judge hadn't known those two lawyers were watching him.

o Some years ago a hospital official in Atlanta, Georgia, after watching the lives of professing Christians in a large denominational hospital, and perhaps on insufficient and hasty evidence, concluded, "They just don't live what they preach. And if they can't, then I couldn't either." Someone mentioned the exemplary life of the pastor of a large church nearby. This hospital official decided to see if this preacher's life measured up to his profession. So he hired a plainclothes detective to follow this pastor everywhere for a week. At the end of the period the detective declared, "He lives it! No flaw there!"

These words were inescapable evidence. They rang in his ears in an hour of great despair when he was about to take his life. With the help of a godly wife, he accepted Christ as his Savior. He spent his spare time thereafter laboring for the Lord in many ways, including the holding of open-air street meetings. His daughter attended Moody Bible Institute in Chicago, where this story was reported in the student newspaper. The article revealed the preacher's identity: Dr. Will H. Houghton, one-time pastor of the Baptist Tabernacle in Atlanta, who by this time was president of Moody Bible Institute. The article ended with the daughter's questions, "Suppose Dr. Houghton had not lived a sincere, true Christian life— one that would bear watching—where would my dad be today?"

Excuses

● A young man frankly said he did not wish to become a Christian. When asked for his reason, he replied, "Several years ago I was selling from door to door and was invited into a house to show my product to the wife and children. While I was demonstrating, the husband came home, swore at me, and kicked me out. He was a professing Christian. From that time I decided never to have anything to do with religion. The young man was asked, "Would you write down your reason in full and sign it." Hesitantly the young man did so. Then the paper was handed back to him with these words, "Keep this, and when you are asked for your excuse on the day of judgment, hand this up."

Faith

o Two boys were watching the sun set. One said, "What father said about the earth moving and the sun not moving can't be true. Look—the sun moves—it's lower in the sky than it was a few minutes ago, and the earth doesn't move, for we've been standing on it all these times."

His brother answered slowly, "You can trust your senses if you want, but I'm going to trust my Father's word."

o "Faith is the bunk," said a skeptic. "I only believe in the things I can see."

Yet in the previous week he had often pressed the light switch without checking to see if the wires to his house were up or down. He had asked the gas station attendant to put ten gallons into his car and hadn't bothered to make sure that ten gallons had actually gone into his tank. He had dropped an important letter in a mail box, and hadn't waited around to see if any mailman picked it up and didn't throw it away. He had flown to a city halfway across the country and hadn't checked the pilot's credentials. He had ridden up and down the elevator without checking to see if the cables were frayed.

✖ ◐ A man who was in great trouble was able to sleep each night. Someone asked him how he could sleep and he answered, "I've handed the matter over to the Lord, who never slumbers or sleeps, and there's no use both of us staying awake all night."

Faithfulness

◐ One night the director of a rescue mission in London invited testimonies from the floor. A sailor told how after his ship had docked in Sydney, Australia, he was approached on the street by an old man who said, "If you were to die tonight, do you know where you would spend eternity?" And with that question the old man melted into the crowd.

Some months later another sailor rose to his feet in the same rescue mission with a similar story of an old man in Sydney, Australia, who had asked him the same question and then vanished into the night. Both men testified that this feeble witness had started them thinking about spiritual matters, so that they eventually found Christ.

A while later the rescue-mission director visited Sydney for an international convention of rescue-mission directors. Hoping to find the old man who had witnessed to the two sailors, he walked the streets of Sydney night after night. On the last night before departure to London, an old man approached him and said, "If you were to die tonight, do you know where you would spend eternity?" Rejoicing in finding the old man, the mission director told him the story of these sailors who had found Christ through his witness.

The elderly gentleman replied, "I have given my witness with stammering tongue for over fifty years, and this is the first time I have heard of anyone affected by my ministry."

○ On board the *Titanic* was a Scotsman by the name of John Harper who was on his way to America to visit Moody Bible Institute in Chicago at the invitation of its dean. Three years after the sinking of the *Titanic*, in Hamilton, Canada, a young Scotsman rose in a church service and said, "I was on the *Titanic* the night she went down. I had been thrown into the waters and somehow managed to grab a spar and drift alone hanging on for dear life. The waters were icy. What an awful night! Suddenly a wave brought a man near me. He said his name was John Harper of Glasgow. He too was holding onto a piece of wreckage. He called out to me, "Man, are you saved?"

"No, I am not," I replied.

He shouted back through the darkness, "Believe on the LORD Jesus Christ, and thou shalt be saved."

The waves bore him away, but strange to say, a little later he was washed back alongside me. "Are you saved now?" he called out.

"No," I replied. "I cannot honestly say that I am."

Once more he repeated the verse, "Believe on the LORD Jesus Christ, and thou shalt be saved." Then losing his hold on the piece of wood, he sank. And there, alone in the night, and with two miles of water under me, I believed. I trusted Christ as my Savior. I am John Harper's last convert." When the dean of Moody Bible Institute heard this story later, he said, "I knew John Harper. He was on his way to this school when he went down.

Today there is a room in Moody Church in Chicago called the Harper Room, named after this man who was found faithful "even unto death."

O A member of the British House of Commons twitted another member about his humble origin. "I remember when you blacked my father's boots," he sneeringly exclaimed.

The statesman thrilled the assembly with this rejoinder, "Well, sir, did I not black them well?"

Faithfulness of God

● An elderly woman used to like to include in her testimony the verse where the Lord promises, "I will never leave thee." Her pastor who knew her delight in the faithfulness of God one day pointed out that the original could be literally translated, "I'll never, no never, leave thee."

When she showed no surprise, the pastor asked, "Doesn't it make you feel better to know that God makes it doubly sure that he won't forsake you?"

"Oh, no," she said. "I know God says it twice, but that was so some of you preachers could understand it! Once is enough for me!"

O Roger Simms, hitchhiking his way home, would never forget the date—May 7. His heavy suitcase made Roger tired. He was anxious to take off his army uniform once and for all. Flashing the hitchhiking sign to the oncoming car, he lost hope when he saw it was a black, sleek, new Cadillac. To his surprise the car stopped. The passenger door opened. He ran toward the car, tossed his suitcase in the back, and thanked the handsome, well-dressed man as he slid into the front seat.

"Going home for keeps?"

"Sure am," Roger responded.

"Well, you're in luck if you're going to Chicago."

"Not quite that far. Do you live in Chicago?"

"I have a business there. My name is Hanover."

After talking about many things, Roger, a Christian, felt a compulsion to witness to this fiftyish, apparently successful businessman about Christ. But he kept putting it off, till he realized he was just thirty minutes from his home. It was now or never. So, Roger cleared his throat, "Mr. Hanover, I would like to talk to you about something very important." He then proceeded to explain the way of salvation, ultimately asking Mr. Hanover if he would like to receive Christ as his Savior. To Roger's astonishment the Cadillac pulled over to the side of the road. Roger thought he was going to be ejected from the car. But the businessman bowed his head and received Christ, then thanked Roger, "This is the greatest thing that has ever happened to me."

Five years went by, Roger married, had a two-year-old boy, and a business of his own. Packing his suitcase for a business trip to Chicago, he found the small, white business card Hanover had given him five years before.

In Chicago he looked up Hanover Enterprises. A receptionist told him it was impossible to see Mr. Hanover, but he could see Mrs. Hanover. A little confused as to what was going on, he was ushered into a lovely office and found himself facing a keen-eyed woman in her fifties. She extended her hand, "You knew my husband?"

Roger told how her husband had given him a ride when hitchhiking home after the war.

"Can you tell me when that was?"

"It was May 7, five years ago, the day I was discharged from the army."

"Anything special about that day?"

Roger hesitated. Should he mention giving his witness? Since he had come so far, he might as well take the plunge. "Mrs. Hanover, I explained the gospel. He pulled over to the side of the road and wept against the steering wheel. He gave his life to Christ that day."

Explosive sobs shook her body. Getting a grip on herself, she sobbed, "I had prayed for my husband's salvation for years. I believed God would save him."

"And," said Roger. "Where is your husband, Mrs. Hanover?"

"He's dead," she wept, struggling with words. "He was in a car crash after he let you out of the car. He never got home. You see—I thought God had not kept his promise." Sobbing uncontrollably, she added, "I stopped living for God five years ago because I thought he had not kept his word!"

Fathers

O One Saturday night a car with a young couple in it crashed off the highway, killing the young man and seriously injuring the seventeen-year-old-girl, who was very popular in high school. The girl's mother hadn't slept very well that night for she thought she had seen a bottle in the young man's pocket as the couple left the home earlier. Reaching the hospital, the girl's parents learned that the couple had been drinking. The bottle they had used had been found in the car. The father left the hospital in a rage, muttering, "If I could find the person who sold my daughter that whiskey, I'd kill him!"

Returning home, he headed for his liquor cabinet to get something to steady his nerves. There on the shelf inside the cabinet was a note in his daughter's handwriting: DEAR DAD, WE HOPE YOU WON'T MIND US TAKING YOUR WHISKEY WITH US TONIGHT.

O A little boy refused to close a door his father asked him to shut. A little girl who overheard was later asked what the little boy needed.

Everyone thought she would say a "whipping" but she answered, "He needed a daddy!"

O A little boy playing with a toy car let loose a blood curdling oath. His horrified mother reprimanded him. "Where did you learn those words?"

"From Daddy," retorted the boy. "That's what he says when he can't get his car going."

O Many years ago a farmer had an unusually fine crop of grain. Just a few days before it was ready to harvest, a terrible hail and wind storm demolished the entire crop. After the storm was over, the farmer, with his little son, went out on the porch. The little boy looked at what had formerly been a beautiful field of wheat, and then looked up at his dad, expecting to hear words of complaint or despair. All at once his father started to sing softly "Rock of Ages, cleft for me,/ Let me hide myself in Thee." Years later, the little boy, grown to manhood, said, "That was the greatest sermon I ever heard. My father lost a grain crop, but I saw the faith of a godly father in action."

O At breakfast time one Sunday morning ten-year-old Johnny was busy with a high stack of pancakes over which a mixture of butter and maple syrup cascaded. In the midst of his delightful meal John's mother said, "Hurry and get through breakfast so you can get dressed and get to Sunday school on time."

But little John said, "I'm not going to Sunday school today. Things are too dry down there, and besides I don't like the teacher."

John's father was sitting in his favorite chair, reading the Sunday paper. After John's remarks, the father added, "I don't blame the boy for not wanting to go to Sunday school. I didn't like to go when I was a boy. I imagine things are just as dry as they were then. John, you don't have to go today."

John's mother was a shrewd woman. She said nothing, but she knew her son. So she waited patiently for Monday morning to come. While John was eating breakfast, and the father was still at home, the mother told John to hurry with his breakfast so he could get ready for school. The mother's expectations were realized. She heard John say, "I'm not going to school today. It's a dead old place, and besides I don't like that crabby old teacher."

In a cool and taunting voice, the mother said, "I don't know that I blame you, Son. If school is anything like it was when I went, things can be dull and teachers can be crabby."

John's father rose to the bait. With whiplike words he commanded John to get his breakfast over and get down to school on time or he would give him a spanking he would never forget. And Johnny went to Sunday school the next Sunday.

Fear

O For years at Disneyland a woman aerialist playing Tinker Bell flew through the air from the Matterhorn, harnessed to a cable. But to reach Disneyland from her home each day she traveled by bus.

"I'm afraid to ride in a car on the freeway," she said.

O A little girl at Camp Hope, New York (a summer camp for mentally and physically handicapped children), rebelled against going to bed each night. The counselors had to struggle with her, for she would fuss and fight. When finally they asked her why she struggled so against going to bed, she explained, "I have a disease that could take my life at any moment. When I go to bed at night, I could go to sleep and never wake up. This is why I am afraid." The counselors knew she was right.

A few days later she accepted Christ as her Savior. She maneuvered her wheelchair down to the front of the tabernacle to make this decision. That night, and every night thereafter, there was no struggle when she went to bed. She said to her counselor, "If I die tonight, I'll go right to be with the Lord."

O John Knox, Scottish reformer, was not held in the highest favor by Queen Mary, known as Bloody Mary. One day on his way to the court, he was warned that it might be better to postpone his visit as she was in an angry mood. He kept right on going, replying, "Why should I be afraid of a queen when I have just spent three hours with God?"

Fools

● On one occasion a nobleman gave his court jester a staff, charging him to keep it till he met a greater fool than himself. "When you meet such a man, you are to hand over the staff to him," he added. A few years later the nobleman fell ill. The court jester came to see his master who said, "I feel I'm going to die and leave the palace."

"And whither will you go?" asked the fool.

"On a long journey," said the nobleman.

"And when will you return—within a week?"

"No."

"Within a year?"

"No."

"When?"

"Never."

"And what provision have you made for your journey?"

"None at all."

"Are you going away forever?" asked the fool, "and you have made no provision whatever for your journey? Here, take my staff, for I am not guilty of such folly as that!"

O A pastor tried to lead a successful businessman to give his life to Jesus Christ and to a more active part in the work of his church. The interview was rather brief because the man practically closed the door to the preacher's pleadings, saying, "My wife and I have set as our goal the accumulation of lots of property, and a sufficient income on which to retire comfortably. She is working in a good position to help carry out these plans. After a few years, when we've finished paying for all the things we want to buy, then we will give our lives to Christ and come into the church and try to do our part." Nothing the preacher said could change the man's decision.

The years passed. The couple prospered. They had a magnificent home and were about to retire. Their lives' ambition was about to be realized. One day the preacher received a telephone call to come to the beautiful residence at once. The wife met him at the door. "Please pastor, go in and talk with him. He has had a stroke. A few days later the minister stood with the wife by the side of the casket in the funeral home.

The pastor tried to offer her words of comfort, and then as he turned away, he said to himself, "How tragic that he was unwilling to put first things first. He paid too much for his little tin whistle."

O A minister took a visiting evangelist out in the country to meet a family whose father was an out-and-out unbeliever. It was late Saturday afternoon. They found the farmer coming down the ladder from the hayloft. The pastor greeted him cordially, then said, "Your son and your wife have become Christians at our special meetings this week, and both of them are praying that you too will accept Christ. And I have brought the evangelist out so you could meet him and perhaps come to the meetings tomorrow . . ."

But that was as far as the pastor got. The farmer angrily interrupted, shouting, "Now, listen, I didn't ask you to bring anyone out here to preach to me! If my old woman wants to get religion that's her business. If my son wants to get religion, that's his business. And if I am not ready to get religion—that's my business!" Sounding mad enough to fight, he went on. "I know where the church is. Anytime I want to hear anybody preach, I'll go to church. Do you think I'm a fool that I don't know what I'm doing? How do you think I got the biggest farm in the whole county? I'm going to be saved sometime, but not till I'm good and ready." He wouldn't even shake the evangelist's hand.

No one from his family came to the services Sunday. It was still dark Monday morning when the phone rang in the parsonage. It was an urgent message to get out to the farmer's home.

When the pastor and evangelist arrived, the ambulance was just taking the farmer away. In a freak accident, he had fallen from the hayloft. The ambulance driver had stuffed a note in the farmer's shirt pocket. It read: DOA ["Dead on arrival."] The pastor and evangelist stood looking up at the hayloft. In that very place just two nights before the farmer had shouted, "I'm no fool. I'll get saved when I am good and ready!"

Forgiveness

O When William Gladstone was Chancellor of the Exchequer, he sent down to the Treasury for certain statistics on which to base his budget proposals. The statistician made a mistake. Gladstone was so sure of the man's accuracy he didn't bother to verify the figures. He went before the House of Commons to make his speech, basing his appeal on the incorrect figures. His speech was no sooner published than the paper exposed its glaring mistakes. Gladstone was embarrassed. He called for the statistician. The man came, full of fear.

Gladstone said, "For a long time you've been handling the intricacies of national accounts and this is the first mistake you've made. I want to congratulate you and express my keen appreciation."

O When a certain Archbishop of Canterbury died, among his papers one bundle was bound apart from all the rest. It contained all the letters he had received that insulted him bitterly for the unpopular causes he had championed.

Over this bundle was written: MAY GOD FORGIVE THEM! I AM SURE I DO.

● George Washington and Peter Miller were good friends. George Washington became the first president of our country, and Peter Miller became a preacher of the gospel. While Washington lived at Philadelphia, Peter Miller had charge of the village church of Ephrata about seventy miles from the capital.

In Ephrata lived a man by the name of Michael Wittman, who caused a great deal of trouble for the preacher. He did everything in his power to make the life of Mr. Miller unhappy. Slanderous stories were told by him. And one day he even attacked the minister and inflicted bodily harm on him.

Some time later it was discovered that Wittman was involved in treason. He was tried and sentenced to death. Mr. Miller decided to go to the president of the USA and plead for this life of the man who had so often persecuted him. He walked seventy miles to the capital.

"Well, Peter, it is a pleasure to see you. What can I do for you?" asked Washington.

"I have come to beg the life of the traitor Wittman," answered Miller. "For old friendship's sake, George, I know you will not refuse me."

"But I cannot do this," replied Washington. "This case is too black. I am sorry I cannot give you the life of your friend."

"My friend!" exclaimed the preacher. "He is not my friend. He is the bitterest enemy I have." And then he told about the suffering and persecution he had experienced at the hands of Wittman.

"That puts another light on the matter," said the president. "I could not very well grant you a favor by giving you the life of a friend. But I will give you freely a pardon for your enemy."

O A few years ago a young Korean, after graduating from the Seoul National University, came to the United States to study at the University of Pennsylvania. On his way to mail a letter one evening he was stopped by a gang of eleven delinquent teenagers, looking for some money. They wanted sixty-five cents each to get into a dance. The Korean boy had no money so the teenagers beat him to death. The murder shocked Philadelphia. Most citizens felt that the severest punishment would be too good for the culprits. But on the other side of the world the parents of the Korean lad viewed the tragedy differently. Their letter to Philadelphia authorities stirred hearts everywhere. In it they said they were establishing a fund to be used for the religious, educational, vocational, and social guidance of the teenagers who killed their son.

The letter also said, "Our family has met together and we have decided to petition that the most generous treatment possible within the laws of your government be given to those who have committed this criminal action."

● A Scottish doctor, noted for skill and piety, died. When the books were examined, several accounts were found with this written across them in red ink: FORGIVEN—TOO POOR TO PAY.

His wife who was of another disposition said, "These accounts must be paid." She sued for the money.

The judge asked her, "Is this your husband's handwriting in red ink?"

"She replied, "Yes."

"Then," said he, "there is not a tribunal in the land that can obtain the money where he has written FORGIVEN."

Formalism

○ At a well-known eastern university when students scheduled to graduate flunk out at the last minute, because parents and friends are present for the big occasion and all arrangements have been made, these students are allowed to march in the graduation procession, walk across the platform and receive a diploma. But when the diploma is opened, it will turn out to be a blank.

○ The new music teacher at the boys' school had just organized a band. The principal decided that the band should give its first concert before the music teacher thought the band was ready. Just before the concert, the music teacher whispered to his nervous musicians, "If you're not sure of your part, just pretend to play."

When at the big moment he brought his baton down with a sweeping flourish, the band gave forth with a resounding silence.

Frailty of Man

◉ A magazine carried a picture of Adlai Stevenson, then Secretary of State, taken on a London street five minutes before he died. At that moment he was smiling and vibrant with life. Five minutes later he was dead.

○ Harry Houdini, regarded as the most fabulous magician of all time, created the illusion that he was a superman physically. As part of his act he permitted people in the audience to strike him in the stomach with a clenched fist. Knowing they were about to strike, he could tighten his muscles and absorb seemingly devastating blows.

On October 19, 1926, after a performance in Windsor, Canada, a group of students visited Houdini's dressing room. While the magician was not looking, one of them suddenly punched him in the stomach. Unprepared for the blow, Houdini winced, but managed to hold himself erect and refrain from audible groan. But the minute they left he dropped on his cot, moaning in agony. Though still in great pain and with a high fever, Houdini went to Detroit and gave a scheduled performance. He didn't want to destroy the illusion that he was physically superhuman.

But the next day the fever and the pain were both worse. A doctor was called, who carefully examined Houdini but could find scarcely a trace of a bruise. Alarmed because the discomfort of the blow should have subsided now, he called in other doctors. An X-ray and blood count were ordered and the incredible truth came out—Houdini had a ruptured appendix. Though the symptoms indicated this, he had been struck on the left side. And an appendix is almost always on the right. The doctors did their best, but Houdini died.

Free Will and Determinism

● One day in San Francisco a Christian heard the testimony of a young Chinese. Thinking that perhaps he might know missionaries in a certain part of China, the Christian approached the young man after the meeting and asked him where he had found Christ.

The young man looked up with a smile, "I not find Christ; Christ find me."

● The young boys of the village laughed at a wise, old hermit. "I know how we can fool him," one said. "I'll take a live bird and hold it in my hand and ask him if it's alive or dead. If he says it's dead, I'll let it fly away; if he says it's alive, I'll crush it."

So they found him at the door of his hut. "Old man, I have a question for you. What is it I hold in my hand?"

"Well, my son, it looks like a bird you have caught."

"Right. Now, tell me, is it alive or dead?"

The old man fixed his eyes on the boy. "It is as you will, my son."

Fruitfulness

○ A woman, whose beautiful rose bush withered, phoned an expert. He offered to come on two conditions: first, half the price had to be paid in advance; second, she had to be out the day he came to do the job. These stipulations bothered her, but she finally consented.

Returning the day after the job was done, she expected to find her bush filled with buds and blossoms, but there were none. The dead vines were cut down and burned. Nothing was left but a lot of dry stubs. She flew into a rage, repeating, "Now I see why he wanted the money in advance. Now I know why he didn't want me around."

But when sun, wind, and rain came, before long new life began to appear, vines grew and little buds came out here and there. Day after day the woman would go out to watch until one day the vine was filled with beautiful roses.

Future Unknown

\● A few autumns ago a fellow from Pottstown, Pennsylvania, was acclaimed a wonder at guessing sports results before they happened. He astounded the nation by guessing to the exact digit the total number of points which would be scored in major football and basketball games. The Sporting News, a paper published in St. Louis, Missouri, wrote and asked the gentleman how he picked the winning number of 404 which was correct to the point for the combined total of scores for the major games the previous Saturday. He replied he picked 404 on a hunch when he noticed that number on a pencil he was using. The paper asked him to send a picture of the pencil, but the fellow, a postal clerk, replied he had lost it. But this is how he did it, as told to the federal government agents who ordered his arrest. He addressed his letter the day before the games and postmarked it, for he worked in the post office, then waited till the games were over, filled in the total of all scores, and then mailed it. The contest editors received the letter a day late, but since it had been postmarked on this set day, thought it had been merely delayed in transit.

Giving

O A clergyman who wrote to a wealthy and influential businessman, requesting a donation to a worthy charity, received a curt refusal that ended by saying, "As far as I can see, this Christian business is just one continuous give, give, give."

After a brief interval the clergyman responded to his note: "I wish to thank you for the best definition of the Christian life that I have yet heard."

⊘ The premier of France, referring to a large gift made some years before by John D. Rockefeller for help in the restoration of the Rheims Cathedral, quoted Rockefeller as saying, "Use it in the unseen parts of the work, for you will find enough people who want you to use their money for what can be seen."

Glorifying Christ

● A man, his wife, and little daughter stayed at the home of a friend. On the bedroom wall, just over the head of the bed in which they slept, there was a picture of the Lord Jesus, which was reflected in the large mirror of the dressing table standing near the bedroom window.

When the little girl woke on her first morning there, she saw the picture reflected in the mirror while she still lay in bed and exclaimed, "O Mummy, I can see Jesus through the mirror." She quickly raised up to take a better look, but in so doing brought her own body between the picture and the mirror, so that instead of seeing the picture of Jesus reflected, she now saw herself.

So she lay down again, and again she saw the picture of Jesus. She was up and down several times after that with her eyes fixed on the mirror. Then she said, "Mummy, when I can't see myself, I can see Jesus; but every time I see myself, I don't see him."

Good Samaritan

O On a trip a man's car got a flat tire on a steep hill. The driver behind slowed down and told the driver that he had seen the tire going down and that he was fortunate to be able to stop before it caused an accident. He passed on. Then a clergyman stopped, looked at the tire, and remarked, "Someone will be along to help you."

The driver started on the job himself. Just when he got the jack under the car, a third man came along and changed the tire. It was then that the thought came, concerning Christ's words, "Which now of these three, thinkest thou, was neighbor . . . ?"

❿ One day on a train an intoxicated man with a black-and-blue eye recognized the famous evangelist, D. L. Moody and began bellowing out hymns. Moody decided to move to another coach, but learned that the other coaches were full, so was stuck. When the conductor came along, Moody informed him of the drunk.

Whereupon the conductor gently and quietly took the fellow, bathed his swollen eye, and sent him back to his coach where he fell asleep.

After a while Moody thought, "What a rebuke to me! I preached last night to a big crowd against hypocrisy. I urged people to be like the good Samaritan. Now today when I get a chance to practice what I preached, I imitate the priest and the Levite, and the conductor comes along as the good Samaritan." For the rest of that evangelistic trip he told the story publicly against himself.

Good Works

● A noted psychiatrist was asked what he would do if he felt a nervous break-down coming on.

He answered, "I would go down the street and find someone needy and immediately seek to help him."

● A chaplain with Bible under his arm walked across a battlefield, stopping where needed to minister to the wounded and dying. Coming to a man in great pain, he laid his Bible on the ground, took off his coat and made a pillow for the soldier, then gave him the last drops of water in his own canteen. Finally, he tore up some of his own clothing and made a bandage for the soldier's wound. When he had finished, the soldier said quietly, "Now, chaplain, if there is anything in the book you placed on the ground that made you do all those things for me, please read it to me."

Gossip

O A month after arrival in a different church, the new pastor learned that a rumor had circulated about him. In effect it said that he had taken his wife to a concert after prayer meeting, had bawled her out as they sat on the front row, then had marched her down the aisle before the concert was over, arguing with her all the way down the aisle.

He let the rumor circulate for a few weeks, then decided to spike it. During the announcements on a Sunday morning he said, "The story is not true—for four reasons. First, I wouldn't take my wife to a concert after prayer meeting. Second, I wouldn't argue with her in public. Third, I wouldn't create such a scene by marching her down the aisle while the program was still on. And finally, I'm not married."

Growth

Þ In a testimony meeting a sour, old Christian, noted for his lack of growth in grace, rose to tell of his experience. "Forty years ago," he began, "the Lord filled my cup with the water of life. Since then, not a drop has run in and not a drop has run out."

Just then a little boy on the front row said in a stage whisper, "My, I bet there's a heap of wiggletails in it!"

O A girl, converted, came back to the pastor's study weeks after and said, "It's no good. Religion doesn't work. I'm just as bad-tempered as ever. I'm giving it up."

She had not been gone ten minutes when her father, who did not know she had been to church that evening, came in and put down a generous donation on the table for the work of the church.

"I'm giving you that," he said to the pastor, "because since my daughter started coming here, she's not only a different girl, but my home's a different place. The whole atmosphere's different. It's so pleasant now!"

Habits

● A boy had an oversized Saint Bernard dog on a leash. A passerby asked the boy where he was taking the dog.

Said the boy, "I don't know. I'm waiting to see where he's going first."

O A man kept reading about the danger of smoking. Everywhere he turned there were articles and warnings. He told his wife he had decided to give it up. She was delighted till she discovered that he had decided to give up—reading.

Hands

O An American unit occupied a village in Germany after World War II and decided to restore its bomb-crushed beauty. They worked hard. They restored homes, churches, public buildings, and at last, out of the rubble reconstructed a statue of Christ in the public square. They found all the pieces except two important ones, the two hands. They searched everywhere to no avail.

Then the chaplain had an idea. He said, "Let's carve on the pedestal: I HAVE NO HANDS BUT YOUR HANDS."

O An old saint in a prayer meeting prayed his stereotyped phrase, "O Lord, touch the needy with Thy finger." As he intoned this phrase, he stopped speaking. Others present moved to his side to ask if he were ill.

"No," he replied, "but something seemed to say to me, 'Thou art the finger.'"

Hearing

O During an autumn Sunday-afternoon service, suddenly the preacher's voice was interrupted by another sound. The excited voice of a radio announcer, giving a play-by-play description of a tense moment of a professional football game, blared out in the church auditorium loud and clear, making the preacher stop. This had happened: a man had brought a small, portable radio into the service, hidden in his pocket, from which he was listening to the football game by an ear plug. He hoped people would mistake it for a hearing aid. But when he sneezed and reached for his handkerchief he jerked the ear plug out so that the sound blared out into the audience.

O One preacher said the most painful moment of his career came one Sunday when he was preaching the morning sermon. A woman in a front row scrambled in her handbag and brought out a hearing aid. She put it in her ear. After five minutes she took it out again, put it back in her handbag, and sat perfectly still for the remainder of the sermon.

○ A woman lived on a busy street corner in the heart of a large city. One hot summer night she retired early. The phone rang. She slept through it. Fire engines clanged around the corner. Next door a radio blasted the night with a rock program. She slept through it. Her sister arrived with a group of friends who raided the refrigerator and played the stereo full force. She slept on. Then a remarkable thing happened. From the rear room at the opposite end of the house came the faintest kind of a voice. It said, "Mommy." Like a shot out of a gun, she was out of bed and at the side of her little three-year-old girl.

○ A great naturalist, riding in a noisy subway in New York City, suddenly exclaimed, "I hear a cricket!" His friend could not believe it, for he had heard nothing, but after a short search the cricket was found in a corner of the subway car. The friend marveled that the naturalist could detect such a sound in the midst of all the city noises.

Later, when they were walking up a busy street, someone dropped a dime on the sidewalk. The friend stopped, "Someone dropped some money!"

Whereupon the naturalist remarked, "We hear that which we are trained to hear."

○ A group of applicants were waiting at a steamship office to be interviewed for the job of wireless operator. They spoke so loudly they failed to hear the dots and dashes which began coming over the loudspeaker. About then another man entered the room and sat down quietly by himself. Suddenly, he snapped to attention, stood to his feet, then walked into the private office. A few minutes later he came out smiling. One of the group called out, "How did you get in ahead of us? We were here first."

The man answered, "One of you could have gotten the job, if you had listened to the message from the loudspeaker."

"What message?" they asked in surprise.

"Why—the code! It said, 'The man I hire must always be on the alert. The first man who gets this message and comes directly into my private office will be given the operator's job now open.'"

Heart, Not the Outside, Is What Counts

○ A Quaker woman walking down the street, was accosted by a woman who in a fit of anger proceeded to administer a tongue lashing. But the Quaker woman took it graciously. She did not retaliate even though blameless.

After the episode, a friend said wonderingly, "I marvel that you responded to her with such real Christian grace."

"Ah," said the Quaker woman, "thee did not see the boiling within."

◑ Billy Graham rented special formal clothes for his short stay at a Scottish Castle. "Never in my life have I seen so many top hats and striped trousers," he commented later. "I turned to one of the perfectly attired men at a banquet and said, 'Your grace, I don't believe we've met.' He replied, 'I'm your waiter, sir.'"

○ Dr. Peter Marshall told how in the hills above a European village an old man served as Keeper of the Springs. Patroling the mountainside, he kept the springs pure by cleaning out deposits of silt, leaves, and decay, so the waters that came tumbling down were pure and cold. But one day lack of funds led the town council to abolish his job. "The water has always been there for us to drink freely. Why pay someone to do what nature can do at no cost?"

For a few months all was fine. But strange things began to happen. Some became sick; some died. Doctors and council members worked frantically, looking for clues. They found the source of the problem. The water supply was contaminated. The life-giving spring had become polluted and clogged with leaves, had turned green in color and was covered with scum.

Up in arms, the townsfolk besieged the council to hire back the old Keeper of the Springs. Once more he made his rounds across the mountainside and once again, pure water flowed down to the village. People smiled. Sickness and odors subsided.

O In a story by Hawthorne, *Earth's Holocaust*, people overloaded with worn-out accumulation, called for a general bonfire. A stranger stood all night watching earth's inhabitants bringing the things they considered evil: pornographic literature, cigarettes, liquor, guns, and all instruments of war, to toss on the bonfire. Early in the morning the stranger was heard to remark, "These people have neglected to throw into the fire the one thing that causes all other things to be bad. Without this item all other things are nothing at all."

When asked what that was, he replied, "The human heart. Unless they find some method of purifying the heart, from it will come again all the shapes and forms of evil they have been bringing to the bonfire."

Heaven

◐ A skeptic was trying to comfort a Christian who was seriously ill. "My poor friend, how sorry I am," said the skeptic, "that you have to leave the land of the living."

But the dying man, radiant, replied, "You are wrong. I'm leaving the land of the dying to go to the country of the living."

O A dear old saint lay near death, his body racked with pain and disease. A friend asked him, "How are you?"

He replied, "Almost well!"

O A rich man died suddenly. His servant was asked, "Did your master go to heaven?"

"No, sir," came the reply. "My master always made careful preparation when he was going some place, and I didn't notice him getting ready to go anywhere. I don't think he went to heaven."

O A mother was trying to console her little daughter after the death of her daddy and explained that God had taken him away. The little girl asked her mother if God had told them in advance that he was going to take her daddy.

"No," replied the mother, "we did not know when Daddy was to go. It was a surprise."

"Well, Mummy, if God sends for us and doesn't give us notice, had we not better be ready to go when he calls?"

Holy Spirit

O A Sunday-school teacher had required the class to memorize the Apostles' Creed, and to repeat it clause by clause, with each pupil having his own clause. As the recitation began, the first boy said, "I believe in God the Father Almighty, Maker of heaven and earth." The second boy said, "I believe in Jesus Christ His only Son our Lord." The recitation went on until it reached the point where one of the boys had said, "From thence He shall come to judge the quick and the dead." Then there fell a silence that indicated something had gone wrong. The silence was broken by the next boy in line, who said to the teacher, "Please, sir, the boy who believes in the Holy Ghost is absent today."

Then the teacher commented, "Lots of folks are absent when it comes to that clause."

Honesty

O A young lay preacher, after speaking one Sunday night in a small church, boarded a bus next morning for work. He handed the driver a dollar bill. The driver gave him change. Standing at the back of the bus and counting his change, the young man found a dime too much. The first impulse was, *The bus company will never miss this dime.* But he quickly realized he should not keep it, so made his way to the front. "You gave me too much change," he said to the driver.

To his utter surprise the driver replied, "Yes, a dime too much. I did it on purpose. I heard your sermon last night. Had you kept the dime I would never have had any confidence again in preachers."

O An illustration by Norman Rockwell on the front cover of a *Saturday Evening Post* showed a nice, old lady buying a Thanksgiving turkey from a fat, friendly butcher. The turkey was being weighed on the butcher's scales. He stood on one side of the counter and the nice old lady stood on the other side of the counter. Their eyes were both riveted on the weight indicator. You could see the expression of mischievous delight in the eyes of both customer and butcher. Cautiously the butcher had placed his big right thumb on the scales, pressing down. On the other side the sweet little old lady had placed her chubby forefinger underneath the scales, pressing upward. Each was unaware of the other's deception.

Humility

◉ A statue depicted Christ with open arms extending an invitation to come to him. A man stood and gazed at the statue in disappointment.

A little lad standing near saw his disappointment and said, "To understand the statue you must go close to it, then kneel down and look up into his face."

When the man adopted this posture, the face of Christ took on new beauty.

O Felix Mendelssohn, playing with two other pianists in a three-piano arrangement, found that the other two had to concentrate grimly on the score. Although he could easily play the piece from memory, he placed some music on the rack and asked a friend to turn the pages for him.

O Late one night during a conference at Moody Bible Institute, the famed Moody was walking around the halls to see that all was in order. Turning a corner he came upon the guest rooms where some visiting English preachers were sleeping. Outside each door was a pair of shoes.

Spotting some students he said, "These ministers are following the custom of their country, where they always put their shoes out to be cleaned at night. Would you fellows get a piece of chalk from a class room, put the number of the room on the soles of the shoes, then shine them nicely?"

One student protested, "Mr. Moody, I didn't come to this school to clean shoes. I came here to study for the ministry." The others said the same.

"Very well," said Moody, "you may go back to your rooms." Then Moody himself collected the shoes, took them to his room, polished them nicely, and put them back in place.

O A rider on horseback during the Revolutionary War came across a squad of soldiers trying to move a heavy piece of timber. A corporal stood by with a self-important air, giving lordly orders to *heave*. But the piece of timber was a trifle too heavy for the squad. "Why don't you help them?" asked the quiet man on the horse, addressing the officious corporal.

"Me? Why, I'm a corporal, sir!"

Dismounting, the stranger carefully took his place with the soldiers. "Now, all together, boys, *heave*," he exclaimed. And the big piece of timber slid into place.

The stranger mounted his horse. Then turning to the corporal he said, "The next time you have a piece of timber for your men to handle, corporal, send for the commander-in-chief." The stranger was George Washington!

Hypocrisy

O During a coffee break in a Manhattan factory, a small group of workmen were coaxing one of their number to have a cup of coffee. "Naw, I gave it up for Lent. It's a religious principle with me."

But as the group stood to leave, he turned to the supply clerk standing next to him and said, "Say, I need another pair of work trousers. How about stealing me a pair some time this week?"

O One Christian who owed money to another prayed in prayer meeting, "Lord give us faith—a devil-driving faith."

The brother to whom he owed money prayed quietly, "Amen, Lord, and give us debt-paying faith too."

Idle Words

O A wife persuaded her unwilling husband to go out to dinner at the home of one of her acquaintances. During the evening, when the host and hostess left the room, the irritated husband remarked, "Well, I hope you are enjoying yourself, because I'm not! This man's a bore; the woman's a snob; the meal was awful; the chairs are hard; the room is as drafty as the South Pole. Speaking for myself, this is the last time I am coming to this house!"

A moment later the host returned to the room. Pulling a rather large object from behind the davenport he said with a roguish grin, "I've got something here that will intrigue you. You see—I switched this tape recorder on when I went out of the room. I thought you would be amused to hear what your voices sound like. I'll play it back now." And he did.

The husband was quite right when he said this was the last time he would ever come to that house!

O One night before a church service at which hundreds were present, Jim Vaus, an electronics expert who once worked for Mickey Cohen and syndicated crime, wired mikes in several spots around the church. At the end of the service, he told the congregation that he had recorded several conversations from all parts of the church and would play them back the next night.

When the service was over, several men approached Vaus and offered to buy the tapes. They didn't want words uttered privately played back publicly. Later Vaus discovered that he did not have the switch on, so none of it was on tape anyway.

Incarnation

O Not long after a little boy fell asleep one night, a nightmare woke him up screaming. His father hurried up to comfort him, but the shadows on the wall plus the darkness of the room, kept him shuddering. Finally, his father said, "I must leave you now. But God will watch over you. God's right here."

As the father left, the little boy whispered, "I want a God what's got skin on."

O A young man became a partner with his father in a business with branch factories all over the country. One day this young man disguised himself and applied for a job at a branch factory in a remote site. Hired by the personnel department, he put on working clothes like the other men, punched a time clock, carried his lunch to work, joined the same union, and drew the same wages. Literally, he became one of the employees of the factory. However, he did not cease to be the co-owner of the company. At the same time he was both co-owner and employee.

O An educated Hindu one day stopped to examine a hill of ants. As he stooped, his shadow frightened them into all directions. When he lifted himself up, the ants resumed their usual activities. When he bent down a second time, they again scurried in all directions. The Hindu thought, "I wish I could talk to those tiny creatures and let them know I wouldn't hurt them." His mind toyed with the experience. "Even if I could talk to those creatures, and even if they had intelligence, and if I could learn their language, I probably couldn't communicate with them because my thoughts are not their thoughts. My terms of expression would not be understandable to them." His imagination kept working. "But if I could become one of them, somehow retaining my personality and my self-consciousness, I could then really tell them something of my thoughts."

Then suddenly it dawned on him, "That's exactly what these Christian teachers have been telling us all the time, that God has become man in order to reveal himself to us, and rescue us." According to this story, this educated Hindu became a Christian through his own illustration.

O One winter night many years ago in a European town the steeplewatch of a cathedral tower was sitting in his cozy parlor with his open Bible on the table and his stove burning by his side. To his surprise he heard steps on the stone stairs. The door was opened by a famous astronomer who lived in town, breathless from fatigue and shivering from the cold. "Why, doctor," said the steeplewatch, "how is it you are here on such a frosty night?"

"I have a job that must be done tonight. There'll never be another opportunity for 200 years. A conjunction of certain stars will occur at 12:30. I would regret it the rest of my life if I missed it. It's 11:30 now. I must go up and fix the telescope."

Then viewing the snug, little room, the doctor commented, "A comfortable place this is, but how can you be happy living here alone?"

"I'm not quite so alone as you think sir. You know I'm fond of reading."

"Yes, I never come here but I find you at your Bible. How can you fill up your whole life with the contents of that one book? Contrast that little volume with the infinite book I peruse. The whole firmament lies open before me. Do you readily believe that the Creator of all these magnificent orbs lowered himself to become a man? Can you suppose that the Prince of heaven would bypass those wonderful worlds to take an interest in such a paltry particle of the universe as this earth?"

The steeplewatch replied, "A shepherd will leave his sheep to seek one that is lost. Such a one is Christ. If no way to save his fallen creatures could be found but by coming down here to bear their due, he would do it, even though it cost him his life."

Just then the clock struck midnight. The astronomer seized his lantern and climbed the tower steps. Scarcely fifteen minutes had gone when the steeplewatch was roused by a violent push at the door. There stood the doctor agitated, "Quick, bring your lantern! There's not a moment to lose! Help me hunt! A small screw slipped from my cold fingers when I was fixing my instrument. It must have fallen on the balcony outside your room!"

The two men got down and groped over the cold stone pavement. The doctor, unmindful of the frosty wind chilling him to the bone rubbed his hands over the stones as though polishing them. Suddenly he exclaimed, "Here it is!" He bounded up the steps to his telescope.

An hour later the doctor came down. "I've seen it all! It was most beautiful!"

"I'm glad, sir, for I feared you would miss it altogether. How surprised I was to see you making such a fuss about a tiny screw. I thought to myself, 'There is the famous doctor, the most learned and wealthy man in this town, one to whom everyone bows respectfully, running down our stairs, panting and coughing at this late hour of the night, and all for the sake of a little screw!'

"Well, well," cried the doctor, "don't you see, you simple fellow, that everything depended on that little screw. If I hadn't found it, the telescope would have been useless. My investigation would have been a failure, and I couldn't have reported it to the scientific world!"

"Then, sir," said the steeplewatch, "you yourself have experienced what a man will do to recover what he has lost, insignificant as it is, but connected with the delight of his heart and the honor of his name. If you, the noblest inhabitant of our town, didn't hesitate to lower yourself to the dust of the pavement for the sake of a lost piece of brass, why do you wonder that the great Creator should have humbled himself to find and save his lost creatures, however insignificant and worthless they seem?"

The doctor was silent. Then with a tear in his eye, he rose, "Sir, your book teaches you higher things than the stars ever taught me!"

Infidels

O On an ocean liner crossing the Atlantic a Sunday-morning sermon on "God's Answers to Prayer" made a skeptic react, "Bah, child's talk." Later that day after the noon meal he slipped two oranges into his pocket, intending to enjoy them in a quiet spot. Spotting an old woman in her deck chair, with upturned face, eyes closed in sleep, her arms resting palms upward, he thought he would play a little joke on her, so gently laid an orange in each hand. Returning later, he found her eating an orange with great delight. "Enjoying your orange, Mother?" he asked.

"Oh, sir," she responded, "very much. You see—I was so thirsty with sea-sickness, and I asked my Father in heaven if he would send me an orange. I must have gone to sleep, and when I awoke, I found an orange in each hand. My Father is so good!"

O A girl lay dying. Her father was an infidel, her mother a Christian. The skeptical father had often ridiculed his wife's faith to his children, but now a great sorrow was crushing the father's heart. His little child was dying. Just then her weak voice was heard, a voice soon to be hushed in death. "Father, shall I believe what you tell me, or what Mother teaches me out of the Bible about what comes after I die?"

After a moment's quiet the father spoke, "You'd better believe what your mother tells you."

O In the eighteenth century two men of acknowledged talents, persuaded that the Bible was an imposture, determined to expose what they considered to be a cheat. Their strategy was to attack what they considered the two bulwarks of Christianity: the resurrection of Christ and the conversion of Paul.

Lord Lyttleton, graduate of Eton and Oxford and member of Parliament, who moved on intimate terms with Bolingbroke, Pope, Chesterfield, and Dr. Samuel Johnson, chose the conversion of Paul. His friend Gilbert West took the resurrection of Christ for the subject of hostile criticism.

Neither had read to any extent in the New Testament, so in fairness to their assignments, they began to examine the evidence. Though both began their tasks full of prejudice against the Bible, when they came together with their finished books, instead of exposing the Bible to ridicule, their books have provided for us two of the most valuable treatises in favor of the Christian faith, one entitled *Observations on the Conversion of St. Paul*, and the other *Observations on the Resurrection of Christ*.

O When Dr. Samuel Johnson was paid a visit by a man who denied the existence of God and a moral order, he commented to his friend, Boswell, "If he does really think there is no distinction between virtue and vice, then when he leaves our house, let us count our spoons."

Joy

O On a train from Kansas City to Chicago an evangelist's wife was unable to get a seat. A porter said, "There's a vacant room ahead. I'm going to put three women in it and I want you to be one of them."

Going to the roomette, she found herself in the company of two other women. One was a giddy, young blond with heavily painted face, gaudy dress, filthy vocabulary, and a small bottle of whisky in the pocket of her fur coat. The other woman was a well-dressed woman of culture and refinement whose husband was a prominent businessman.

The ride was long, so the women in the small compartment took down their hair. The giddy blond offered the other two a drink, which they refused, told how she was going to spend the weekend with a soldier in Chicago, how she lived for pleasure. She asked to try on the distinguished woman's large diamond rings and said she would be the happiest person in the world if only she had such rings and a mink coat.

The evangelist's wife told of her life married to a preacher and how happy she was to be a Christian and in the Lord's work.

The other woman then spoke to the blond. "My dear, you say you would be the happiest woman in the world if only you had my rings, my coat, and my home. But I have these and a great many more things and instead of being happy, I believe I am the unhappiest woman in the world. I have found that wealth does not bring happiness. I have a large home, servants, and automobiles, but for years I've not been happy. My husband and I have grown apart; our love has grown cold. Today I believe I have found from our conversation where the trouble lies. I have left Christ out of my life, and so have you."

O A boy often exclaimed, "Hallelujah" in school. Because this disrupted the class, the teacher ordered him to stop saying this word. When he unwittingly kept letting out a loud "hallelujah," the teacher ordered him to the principal's office. The principal, busy for the moment, gave him a geography book to look at, thinking there was nothing in there to excite the lad's religious enthusiasm. Suddenly, the principal heard a loud "hallelujah" and came running to see what made the boy get excited.

Said the boy, "I was just reading in this geography book about oceans, and I came to a sentence which says that the depth of some seas has not been discovered, and my Bible says that my sins have been cast into the depth of the sea— hallelujah!"

A hunter who had been out all winter alone, trapping for furs, tells this story, "It was March, just as the ice was starting to break up. I was hunting for beaver on one of the remotest, wildest lakes I have ever visited. There couldn't have been a human being within eighty miles. Suddenly I heard something walking through the loose ice. I felt sure it was a moose. I had my rifle ready in one hand, and was pushing the canoe with the other. Carefully I rounded a point and saw a man, wading in the ice water. He had nothing on his hands or feet, and his clothes were almost torn off. He was wasted to almost skin and bones. I got this skeleton figure into my canoe, rowed to shore, and built a fire. In his hand he had the bone of an animal which he had gnawed to almost nothing. I gave him hot food and tea.

Next morning I found out from him with great difficulty his hometown. After a week's careful travel, I arrived at the town where he said he lived. I found the town in great excitement. More than a hundred men were scattered through the woods and mountains looking for him. It had been prearranged that if he were found, immediately the bells should be rung and guns fired. Soon as I brought him, a shout went up, his friends rushed to him, and then bells pealed forth in loud notes and guns fired, echoing again and again through mountain and forest till every seeker knew he had been found.

All day long I had to repeat the story. People were crazy with joy. The man came from one of the finest families. His memory returned to him. They dined me and loaded my canoe with provisions. They forgot all except the finding of the lost man."

o A pastor was visiting a mission field. The missionary took him to a building where lepers were soon to come for a service. The pastor watched, as one by one the sufferers came limping in, their swollen faces lifted in happy expectation.

"What shall we sing?" inquired the leader, thinking they would call for "I must tell Jesus all of my troubles."

But to his surprise, the request came at once for something very different:
Singing I go along life's road,
For Jesus has lifted my load!

Judge (To Be Faced Some Day)

o A father whose son was wayward asked a friend, a Christian lawyer, to try to talk sense into him. At an opportune moment, the lawyer witnessed to the boy who laughingly put him off.

One day, the young man, thoroughly intoxicated, was trying to cross a busy intersection, when a speeding car threatened to run him down. In a flash someone pushed him to safety, probably saving his life. It was the Christian lawyer, who seeing who the young man was, again begged him to give his life to Christ. Again he was rebuffed.

Years went by. The young man had gone from bad to worse. Now a middle-aged man, he was on trial for a serious crime. The judge happened to be the Christian lawyer who had been promoted to the judgeship. At the end of the trial, when the young man was asked if he had anything to say, replied, "Yes, I know this judge. He's a friend of my father. And once he saved my life, and I believe he's going to do it again."

After a brief pause, the judge looked at the man, then said, "It's true I'm a friend of your father. And it's true I did save your life once. But now I'm your judge, and I am going to have to pass sentence on you." If we reject Christ as our Savior here, we'll face him as our judge in the hereafter.

O A judge in a Pennsylvania city, walking down the main street, saw two men fighting. When he tried to intervene, one of the fighters punched him in the face. The judge went to his office and issued a warrant for the two men.

When they were brought before him, they exclaimed, "Oh, judge, we didn't know it was you!"

Judging

● A newspaper once printed the pictures of the nine members then serving as justices on the Supreme Court of the USA, without their names underneath. They mixed these pictures with those of nine convicted murderers—criminals who had committed rather vicious killings—and again omitted names. Then the newspaper asked its readers to pick out which was which. People could not tell. They made many mistakes.

● A couple was thinking of adopting a little boy from an orphanage. He was staying with them for several days. They all seemed so happy together until one morning the couple thought the boy had told them a lie. They kept candies in a paperbag at the head of their bed, and some were missing. Neither threat nor promise could draw from the boy a confession of guilt. So the couple sadly and silently drove him back to the orphanage and left him.

That night they could not sleep. Suddenly, in the stillness, they heard the rustling of the paperbag containing the candy. Turning on the light, they saw a mouse scurry across the floor and disappear down a hole. A mouse was the thief. Deeply grieved that they had so harshly misjudged him, long before daylight they rose and sped back to the orphanage to bring the child back home.

● An opinionated young man stood in front of a taxidermist store. In the window was an owl that had attracted many sightseers. Anxious to display his knowledge, he said with pompous air, "If I couldn't stuff an owl better than that, I would quit the business. The head isn't right. The pose of the body isn't right. The feet are not placed right."

But before he could finish his evaluation, the owl turned his head and winked at him. The crowd laughed, and the critic moved on.

O A lady was showing a friend her neighbor's wash through her back window. "Our neighbor isn't very clean. Look at those streaks on the wash!"

Replied her friend, "Those streaks aren't on your neighbor's wash. They're on your window."

O A missionary gave an impassioned plea for young people to consider service on the mission field when they grew up. After the service a small boy asked to see him.

"I think I can guess why you wish to see me. You want to be a missionary when you grow up, don't you?"

"Oh, no, sir," answered the boy, "I just wondered if you had any foreign stamps you could give me."

O An English newspaper ran a contest in which the contestants were to write a piece in the style of George Bernard Shaw. Shaw sent in some of his writing under an assumed name.

He was quite amused to receive a consolation prize with the comment "Mediocre."

Judgment

O In September 1938, a man who lived on Long Island was able to satisfy a long-time ambition, which was to own a very fine barometer. But when the instrument arrived by mail in his home, he was extremely disappointed to find that the indicating needle appeared to be stuck, pointing to the sector marked HURRICANE. After shaking the barometer vigorously several times, he sat down and wrote a scorching letter to the company from which he had purchased the barometer and mailed the letter the following morning on his way to his New York City office.

That evening he returned to Long Island to find his house severely damaged. The barometer's needle had not been stuck after all. There was a hurricane—and a severe one.

O The railroad station agent at Chappaqua, New York, was selling six hundred newspapers a day from his newsstand concession. He began to worry when his receipts were off several dollars a day. So he bored a hole in the ceiling above the coin box, and with his helper watched the morning commuters, as they made their own change. He noted four well-dressed men and a woman dropping in small coins and taking out quarters and fifty-cent pieces. The next day he made a movie, filming the actions of the light-fingered five. When the film was developed, he posted a sign in the station warning the culprits and commenting, "Shall we have an early movie some morning, or do I rate reimbursement?"

A great flurry of newspaper publicity greeted the announcement. The pilfering abruptly ceased. The station agent publicly burned the secretly made picture film.

O On a vacation trip to the Adirondacks a man and wife from Vermont met a quiet, pleasant couple from New York. All four of them had a grand time together. Later the gentleman from Vermont made up a nice album of snapshots he had taken of the other couple and mailed it to them in New York. The gift was never acknowledged, until one day a big city lawyer appeared and asked the gentleman if he had prepared the album.

"Sure," was his reply. "Did they get it?"

"It was received all right," said the lawyer. "And I'm representing the man's wife in a divorce suit. You see—she wasn't the woman in the album!"

O The gifted poet, John Donne, was walking one day in a churchyard in England. He saw the sexton digging a grave. As he lifted up spade after spade—full of dirt, suddenly a skull was tossed up along with the dirt. John Donne picked it up in his hands and examined it. In the skull, sticking in the temple, he saw a headless nail. Quietly he drew it out and wrapped it in the corner of his handkerchief. Then he asked the gravedigger if he knew whose skull it was. The grave digger said he did. It had been a man's who kept a rum shop, a dissipated fellow who one morning was found dead in bed after he had taken two quarts of liquor the night before. "Had he a wife?" Donne asked.

"A very good one," responded the gravedigger." "Only her neighbors often wonder about her because she married the day after her husband was buried."

A few days later John Donne paid a visit to this woman. He asked her a number of questions, among others, what sickness her husband had died of. She told him about his having taken the two quarts of liquor and how he was found dead in bed the next morning. Whereupon Donne opened his handkerchief and holding up the nail, said, "Woman, do you recognize this nail?"

The woman suddenly turned white and immediately acknowledged the crime, for which she was later punished.

Justification

● A man resigned from the official board of a large Canadian church. His besetting sin before conversion had been alcohol. Now he had slipped and had been seen intoxicated on a crowded streetcar. He was removed from the elder board.

A few months later he came to the business meeting of the church, confessed his fault, and for many months lived an exemplary life. Thereupon he was voted back on to the elder board.

At one of the board's later meetings, his fellow elders voted to expunge from the minutes every mention of the incident, so that today no record can be found in their official transactions. It was just as if he had never sinned.

Kindness

● A plainly dressed woman was noticed picking up something in the street in a slum district where ragged, barefooted little children were accustomed to play. The policeman on the beat noticed the woman's actions and watched her very suspiciously. Several times he saw her stoop and pick up something and hide it in her apron. Finally he went up to her and in a gruff voice demanded, "What are you carrying off in your apron?"

The timid woman did not answer at first, whereupon the policeman, thinking she must have found something valuable, threatened her with arrest if she did not show him what she had in her apron.

The woman opened her apron and revealed a handful of broken glass.

"What do you want with that stuff?" asked the policeman.

The woman replied, "I just thought I'd like to take it out of the way of the children's feet."

● A young girl in a small German town had advertised a piano recital, stating untruthfully that she was a pupil of Liszt. The day before the recital the young pianist was suddenly terrified to learn that the great musician himself had arrived in the area.

O Not knowing what to do, she finally decided to see the famous composer and tell him her story. In great agitation she gained admittance to his room and sobbed out her confession, explaining that she had been left an orphan, that she had no means of earning a livelihood other than by her musical ability, and that she had pretended to be his pupil to win recognition.

Liszt looked at her with kindly eyes. "You have done wrong, but we all make mistakes, and then the only thing left for us to do is to be sorry. I think you are sorry. Let me hear you play."

Very timidly the girl obeyed, faltering at first, though she won confidence as she went on. She played very well, but Liszt corrected her in one or two points, and then said, "My dear, I have now instructed you a little. You are a pupil of Liszt. You may go on with your concert, and as you tell me the programs are not yet printed, you may add that the last number will be played, not by the pupil but by the master."

Knowledge

O A science professor in a boys' school possessed an uncanny knowledge of life. You could show him the bone of any animal, and he could name the animal. Give him the scale of a fish, and he would not only name the fish but tell you where it lived and when it spawned. His was the world of animals. One day the boys tried a trick on the professor. They got the skeleton of a bear, stuffed it with cotton, sewed over it the skin of a lion, fastened on its head the horns of an ox, and on its feet they glued the hooves of a wild buffalo. They made a good job of it.

Then one afternoon, when the professor was taking his after-lunch nap, they opened the door of his study, and carefully set up their monstrosity. Behind the door, they let out an unearthly growl.

The professor stirred, then tumbled off his bed and bolted to his feet, alert with fear. Then through their peepholes, the boys witnessed a surprising change. The old professor rubbed his eyes, looked at the fierce teeth, the horns, and finally at the split hooves. He exclaimed, "How wonderful—it's herbivorous, not carnivorous!" And he went back to finish his nap. His knowledge had rescued him.

Lamb of God

O A man traveling in Germany saw the carved figure of a lamb near the top of a church tower. Asked why it had been placed in this position, he was told this story:

When the church was being built, a workman fell from the high scaffold about the tower. The men working with him, transfixed with fear, reached the ground as quickly as possible, expecting to find the body dashed to pieces. To their surprise, their companion was virtually unhurt. A flock of sheep was being driven past the church at the moment of his fall. He had fallen on one of the lambs. The lamb was crushed to death, but the man was saved.

The carved figure of a lamb was placed on the tower, not only to commemorate the event but to remind all of Jesus, the Lamb of God.

Leisure

O An Oriental gentleman on a tour of an American house listened patiently to explanations of each time-saving gadget. At the end he asked, "And what do you do with all the time you save?"

Life

O Schopenhauer, pessimistic European philosopher of the nineteenth century, sat on a park bench at 2:00 A.M. one morning with chin in hands and elbows on his knees, when a policeman came along. Not recognizing the distinguished philosopher, the officer asked, "Who are you, and what are you doing here?"

After a minute of silence, Schopenhauer replied, "I wish I knew."

O What is the best age of life to be alive?

This question was asked of a dozen people on a television program. One little girl said, "Two months, because you would be carried around. And you had lots of love and care."

Another child answered, "Three years, because you didn't have to go to school. You could do pretty much what you wanted, and could play most of the time."

A teenage fellow said, "Eighteen. Because you are out of high school and you can drive in New York City."

One girl said, "Sixteen, because you can have your ears pierced."

One man replied, "Age twenty-five. Because you have more pep." The man who answered was then forty-three. He said he found it hard to walk up a hill now. He said that at twenty-five he used to go till midnight, but now he is asleep by 9:00.

A three-year-old girl said the best age to be alive was twenty-nine. Because at that age you could lie around the house, sleep, and loaf most of the time. She was asked, "How old is your mother?" She replied, "Twenty-nine."

Someone thought forty was the best age because you are in the prime of life and vitality.

One lady answered fifty-five, because you are over your responsibilities of raising your children and can enjoy life and grandchildren.

One man said sixty-five, because after that you can enjoy retirement.

The last person, an elderly woman, commented that all ages are good, so enjoy the age you are now.

O A country woman at a county fair was angry at her husband who somehow managed to get hold of a nickel and go on the merry-go-round. She guarded the family purse strings in miserly fashion, and felt this a foolish waste of money. When the merry-go-round came to a stop, she was waiting for him. "What's the big idea! You got off where you got on! You spent a whole nickel and you ain't been nowhere!" Sometimes life seems like a merry-go-round.

Little Things

O A fine cathedral clock in a great European city ceased to sound its chimes. The citizens were disturbed. Some said it was a warning of impending ill fortune. Some thought it the work of enemies.

The caretaker climbed up and examined the works—the wheel and springs had not been tampered with. Then an old watchmaker climbed up. Finally he found in one of the most delicate springs of the old time piece a tiny bit of crushed butterfly.

O A small thing played an important role in sending a murderer to the electric chair.

One witness was a taxi driver who remembered him on the night of the murder. Why? Because on a three-dollar-and-fifty-cents fare the accused man had given him only a five-cent tip.

"Five cents," the taxi driver repeated. "I took a good look at his face, and I'll never forget him. There he sits, right over there."

And he pointed at the accused man.

O Many years ago Queen Victoria was returning to London from Balmoral Castle. There was snow in the highlands, but a torrential rain was falling. The train bearing the Queen, the Prime Minister and other dignitaries was rushing through the night when suddenly, outlined against the snow in the glare of the headlights, a black figure appeared waving its arms frantically. The engineer jammed on the brakes. The Queen and her companions were thrown from their seats. The train crew ran ahead and there fifty yards ahead, was a bridge fairly washed out by the storm. Another minute and the crew, the Queen and her retinue would have been engulfed in the waters of the river.

Breathing a prayer of thanks, the crew looked about for the warning figure, but it had disappeared.

Later, the engineer discovered a moth had somehow been caught in the headlight.

Lord's Supper

O A Christian woman, a faithful tither for many years, came to church early one Sunday morning with her heart set on buying some lovely clothes. When her husband's check had arrived Saturday, she had thought, "This one time I'll not put in the tithe. I'll give only one dollar so I'll have money to purchase that dress."

But that Sunday morning she was helping on the committee to prepare the elements for the communion table. As she started to fill the little glasses, the Lord began to speak to her about her plan to withhold the tithe to use for her own self. Examining herself, she cried out, "O Lord, I cannot take the Lord's Supper till I know you are pleased with me."

She solemnly promised God that when she cashed that check she would give the tithe to him. Later in the service, in sweet peace and remembrance of the One who sacrificed all for us, she partook of the elements which pictured his broken body and shed blood.

Long-Suffering of God

● The infidel Bob Ingersoll thought he had once proven there was no God when he challenged God by giving him five minutes to strike him dead.

An old saint in England hearing what the infidel had done, remarked, "Does the gentleman from America think he can exhaust the patience of God in five minutes?"

❿ A deacon, usually noted for his poise and patience, was feverishly pacing the floor one day. A friend asked, "What's the trouble?"

His answer, "I'm in a hurry—but God isn't."

✘❿ After an atheist had challenged God to strike him dead in five minutes, and nothing had happened, he boasted, "What did I tell you?"

An elderly woman standing by said, "Sir, have you any children?"

"Yes," replied the man. "Why?"

Said the lady, "If one of your children handed you a knife and said, 'Kill me, Daddy,' would you do it?"

"Why, no," replied the astonished man, "I love them too much."

Retorted the lady, "That is exactly why God did not strike you dead. He loves you too much!"

Love

✱❿ A missionary returned after several years of service. His friend said to him, "Tell me what you found at your station."

"Found! I found people who seemed utterly devoid of moral sense. If a mother was carrying her little baby, and the baby began to cry, she would throw it into the ditch and let it die. If a man saw his father break his leg, he would leave him on the roadside to die. They had no compassion whatever. They did not know what it meant."

"Well, what did you do for people like that? Did you preach to them?"

"Preach? No! I lived."

"Lived? How did you live?"

"When I saw a baby crying, I picked it up and comforted it. When I saw a man with a broken leg, I mended it. When I saw people in distress, I took them in and pitied them. I took care of them. And those people began to come to me and say, 'Why are you doing this?' Then I had my chance and I preached the gospel."

"Did you succeed?"

"When I left, I left a *church*!"

❿ A little, barefoot boy was being taunted continually by children in his neighborhood with these remarks, "You are a little Christian. Why doesn't God tell his friends to send you some shoes?"

The boy's Solomonlike answer was, "I think God does tell them, but they don't listen."

O It was a hot Sunday afternoon. A little boy was seen trudging along the road. "Where are you off to?" said someone.

"My old Sunday School," was the reply.

"But that's a very long way from where you are living now!"

"Yes, it's a good three miles!" said the sturdy little chap, "but I still go every Sunday, because they love a fellow over there."

● A Sunday school teacher was much exasperated at the inattention of her class. "Will you shut up while I teach you about the love of God?" she shouted.

Lukewarmness

O The new minister announced that there would be no more *amens* or *hallelujahs* in the church service. In fact, he instructed the ushers to remove from the sanctuary any one who persisted in saying *Amen* or *Hallelujah* during the sermon.

The very next Sunday a little old woman got carried away. Right in the middle of the service she began to shout "Amen, Hallelujah!" Two ushers hastened to her aisle, lifted her gently but firmly out of the seat and half-carried her down the center aisle.

She waved her handkerchief the entire route, saying, "Jesus rode one into Jerusalem, and it takes two to carry me out!"

Lying

O Some schoolteachers were taking a periodic efficiency test. On the final page was a long list of books. CHECK BOOKS YOU HAVE READ, advised the printed directions.

Later the examiners discovered to their amazement that one-third of the teachers had checked almost every book. Some had checked every one.

Were they well read? No, they were liars. Twenty-five of fifty titles did not exist. They had been invented by the examiners to test honesty.

O "Nancy," said the teacher sternly, "you know you shouldn't tell lies. Your mother wouldn't like it!"

"Oh, my mother doesn't care," replied Nancy. "She does it herself. Last night she told me she would be right in the next room all evening while I slept, and when I peeked through the door I saw a strange lady there. My mother had gone to her club!"

O On a warm summer morning a preacher noticed that many in the congregation were drowsy. He paused in his sermon, then said, "Once I called at a farm and beheld a most unusual sight. I saw four little lambs, and each lamb had a long five-foot curved horn growing out of the middle of its back." The clergyman paused again. Everyone was wide awake.

"How strange," he said. A few minutes ago I was preaching truth. Most of you dozed. Now I tell you a whopper of a lie, and you are all awake."

O A lady, who never went to church, sent her ten-year-old boy to Sunday school. He learned many things that seemed so different from the way his mother lived. In the spring she planned a trip east, deciding to take the boy with her.

At the railway ticket office she quietly told him to lie about his age and say he was nine, thus saving her twenty-five dollars in fare. But the boy unexpectedly and earnestly blurted out, "No, Mom, I'm not going to hell for twenty-five dollars."

Man

o A friend of the late Teddy Roosevelt reported that he and Roosevelt used to play a little game when they were visiting each other. After an evening of conversation they would go outside on a clear night and search the skies until they found a faint speck of light-mist in a certain spot in the heavens. Then one or the other would recite:

That is the Spiral Galaxy in Andromeda.

That speck is as large as our Milky Way.

It is one of a hundred million galaxies.

It consists of one hundred billion suns, each larger than our sun.

Then Roosevelt would grin and say, "Now I think we are small enough! Let's go to bed!"

o A young man left Wales to live in America. His parents, late in life, had a son whom the Welshman, now in America, had never seen. When his mother died, he returned home to Wales to see how the little lad and his aging father were getting along. On arrival he found out that father and son were getting along beautifully, despite the big generation gap. Each was devoted to the other. By the hour the son would listen to his father read stories.

One night, after the lad had gone to bed, the older son asked his father, "Suppose something should happen to you?" The old man admitted thinking of this many times.

Knowing he could never succeed in getting his father to leave Wales, the older boy suggested, "Let me take the lad with me back to America. He'll be sure of a home with me. Then you won't have to worry."

Although it broke the father's heart, he agreed to let the boy go. As father and son said good-bye in heart-rending embrace, the older son pushed a new toy into the lad's hand to get him aboard the train. During the train ride to the coast, despite his new toy, the lad kept falling into a sad stare. On board ship things were no better. He ate little, cried himself to sleep. In America he was surrounded with the best wealth could buy. He had a finely furnished room. Every effort was made to make him feel at home. But he had no appetite and lost weight.

The doctor, learning the facts, said there was only one cure—the boy had to be taken back to his father. The Welshman found a nurse going to Wales. He learned later that back in his familiar surroundings with his father, his appetite came back as did color to his cheeks. The old father and the lad continued as before, devoted to each other. Man was made for God and finds no rest till back in fellowship with the father.

Marriage

o According to psychologist Alfred Adler, a test for marriage compatability was observed for years in a certain district of Germany. A prospective bride and groom were taken to a clearing where a tree trunk had been cut down. The couple were given a two-handed saw and told to saw the trunk in two. If they pulled against each other and got nowhere, it showed lack of cooperation. If one wished to take the lead and do it by oneself, it took twice the time. Both needed initiative, but their initiatives had to be combined.

○ A different kind of announcement was placed in a newspaper on the twentieth anniversary by a proud husband.

It read: "I WILL BE RESPONSIBLE FOR ALL THE OBLIGATIONS OF MY WIFE. DURING TWENTY YEARS OF MARRIAGE SHE HAS GIVEN ME GREAT HAPPINESS, COMFORT, COUNSEL, AND TWO FINE CHILDREN. AS WE BEGIN OUR TWENTY-FIRST YEAR, I AM PROUD TO ASSUME ANY AND ALL OF HER WISHES.

○ A seven-year-old was asked, when attending a wedding, what kind of wedding he was going to have. Solemnly he answered, "I'm never going to marry. I've lived with married people too long."

● The teacher was making out a registration card. "What is your father's name?" she asked.

"Daddy," answered the little girl.

"Yes, I know, but what does your mother call him?"

"Mother doesn't call him anything," the little girl replied, "She likes him."

Mary/Martha

○ Two preachers were discussing the relative merits of Mary and Martha. They noted how Martha took pains to prepare a good meal, while Mary sought fellowship with Jesus. Finally, one said to the other, "Which would you prefer for a wife?"

Came his quick reply, "I would like Martha before dinner and Mary after."

Master

○ A soldier, transferred to a new base, contacted his superior officer and told him all the things he could do.

After letting him talk for a few minutes, the officer said, "Private, your only responsibility is to report for duty."

● Henry Ford and three companions, on a short trip in the early days of the automobile, stopped by the roadside when a man came along, quite disturbed, explaining that his car had gone dead a mile away. "Do any of you know how to fix a Ford?"

One of the men pointed to Ford. "That old fellow there knows something about Fords."

Driving down the road in his own Model-T to where the car was stalled, he soon had it going. The man exclaimed, not knowing that the man who fixed his car was the man who had designed it, "You've fixed my car so it runs better than it ever did."

○ A retired jockey appeared at a mission service on Palm Sunday. The lesson was that of Jesus entering Jerusalem.

After the service the jockey commented, "What a jockey he would have made! I know what he was riding. It was a Syrian colt. I had a drove of those beasts to break once. Jesus sat on one that nobody had ever ridden before. And all those youngsters were running in front and waving palms. Yet Jesus was holding him as meek as anything."

The jockey paused a moment, and then said, "I say, if he could do that with a bit of horseflesh, I reckon he could do something with me."

Missions

● One day Dr. Wilfred Grenfell, medical missionary to Labrador, was a guest at a dinner in London together with a number of socially prominent British people. During the course of the dinner the woman seated next to him turned and said, "Is it true, Dr. Grenfell, that you are a missionary?"

Dr. Grenfell looked at her for a moment before replying, and then he said, "Is it true, madam, that you are not?"

o Through the quiet streets of a fishing village at the mouth of a turbulent river, a cry rang out, "Boy overboard!" Quickly a crowd gathered, and anxious eyes looked out over the rushing water to the figure of the drowning boy. Each anxious mother's heart was asking, "Is he *my* boy?"

A rope was brought, and the strongest swimmer in the village volunteered to rescue the drowning lad. Tying one end of the rope to his waist, he threw the other among the crowd, and plunged in. Eagerly they watched him breast the tide with strong, sure strokes, and a cheer went up when he reached the boy and grasped him safely in his powerful arms. "Pull in the rope!" he shouted over the swirling waters.

The villagers looked from one to another. "Who is holding the rope?" they asked.

But no one was holding the rope! In the excitement of watching the rescue, the end of the rope had slipped into the water. Powerless to help, they watched two precious lives go down because no one had made it his business to hold the shore end of the rope.

o Back before the Communist takeover of China, a large company was looking for someone to represent their interests in that country. A board member exclaimed, "I know just the man for the job. And he knows the language and customs of the people. And on top of that, he's in China now. You see—he's a missionary there."

The board member was authorized to track down the missionary and offer him a large salary to secure his services. Finding him in the heart of China, he offered him ten thousand dollars if he would take the job. The missionary refused. The offer was increased to twelve thousand, then fifteen thousand dollars. Finally the missionary was offered twenty thousand dollars, an enormous amount in those days. When he refused, he was asked, "Isn't the salary large enough?"

He replied, "The salary is large enough; in fact, it's too big. But the job isn't big enough."

O A young man and his bride went out to Africa as missionaries. A baby was born to them. The work flourished. Then the baby became sick and died. Later the wife passed away. A few years later the work began to decline. The missionary came home on furlough, and slipped into his church's prayer meeting one night. As the meeting ended, he let out a sob. Someone recognized him, "Why it's our missionary. What's the matter?"

With tear-filled eyes, he said, "When my wife and I left, you said, 'We'll pray for you till our dying day.' While you prayed the work progressed. But you stopped praying, my wife and baby died. The work declined. Tonight I have sat through your prayer meeting and never once have you mentioned your missionary in prayer."

O A young couple in an earlier generation began to see a lot of each other. He moved to another city, but carried on the romance by correspondence. Finally, he got up enough courage to propose to the girl in writing. He worded the letter carefully, telling her of his deep love for her, and asking for her hand in marriage. He gave the letter to his brother to mail, then waited anxiously for the postman to bring her answer.

A week went by and no reply. Then two weeks. His heart sank. When a month, then three months, he gave up in utter hopelessness. A year went by—thirty years passed by. His brother passed away. Going through his brother's discarded clothes, he came across the pocket of an old overcoat in which something seemed to be lodged. Closer examination revealed it to be the letter of proposal he had written thirty years before. It had never been mailed. His brother had forgotten it, and it had fallen into the lining to go unnoticed.

Money

● On a Florida golf course a small boy was hired to caddy for an older man. The youngster, hungry, hauled out a brown paper bag. As he bit into his sandwich with zest he was surprised to see the golfer looking enviously at him. "Does that hamburger have onions on it?"

"You bet, sir, and mustard and pickles too."

The man sighed, "Son, you don't know how lucky you are. All my doctor lets me eat are crackers and milk."

Not till later did the boy learn he had been caddying for one of the richest men in the USA.

O "As you know," the minister was preaching, "John Jones passed away last week. The newspapers say he was worth a million dollars. No man should be allowed to leave so much money!"

The chauffeur's reaction was immediate. "Pastor, you'll pardon me. But I was with Mr. Jones when he died, and let me tell you something—he didn't want to leave it!"

O A businessman pulled out his change from his pocket. Among the coins was a small cross. "What a place to carry it," someone remarked.

"Oh, not a strange place," was the reply. "When I'm tempted to spend money foolishly, I'm reminded that the cross has first claim on it."

Mothers

O A teacher was giving a lesson in fractions. "Johnny, suppose there were seven in your family—five children, mother and father—a total of seven. And suppose there was pie for dessert. What fraction of the pie would you get?"

Johnny answered, "One-sixth."

"But you don't understand," replied the teacher. "Don't you know about fractions?"

"I know about fractions and I know about mothers too," remarked Johnny. "Mother would say she didn't want any!"

When a young man left for college years ago, his mother gave him a Bible. On the flyleaf she wrote his name, her name and a Bible verse. The young Scotsman became a successful doctor, then head of the largest hospital in Edinburgh. A committed infidel, he was elected president of a society of atheists in the capital city. One day an accident victim, learning he had only a few hours to live, asked the doctor, "Will you please send at once to my landlady and ask her to send me the book?"

"What book?" questioned the doctor.

"Oh, just ask her for the book. She will know." Then he added, "I am ready to die. I am going to be with the Lord Jesus."

A few hours later, back in the ward where the injured man had just passed away, the doctor asked the nurse in charge, "Did he get the book in time?"

"Yes, just a few minutes before he passed away."

"It was his bank book, wasn't it?"

"No. The book is under his pillow. It's still there. Go and look at it."

The doctor reached under the pillow and drew out a Bible. Opening to the flyleaf he spotted in his mother's handwriting his name, her name, and a Bible verse! It was the very Bible he had received from her years ago as he was leaving for college. Long ago, on a drunken spree, he had pawned it to get money for more liquor. Overwhelmed by tremendous memories, he hurried to his private office, fell to his knees, and prayed for mercy. The doctor became a lay preacher, also author of a well known gospel song "Revive Us Again."

O During a drought in Australia, the creatures of the bush became so thirsty that they braved even the dangerous dooryards of settlers for a drink of water. So the settlers, whose sheep died like flies for lack of water, were constantly on the alert lest these wild creatures drink what little water was left. Each man hung a loaded gun near the doorway.

Suddenly one hot, summer day, a settler noticed movement in the brush. Instantly he seized his gun and stood ready. Out of the bush a mother kangaroo, with a young one in her pouch, came loping across the brown, parched open space surrounding the house. Nearer and nearer she came, her beautiful brown eyes fixed beggingly on the settler. She made her way straight to the tub of water placed there for the use of the few domestic animals that had thus far survived. Still the settler did not shoot.

Reaching the tub, the kangaroo waited, her soft gaze still fixed on the man, while the young kangaroo in her pouch drank its fill. Then she turned without taking a drop for herself and loped back across the arid, open space and on into the tangled depths of the bush. The settler watched till she disappeared. Then he hung up his gun and with a lump in his throat, went back to work.

O Two men were playing cards in a gambling den in the Orient. They were godless man, swearing and cursing as they gambled. One began to whistle. The other looked up surprised, "Say friend, do you know what you're whistling?"

"No, said the other, "I did it without thinking."

"Well," said the first, "you were whistling a hymn—a Christian hymn—'One sweetly solemn thought comes to me o'er and o'er; I'm nearer home today than I have been before.' Where did you pick up that thing? I didn't know that you knew about church hymns."

The other lay down his hand of cards. "Oh, yes, I know lots about church hymns, my friend. I was not always what I am now, thank God. I used to go to church and Sunday school. And I used to know many texts out of the Bible too. My mother, sir, was one of the finest Christian women that ever lived."

"Well, sir," said his companion, "that's funny. But do you know it reminds me that I used to go to church and Sunday school. And that I too had a Christian mother. Strange we should meet in this place, isn't it?" And so they talked on, and as they talked a sense of their sin came upon them and one said to the other, "Say, pal, this is no place for us—this gambling den—for two men who have had Christian mothers and Christian training. Let's get out of here."

So they left. They sought out a missionary whom they knew was working in those parts of the Orient and through him they sought the Christ of their mothers.

O Mrs. Plitt knocked at her neighbor's door. Gene, a six-year-old, appeared. "Hello, Gene, are you all alone here?"

"Yes," said the youngster sadly. "Mother's in the hospital, and me and Daddy and my two sisters and two brothers are here all alone."

O A lady watching a mother with her four grown sons commented, "I'd give thirty years of my life to have four boys like yours."

The mother answered, "That's about what it took."

Motivation

O An Omaha, Nebraska, clergyman was pleased at the sudden interest in religion shown by a young housewife who phoned to ask for another word for the first part of the Sermon on the Mount. "Beatitudes," the pastor told her.

"Oh, thank you, thank you," came the happy reply. "If that radio quiz program calls me now, I can win twenty-five thousand dollars."

○ Two boys had set up two viewing positions in competition with each other down in the Shenandoah Mountains. The first boy charged twenty-five cents to look through his telescope. But the other boy charged only a dime. This seemed so unselfish and so magnanimous to one tourist that he gave the second boy his business, and then overwhelmed by the view, handed the lad fifty cents. "How in the world can you afford to be so unselfish," the tourist asked.

The lad replied, "After people see my breathtaking view, they usually give me far more than twenty-five cents, and so I make more money than the other boy by offering my view more cheaply."

○ Dr. Eric Frykenberg, veteran missionary who spent half-a-century in India, could regale friends with incidents of his life on the field. One day someone asked, "Dr. Frykenberg, what was the most difficult problem you ever faced?" Without hesitation he answered, "It was when my heart would grow cold before God. When that happened, I knew I was too busy. I also knew it was time to get away. So I would take my Bible and go off into the hills alone. I'd open my Bible to Matthew twenty-seven, the story of the crucifixion and I would wrap my arms around the cross. And then I'd be ready to go back to work."

Nails

◉ A man who owned a restaurant in London gave generously to the Lord's work.

One day he happened to open his cash register in the presence of a missionary. To his surprise, the missionary saw a six-inch nail among the bills and coins. "What's that doing there?" he asked.

"I keep this nail with my money," he replied, "to remind me of the price Jesus Christ paid for my salvation and how much I owe him in return."

○ A few years ago a missionary was telling the gospel story on the Island of Sumatra. As he told about the cross, the chief frowned. "What is a cross?" he asked.

The surprised missionary wondered how he might describe a cross to people who had never seen or heard of one. He cut down two branches of a tree and formed them in the shape of a cross. But the chief wanted to know, "How was Christ fastened to the cross?"

The missionary laid the cross on the ground and stretched himself on it, and told how the soldiers had driven nails into Christ's hands and feet.

Then the chief asked, "What is a nail?"

The villagers had never seen a nail. How could one describe a nail? The missionary searched for something to resemble a nail. The people seemed to lose interest in the missionary's message. That night the dejected missionary began his evening meal. Picking up a can of Japanese oranges, he poured its contents into a dish and was about to throw the can out, when he heard a rattling sound inside it. Curiously he looked inside. His eyes opened in amazement. There in the bottom of the can was a nail! With nail in hand he rushed to the village where he continued the story of the cross, showing how Christ was crucified.

That night the chief and many others accepted Christ.

Neglect

Playboy ex-King Farouk of Egypt moved into the same Paris hotel where Billy Graham and his team were staying. Friends of the evangelist thought it would be a wonderful thing if Billy could tell Farouk about the new life offered by Jesus Christ. Billy was willing.

One of the friends knocked on Farouk's door. A cold-faced aide answered and listened stonily to the request. "Just a minute and I will see," said the aide, who left the friend shifting from one foot to the other in the hallway. He came back in a few seconds and said, "King Farouk cannot see Billy Graham."

"Will it be possible for them to talk tomorrow?" asked the friend.

"King Farouk cannot see Billy Graham tomorrow or any time," replied the aide.

Noisy revelry could be heard from inside the room. Farouk was engaged in his favorite pastime of wine, women, and song. He had no time for the things of God.

● A little lad went home from Sunday school all excited. His mother who never bothered with spiritual matters asked him why he was so excited.

He said that his Sunday-school teacher had told him that the Bible was God's Word, God's Book.

His mother readily agreed, "Why, yes, my boy, the Bible is God's Book."

The little fellow, with puzzled expression, said, "Mom, do you really mean the Bible in the parlor is God's book?"

"Yes, my boy," replied the mother.

Then the little fellow excitedly exclaimed, "Then don't you think we ought to send it back to God, because we never read it?"

New Birth

O A census taker called at a home of a Christian man who showed the census taker the family Bible in which were recorded the names of the various members of his family. After looking down the list of names, the officer was visibly puzzled. He said, "I cannot understand it. For instance, here is R. T., born on such-and-such a date, and on the next line he is said to have been born on such-and-such a date. Is it the same person or does it refer to another member of the family with the same name?"

The Christian explained that Jesus said to Nicodemus, "Ye must be born again," you must have a second birthday. And when a member of the family received Christ and new life though him, that date was placed in the family Bible. It was the date that person had received a new life.

O A Marxist, speaking in Hyde Park in London, pointed to a man in rags and called out, "Communism can put a new suit of clothes on that man."

A Christian, standing nearby, pointed to the man and shouted, "Christ can put a new man in that suit."

O A small but beautiful plate-glass window in a large church was smashed to pieces, which were collected into a box. One day a visitor asked permission to take the box. Months later he invited the church officials to his studio, where he showed them a window more beautiful than the original.

"Where did you get it?" they asked.

"From the broken fragments you gave me."

● Not long after Augustine was converted, he saw on the street a pretty companion of his former unprincipled life. When he ran swiftly from her, she pursued, crying, "Augustine, why did you run? It is I."

Running faster, Augustine called over his shoulder, "I run, because it is not I."

Nonretaliation

O Back in the days of Prohibition a young comedian by the name of Happy MacDonald, known to his acquaintances as Happy Mac, made friends with the barkers who worked on South State in front of the burlesque shows. He often bought them drinks in speakeasies, illicit drinking places of that era. There were eight friends in particular, including Happy Mac's special pal, whom he called Big Jim. Big Jim, also called Doc, middle-aged, almost six-feet-tall, big-boned, with heavily lined face, used to bark outside a show: "See the girlies. You're just in time for the next show. Come in and see the girlies!" Often when Happy Mac and these eight were sitting in a speakeasy, Big Jim would lean over and with real menace in his voice say, "We've got to do something about that Pacific Garden Mission." When asked why, he would reply, "We lost another one of our showgirls to them last week. She went in the mission, got converted, and quit her job. It's unhealthy for our business to have that mission right in the same block."

Whenever he did that, Happy Mac changed the subject, for his friends did not know that he had been attending the mission every night. Happy Mac wanted desperately to save face with his barker friends so didn't mention it. But came the night of May 29, 1925, when after weeks of struggle and resistance, Happy Mac, a successful dancer and comedian, received Christ as his Savior, and decided to live another kind of life. Hard-drinking, hard-dancing, big-time Happy Mac began to see what it meant to have real joy in his heart. He thrilled to see the new power to live a victorious life which was his almost immediately. Soon Happy Mac became songleader at Pacific Garden Mission. He wondered what his friends would say when they found out. He avoided them for a week or so, but knew sooner or later he would have to face them. Finally one night he started down South State Street. There was Big Jim barking away, "Come in and see the pretty girls. The grr-reatest and biggest show in all Chicago!" Then seeing Happy Mac he broke off, "Well if it ain't little Reverend Happy Mac. Happy, say it's a lie! Say it ain't true that them mission people got my old pal!"

Happy Mac replied, "No, Doc, it isn't a lie. I've become a Christian. I'm through with the old life."

Doc wouldn't hear any more. As Happy Mac walked on, Doc warned, "Some of us boys might drop in on you at the mission some night."

That scared Happy Mac. Sure enough that very night when Happy Mac led singing, Big Jim stood outside the big storefront window, flapping his arms, mimicing Happy Mac's every move. Happy Mac's normal reaction would have been to become very angry, but the fact that he carried on with his song leading proved to him that he had been truly changed by Jesus Christ from the old hot-tempered Happy the boys had known.

A few days later Happy Mac was walking down South State, wearing a new tan suit and shoes. Suddenly, all eight friends loomed in front of him, lined up four on each side, so Happy Mac had to walk between. Big Jim went, "One, two, three—" then they all spat tobacco juice on Happy Mac's new tan suit and shoes.

Unlike the Happy of old, he responded pleasantly, "Your aim is excellent, Doc. Caught my new trouser leg and my shoe."

"That's all you got to say?" Doc growled.

"Not quite, Doc. There's this. When you get to know Jesus Christ the way I've come to know him, you'll be able to unclench your fists. You'll let a guy spit on you, and it'll be all right."

Three weeks later Doc walked into the mission as Happy Mac began to lead singing. When the service was over, Happy Mac dropped down to the front row where Doc was sitting. "You're not mad at me," Doc asked Happy.

"The Lord won't let me get mad anymore, Doc," said Happy.

Then Doc asked, "Happy, have you been a Christian long enough to know how to lead a guy to Jesus?"

When Happy assured him he had, Doc said, "Then I'm your customer." That night Doc called on the Lord Jesus to forgive him his sins and to help him lead a new kind of life.

He showed Happy Mac a letter that had made him come to the mission. It was from his aged mother who was dying, and Doc was preparing to go to her bedside. But to prepare, he first had to become a Christian. Said Doc, "I promised my mother I'd become a Christian before she died. She's waited fifty-four years. But now that you've led me to Jesus, I'm gonna beat it home."

Two weeks later, Doc was back in Chicago. He'd had three hours with his mother, and his news had brought great joy to her heart. Doc continued on the street, barking, but now instead of barking in front of the burlesque show, it was in front of the Pacific Garden Rescue Mission, inviting people to come in and find Christ and forgiveness in him. And then one day a couple weeks later Doc dropped dead on the sidewalk. Said Happy Mac, "I thank God from the bottom of my heart for the day old Doc spit on my new tan suit and shoes. What if I had lost my temper and had resentment and couldn't forgive?"

o When two prize chickens wandered into a neighbor's vegetable patch, the neighbor wrung their necks and tossed them over the fence whence they had come. The woman next door, seeing her chickens fly over the fence and land with a thump on her lawn, ran out to the still-flapping birds. Her children wondered what their mother's reaction would be: angry denunciation of the ill-tempered neighbor, tears, or crying on father's shoulder when he came home. To their amazement she proceeded to make two delicious chicken pies, one of which she took to the neighbor with an apology for the damage her chickens had done to the vegetable patch. The children hid behind a bush to see the neighbor's expression. He who never lacked words to express his anger stood speechless and ashamed.

Offering

O A visitor in a large New York City church reached into his wallet at offering time and chose a one-dollar bill. Suddenly he noticed that the usher coming his way was a business acquaintance. Wishing to make a good impression, he switched the one-dollar bill for a ten-dollar bill, and placed it on the plate.

O One night during an appeal for money, a little lame girl walked slowly up the aisle, leaning heavily on her crutch. At the front she pulled a ring from her finger and laid it with the many other gifts. Adjusting her crutch, she returned to her seat.

After the service the preacher said to her, "My dear, I saw what you did tonight. It was beautiful, but you know, the response has been so large that we want you to have your ring back."

The little girl looked up and firmly said, "I didn't give that ring to you."

O During a Sunday-morning church service the preacher made his usual announcements, then asked the ushers to come forward to take up the offering. Soon as the ushers picked up the plates and walked to the first row, the pastor left the pulpit, stepped over behind an usher, and looked over his shoulder and watched as people made their gifts. He saw every penny, every nickel, dime, quarter, and dollar which the people on the first row gave. (This church did not use church envelopes.)

Then he followed the usher all the way down the aisle, as he moved from row to row, noting what each person dropped into the plate. Some were taken by surprise, some embarrassed, others mad, and a few delighted.

Back in the pulpit, the pastor said, "Please forget that I have seen what each of you put on the plate, but do remember that there is an all-seeing eye that watches every gift placed in the offering plate at all times.

O A little boy was given a quarter and a dime one Sunday morning and told to put the quarter on the offering plate at church and to spend the dime on himself.

Later at home he confessed, "I put the dime in the church offering and spent the quarter on myself. You see—the preacher said the Lord loves a cheerful giver, and I felt I could much more cheerfully part with a dime than with a quarter."

O At a service on the island of Jamaica held for the purpose of taking a missionary offering, the following resolutions were adopted. "*One:* **Resolved,** that we will all give. *Two:* **Resolved,** that we will give as the Lord has prospered us. *Three:* **Resolved,** that we will give cheerfully." It was local practice for each person to walk individually to the communion table and deposit his gift under the eye of the presiding officer.

One well-to-do member delayed until he was painfully noticeable. When he finally came forward to deposit his gift, the presiding officer said, "That is according to the first resolution, but not according to the second."

The member returned indignantly to his seat, taking back his money. But either conscience within or pressure without kept working, until he came forward again, doubling his contribution and muttering, "Take that, then."

The presiding officer commented, "That may meet the first and second resolutions, but it isn't according to the third."

Again the giver retired to his seat. A few minutes later, accepting the rebuke, he came up the third time with a still larger gift, and a good-natured smile.

Then the chairman exclaimed, "That's according to all resolutions!"

Old Nature

● A man was charged in court with a violation of the law. He pled, "Your honor, I'm a Christian. I'm a new man, but I have an old nature too. It was not my new man but the old man that did wrong."

To the self-excusing lawbreaker the judge replied, "Since it was the old man that broke the law we'll sentence him to thirty days in jail. And since the new man was an accomplice in the wrong, we'll give him thirty days also. I therefore sentence you to jail for sixty days."

○ For six years a cat and a parakeet lived in the same house. The cat never bothered the bird, which was always kept in its cage. One day the people returned to find the cage on the floor. The cat had apparently made a lunge for the bird, knocking the cage on the floor. But the bird was safe inside the cage. For the safety of the bird, the people had to get rid of the cat who had shown its old cat nature after six years.

○ The owner of a famous racing stable one day passed a place where a farmer was building a high fence around his pasture. The sportsman, curious, asked the farmer, "why are you building such a high fence?"

The farmer replied, "I've got a mule that can jump most any kind of fence. I've got to contain him."

The sportsman said, "Do you mean you have a mule that can jump that fence?"

"Sure."

"Then I'd like to buy him," replied the sportsman.

When the sale was completed, the new owner placed him among his thoroughbreds. He then sent for a famous veterinary surgeon who trimmed the mule's ears to resemble those of a horse, let his mane and tail grow, and put shoes on his feet. By springtime, outwardly the animal had been transformed into a fine race horse, especially for the hurdle races. The experiment proved successful. Prizes were won in many places.

After winning the last race of the season, just as the judges were beginning to distribute the prizes and were approaching the winning hurdle to award him the blue ribbon, he suddenly reared back on his haunches and with all stops open, brayed like the mule he was.

○ Out of Morocco comes the story of a remarkable cat. According to the tale, one day in Sultan's court an argument arose as to which was better, a man *born* to nobility, or one who through self-improvement and discipline *became* a "gentleman." The Sultan appointed the opponents to debate the question a month later.

Soon after, the proponent of the "work-your-own-way-up" theory started on a business trip, where he learned of a cat that walked in on its hind legs. On its front paws the animal balanced a small tray on which was a cup of coffee. "Oh," said the man, "what convincing proof of the effect of teaching and training!" The traveler was able to buy the cat.

Somehow, after his return his opponent learned about the cat. The month soon passed. Again the Sultan sat in his court. On either side of the hall stood the two leaders with their friends. The Sultan said, "Now we shall decide which is the better, a man *born* to the life of a gentleman or one who has *become* a gentleman by working his way up." Thereupon the first man opened his basket. The cat climbed out. Then standing on its hind legs it held a tray on its paws, waiting till a cup of coffee was put on the tray, and carried it to the Sultan. Everyone was astonished at this display of the power of training.

The cat returned to its master who put a second cup of coffee on the tray to carry to the opponent on the other side of the hall. The clever animal was half way across when his opponent took from under his loose jacket a small box and from it released several mice. In a moment the tray and the cup of coffee crashed to the floor, as the cat, on all fours, dashed after the scampering mice. In a flash, all the education and training of the cat had disappeared as the old cat nature triumphed. It acted like a cat because it was a cat.

Omnipotence

O A sultan once boasted that he was the most powerful king, and that no one had the power to change anything he planned to do. His subjects were afraid of him because of his cruel, despotic rule.

The sultan had a son whom he loved very much. The son had a close friend who came to visit from time to time. One day the prince and his friend went for a stroll around the palace. "My father is the most powerful king," said the prince.

"Your father is a powerful king, but he is not the most powerful," said his friend. There is one King who is all-powerful."

"Who is that?" asked the prince.

"God!" came the friend's answer.

The sultan chanced to overhear the two lads. He was pleased that his son praised him. But he thought, "This friend of my son is blaspheming. Does he think God is greater than I? I'll see if he will save him."

He made up his mind to kill the boy without his son's knowing the plot. When the two boys returned to the palace grounds, he called them. "Boys," he said, "I'm going to send you to the neighboring village."

They were happy to hear the news for they liked the walk to the next village. "Because you have been so obedient I'll give you both new clothing." The boys beamed. He gave his own son a green-silken, long-sleeved shirt, and the other boy a short-sleeved maroon shirt. Then he sent them on the errand.

A little later he called one of his soldiers. "Put on your civilian clothes," he said. Take your small spear and hide it underneath your clothing. Then go to the bottom of the valley on the way to the next village. Hide in a thicket. You will see two boys coming from the village. One will be wearing a green-silken long-sleeved shirt. Kill the boy who is wearing the maroon shirt. Don't let the other recognize you."

While the two boys were returning from the village, the prince said to his friend, "Your shirt is more beautiful than mine. Please let us exchange."

So they exchanged shirts. When they came to the spot where the soldier was hiding, he seized the boy in the maroon shirt and speared him. The other boy came running to the sultan, "The prince is dead. A man killed him!"

The news struck the sultan like a thunderbolt. He fainted. That day he learned a grim lesson. There is One more powerful than any earthly ruler.

O The day after the major earthquake and fire of San Francisco a newsboy was directing a dazed man through the debris. As they walked, the lad philosophized, "It took men a long time to put all this stuff up, but God tumbled it over in a minute. Say, mister, 'taint no use for a feller to think he can lick God."

Omniscience

O The father of Woodrow Wilson, a minister, was once in the midst of a group of men who were having a heated discussion. Suddenly one of the men uttered an oath, then noting Dr. Wilson, began to apologize, saying, "Sir, I had forgotten you were present."

Wilson's reply was, "It's not to me that you owe your apology but to God."

O A father took his small son with him when he went to steal potatoes from his neighbor's field. When they came to the boundary fence, the father stopped and listened while his eyes searched from right to left. Silently he began to climb the fence.

Then the child spoke. "Dad," he said, "you forgot something—you didn't look up."

O An astronomer was engaged in making some observations on the sun with a great telescope. As the sun descended toward the horizon, there came within view the top of a hill seven miles away. On the top of that hill were a large number of apple trees, and in one of them were two boys stealing apples. One was getting the apples, and the other was watching to make certain that nobody saw them, feeling certain they were undiscovered. But there sat the astronomer, seven miles away, with the great eye of the telescope directed fully upon them, seeing every movement they made as plainly as if he had been under the tree.

Original Sin

O A lady was being shown the sight of a bombed and blitzed city. As she saw the pile of human bodies half-buried, and smelt the decay of corpses, the man showing her around said, "This is what original sin has done."

She asked, "Need you bring in that horrible doctrine?"

He replied, "Anything so horrible as this requires a horrible explanation."

Pardon

O The son of a very wealthy man registered in a hotel, letting the owner know who he was. The hotelkeeper thought everything would be all right. The boy bought whatever he wanted, charging it to his hotel bill. By and by the proprietor asked for payment, but the boy had no money. He was asked several times, then suddenly disappeared. He went to another city, doing the same thing, running up big bills everywhere.

One day he felt a firm hand on his shoulder. He expected to see a policeman, but looked up to discover that his father was at his side. "I have found you at last, my boy." The boy, genuinely repentant, dropped his head in shame as the father told him how he had trailed him from city to city, in each of which he had found huge debts the boy had incurred. "And my boy, I have paid it all."

Parenthood

O Two of the three young men who pioneered the Sudan Interior Mission before the turn of the century lost their lives through disease, coming to a lonely end far from home in inland Africa. Roland Bingham, the survivor and founder of the mission, took the belongings of one of the boys to his mother.

Learning of her son's death, she said, "Well, Mr. Bingham, I would rather have had Walter go out to the Sudan and die there, all alone, than have him home today, disobeying his Lord."

O One mother mentioned to a new acquaintance that she had a daughter who was a missionary. The friend exclaimed, "It must worry you to have a girl on the other side of the world."

The mother replied, "She doesn't worry me at all. The daughter that gives me anxiety is the one at home."

O A group of workers gathered one day to bid farewell to a young Japanese Christian embarking for missionary service in Laos.

One of the American missionaries went to the aged father and said, "Honorable sir, you must be grieved at this parting with your son. But be of good cheer! You will see your son again when he returns to Japan for his furlough."

But the old Japanese Christian replied, "Pastor, when we Japanese people sent our sons to war to fight for our country, we did not expect to see them again. In fact, we told them: 'Give your lives for your country.'

"No, I am sending this young man of mine across the seas for a better, nobler purpose, a more glorious conflict in the service of the King of kings. Should I hope to see him again on the shore of Japan? No. I gave a son once for a futile, hellish war. I gladly give this son now to service in Laos for Jesus Christ and eternal things. I do not expect to see him again on this earth."

And then the grand old Christian father turned his face away—but heavenward!

Pass It On

O Over twenty years ago in Vineland, New Jersey, Nicholas and Tessie Pennino and their two-year-old daughter, Marjorie, were nearly asphyxiated by coal gas fumes from a stove in their home. With mother and daughter unconscious, the father managed to crawl to the telephone and ask faintly for help before overcome by the deadly fumes. An alert operator contacted a doctor. The family recovered.

A sequel was played nearly twenty years later. The situation was the same: a home filled with poisonous gas, a weak voice calling into a phone for help, and a fast-thinking operator on the other end. Though the cast was different, one player was the same. For the operator who traced the desperate call and notified the police within minutes, was none other than Marjorie Pennino.

Marjorie had grown up and joined the telephone company shortly after high school graduation. So twenty years later, by the same kind of quick thinking that had helped save her own life, Marjorie helped to save the life of another.

Pastors

O A pastor in a tough situation was asked how he slept at night. "Like a baby," he replied. "I sleep an hour, wake up and cry a while. Then I sleep another while, then wake up and cry again. And so on through the night."

O A new, youthful preacher had recently arrived in his first church in Philadelphia. To get better acquainted, one of the laymen visited him in his home, remarking, "You do not seem to be a strong preacher. From all surface appearances you will fail here. But a small band of us have covenanted to gather every Sunday morning to pray for you."

The young pastor saw that group grow to more than one thousand persons all praying weekly for their minister. No wonder J. Wilbur Chapman became not only one of the greatest preachers in the USA, but a world-renowned evangelist as well.

O A young pastor came to a New York City church. When he didn't do so well during the first year, the deacons met and decided that he had been a flop and should leave. However, before they asked for his resignation one deacon suggested, "Let's pray for him for a while."

They began praying for their preacher. He stayed the next year. His preaching talents were sought across the nation. He stayed fifty years. His name: the well-known Dr. Robert Stuart MacArthur, long-time pastor of Calvary Baptist Church.

Patience

O A phone operator at work said to the operator next to her, "I wonder who that man is on my line."

When she named him, the second operator replied, "That's one of the deacons in our church! Why do you ask?"

Replied the first operator, "Because he's so patient. I got him the wrong number three times in a row, and he only said, 'That's all right. Try again.'"

O At three o'clock one winter morning a missionary candidate rang the bell at the examiner's home. He was ushered into the study where he waited till 9:00 A.M. for an interview. The examiner, an elderly minister, asked him a few simple questions, such as, "Spell *farmer*," and "What are *three* and *three*?"

"That's excellent," said the old pastor. "I believe you have passed. I'll be recommending you to the board tomorrow."

At the board meeting the pastor began, "He has all the qualifications of a missionary. First, I tested him on self-denial. I told him to be at my house at three o'clock in the morning. He left a warm house to come out into the cold without a word of complaint. Second, he was prompt. He was there on time. Third, I examined him on patience. I made him wait six hours to see me, after telling him to come at three. Fourth, I tried his temper. He didn't show the slightest sign of irritation. And fifth, I tested his humility. I asked him questions a six-year-old could answer, and he showed no indignation. So I believe the lad meets the requirements. He'll make the missionary we need."

O At a Thanksgiving dinner a mother spoke to her guests about her blessings, mentioning first of all, her four healthy children. Later when pandemonium reigned in the house, a friend noticed the mother with her eyes closed. The mother explained, "I'm just praying for patience to endure my blessings."

O In a crowded department store a young mother had the added difficulty of a small girl pulling and tugging at her side and whispering incessantly. Suddenly the harassed mother pleaded softly, "Quiet, Susan, just calm yourself, and take it easy."

An admiring clerk commented on the mother's psychology, then turned to the child, "So your name is Susan."

"Oh, no," interrupted the mother, "her name's Joan. *I'm* Susan."

Peace

O The good citizens of a city in southeast France summoned the police to break in the doors of a university room from which were coming sounds of argument and battle. The policemen found the windows broken, the furniture overturned, the curtains torn down, one man dying and another dead.

They lifted the dying man who whispered, "We are two doctors of philosophy. We had agreed on our desire for universal peace, but we have disagreed somewhat on the proper methods for attaining world peace."

O During the riots in Detroit one summer, a bedsheet fluttered down from a third-floor window, on which was scribbled what was probably meant to be a prayer. In the midst of rubble and smoldering ruins were these words PEACE ON EARTH.

O Around Christmas 1944, Burt Frizen was fighting in the Battle of the Bulge. Hit by enemy shrapnel, badly wounded, and unable to move, he lay out on the battlefield, waiting for death or whatever was to come. Much of the time during those six long hours he sang softly, over and over again, the words of the song he had learned from his mother, "There is a name to me most dear . . . like sweetest music to my ear . . . for when my heart is troubled, filled with fear . . . Jesus whispers peace."

He heard a sound nearby. Opening his eyes, he saw a German soldier standing over him with a gun. *This is it,* thought Burt as he waited for the shot.

But the German soldier didn't shoot. He said in English, "Sing it again."

As Burt began to sing the song again, he felt the German lift him in strong arms and place him on the ledge of a rock. His own medics spotted him a few minutes later and took him to safety. Jesus had whispered peace in the midst of war.

Penalty Paid

◖ When Billy Graham was driving through a small southern town, he was stopped by a policeman. "You were doing forty in a thirty-mile zone," charged the officer.

"Sorry," replied Graham, "I am guilty. How much is the fine?"

"It will be ten dollars," said the policeman, "but you'll have to appear in court."

Court turned out to be a barber shop, where the judge, a justice of the peace, was plying his trade of haircutting. Graham had to wait till the barber finished cutting a customer's hair. Then laying down his clippers, the barber assumed the dignity of his office, calling the court to order and asking, "Guilty, or not guilty?"

When Graham pleaded guilty, the judge replied, "That'll be ten dollars, a dollar for every mile you went over the limit."

Suddenly the judge recognized Graham. It turned out he had been a regular listener to Graham's broadcasts for years. Though warm at first, suddenly the judge's attitude cooled. "You have violated the law, and the penalty must be paid."

Graham was about to peel off a ten-dollar bill from his wallet, when the judge motioned for him to put his money back. "The fine must be paid," he said, "but I am going to pay for you." And he took a ten from his own pocket and attached it to the ticket. Then he took Billy out and bought him a steak dinner.

"That," said Graham, "is how our heavenly Father treats repentant sinners!"

Persecution

○ A preacher confided in a friend, "I'm going to resign. I've been mistreated by members of my church!"

The other asked, "Have they crowned you with thorns yet? Or did they spit on you? Have they nailed you to a tree?"

The preacher saw the point and continued his pastorate.

○ A college president, whose job demanded the procurement of large gifts for the school, radiated charm and affability. Because a new young professor often blurted out the truth rather bluntly, the president invited the young professor to a chapel service. The president spoke on the theme of how Jesus found common ground with his hearers to win them to his way.

After the service the young professor thanked the president. "I shall try to profit by your address. But one thing bothers me, if Jesus was so tactful and diplomatic, how did he manage to get himself crucified?"

Perseverance

O A retired missionary was telling a visitor about his son. "Henry has tried several times to get a magazine going, but his journalistic efforts have always failed till recently. He had failure after failure. Finally he and a friend got an idea for a new kind of magazine but didn't have the money to finance it, so asked me to lend the money. I gave Henry six hundred dollars, my entire life's savings."

The visitor was beginning to form an unfavorable image of Henry, when the father asked, "You know my son, Henry, don't you? Henry Luce?"

The visitor suddenly realized who his host was—the father and financial backer of Henry Luce, founder of *Life, Time,* and *Fortune* magazines.

O Two friends were discussing a mutual acquaintance. Said the first, "I think his only trouble is that he lacks initiative."

The other replied, "I don't quite agree. He gets some good ideas. He has originality, but sooner or later he bogs down and is off on something else. What he needs is *finishiative!*"

Personal Confession of Sin and Faith

O The English paper, the *Manchester Guardian,* reported after World War II that a new stained-glass window in a church in Vienna had been discovered that showed Hitler and Mussolini as onlookers among the crowd at the crucifixion. On purpose that artist had placed the faces of these two whose features were unquestionably those of Hitler and Mussolini. Hitler's toga is decorated with swastikas. The faces are not distinguishable to the naked eye, but are easily recognizable with binoculars. The discovery was confirmed by pictures taken by telephoto lens. It will be ultimately revealed that among the crowd at the Savior's death are all faces.

O Some years ago a visiting minister preached in the church where the late John D. Rockefeller, Sr., was a member. At the close of the service Mr. Rockefeller spoke to the preacher and slipped him his personal check for one hundred dollars as a token of his appreciation. The minister, proud to have a check from so rich and so renowned a man, presented it next day at the bank named on the check.

The teller looked at it, then handed it back. The preacher was a little put out. "What's the matter?" he asked. "This is the right bank! The check is made out to me. The signature is genuine, and surely Mr. Rockefeller's check is good for one hundred dollars."

The teller smiled, "Yes, this is the right bank. The check is made out to you. And I would know the signature anywhere. It would certainly be good at this bank for a million dollars and more. There isn't anything wrong with the check, my friends, except that you forgot to endorse it. You will have to turn it over and write your name on the other side."

The embarrassed clergyman quickly endorsed his name on the check and received immediate payment in full.

O A little girl visiting her Christian aunt memorized the first verse of the Twenty-third Psalm. Her aunt taught her the words by use of her thumb and four fingers. The little girl would repeat the verse, "The," putting her finger on the thumb of her left hand; "Lord," touching the 1st finger; "is" touching the 2nd; "my" touching the 3rd; and "shepherd," touching the 4th.

"Which one of these words do you like best?" asked the aunt.

Her niece went over and over the words on her little fingers until at last she paused. Her mind was made up. It was her third finger, that stood for "my."

Back home after the visit to her aunt the little girl suffered a terminal illness that robbed her of her speech. As the end drew near, her mother asked her if she had really found peace through faith in the Lord Jesus.

The only response was the moving of the right hand to clasp the third finger of the left hand. Still clasping that finger she passed into the presence of the Lord Jesus.

The parents did not understand why their little girl had clasped her third finger that way till in conversation with the aunt they told her about it.

The aunt exclaimed, "I know what she meant." Then she told the sorrowing parents about the lesson on the first verse of Psalm 23. She meant by it, said the aunt, that the Lord was her shepherd. She was saying, "The Lord is *my* Shepherd. The Lord is *my* Savior."

Pharisaism

O A missionary on furlough was reprimanded one Sunday by a lady who had opened up her home to him between morning and evening services, because he was typing letters on his portable on Sunday.

Later he walked into the living room and found her writing a letter by pen and ink.

O On Thanksgiving Day 1713, the governor of Connecticut and the king's commissioners were just preparing to dine when it was announced that the bear prepared for the occasion had been "shot on ye Lord's Day."

At that sad news none would touch a morsel of the roast bear, until it was decided that the Indian who shot the animal should be whipped and made to restore the price paid for the bear.

Then, having inflicted a "just and righteous sentence on ye sinful heathen," the company fell upon the roast bear with clear conscience and left nothing but the bones.

O When Dr. Wilbur M. Smith was visiting a Hebrew scholar in Jerusalem, he asked the scholar to give his autograph. The Hebrew scholar politely refused, explaining that, because it was the Sabbath, the writing of a signature, which involved two words in succession, would be considered work.

Later that day when Dr. Smith and the scholar became involved in a discussion of a psalm, the scholar stood up, then climbed a three-story ladder, reached for a large folio on the eighth shelf, brought it down, opened it up, and then began to discuss the particular question.

The action of climbing and reaching to the top shelf involved much more work than writing two words in succession, yet was not forbidden.

Practicing What You Preach

O A doctor of divinity lived in the same house with his son, who was a medical doctor. One day when the phone rang, the maid answered. The voice on the other end asked, "Is the doctor in?"

She replied, "Which one do you want—pills or prayer?"

Another time when a call came for the doctor she was heard to ask, "Do you want the one who preaches, or the one who practices?"

O While a missionary was addressing a group, a woman in the audience rose and left. She came back a few minutes later. After the lecture, the missionary asked the woman if she had left because she had lost her interest.

"Oh, no," she replied. "You said many wonderful things, and I went out to ask your driver if you lived them. He said you did so I came back to listen."

O A certain graduation class at the College of Physicians and Surgeons in New York City numbered 175. Forty years later when those men should have been at their prime, 60 had died, 7 of them in that past year. At the annual reunion, a distinguished member asked, "How many of you have had a complete physical checkup in the past 12 months?"

Not a single hand went up, not even his own.

Then he made a motion that the class choose from its number a committee, whose business it would be to keep its members alive. The motion passed, the committee was chosen, and it went to work. Those experts found that the gall-bladder man had a gall-bladder infection, the hernia man needed an operation for a hernia. Happily, the checkups did not bring all bad news. The heart man did not have heart trouble. Because of those expert findings, and the resulting discipline, the death rate among those men began to drop.

O A sign painter in Saint Joseph, Missouri, was in police court on a charge of smoking in bed. The fire department charged his smoking started a blaze in a hotel room.

Asked if he knew it was against the law to smoke in bed, he replied, "I'll say I do. I painted fifty signs saying it was against the law to smoke in bed. I painted them to be placed in hotel rooms!"

The sign painter was fined twenty-five dollars.

O Bozo, the noted clown of Ringling Brothers, Barnum and Bailey Circus, spent his later years performing for the American Cancer Society. He said, "I guess I've made a billion people laugh." His customary close of a show would be "Bye, Bye now . . . and be sure to have your doctor check you for cancer." He knew the warning could mean life—or death.

But he fell ill himself and learned at his first checkup that he was hopelessly beyond help—with cancer—and passed away soon after.

Prayer

○ A kneeling marble-cutter, with chisel and hammer, was changing a stone into a statue. A preacher looking on said, "I wish I could deal such powerful blows on stony hearts."

The woman answered, "Maybe you could, if you worked, like I do, on your knees!"

● A little boy, dressed up in his Sunday best to see his grandmother, was told by his mother to wait (while she got ready) on the porch and not to dare go down the steps to the street which was full of mud puddles. He did well for a while, but when the neighborhood pals engaged in a mud fight, he couldn't resist. He went down the first step, then the second, and before long was right in the thick of the mud battle. Just then down the street came the ice-cream man, jingling his bell. The lad rushed into the house and asked his mother for money for a cone.

She took one look at the lad, and angrily answered, "Look at yourself. You're in no condition to ask for anything."

○ A little lad, saying his prayers at grandmother's knee, prayed, "If I should die before I wake," then paused.

"Go on," urged Grandmother.

Suddenly the little lad scrambled to his feet, hurried downstairs, then in a few moments was back at his place again, taking up his prayer where he had left off.

When the little fellow was tucked in bed, the grandmother questioned him lovingly about the interruption.

"I was thinking what I was saying," insisted the boy. "That's why I had to stop. You see, I'd mixed up my little brother's zoo, and stood all his wooden soldiers on their heads, just to see how angry he would get in the morning. But, if I should die before I wake, why, I wouldn't want him to find them that way so I had to go down and fix them up."

With a quiver in her voice the grandmother commented, "I imagine there are a good many prayers that would not be hurt by stopping in the middle to undo a wrong."

● A military cadet who had just given his life to Christ was in his room pouring out thanksgiving for pardoned sin. A heavy knock sounded on the door. Before the cadet could get to his feet a colonel entered.

"What," he asked, "do you pray? I gave that up long ago. I have all I want, so there's nothing to ask God for."

"Well, sir," replied the cadet, "you must have a lot to thank him for!"

Prayer Meeting

○ Michael Faraday lectured to a group of distinguished scientists on the magnet—its nature and properties. When he finished, the spellbound audience rocked the house with enthusiastic applause. The then-Prince of Wales proposed a motion of congratulation, which was carried with applause. The audience waited for Faraday's response but the lecturer had vanished!

The renowned scientist was a faithful Christian. Elder of a small congregation, he never missed prayer meeting. The hour at which Faraday finished his lecture was the hour at which the midweek prayer meeting was scheduled to begin.

O Stonewall Jackson never used to take a glass of water to his lips or seal a letter without asking God's blessing. But it wasn't always so. Jackson was a timid man. Shortly after his conversion he attended a midweek prayer meeting. The pastor asked him to pray, without consulting him. He tried but broke down completely. He made a failure at this first attempt at public prayer.

The pastor rebuked himself for placing Jackson in this predicament. The next morning before breakfast a loud knock at the door was heard. It was Jackson. The pastor timidly opened the door. With tears in his eyes Jackson said, "Pastor, I'm sorry I made such a miserable failure at my first public prayer. I came over to ask you if the Christians would be willing to have you call on me for prayer every Wednesday evening until I overcome this foolish timidity and fear of man."

O The preacher stood up and sadly said, "Brethren, I feel we may as well drop the midweek prayer meeting." This caused an uproar among the congregation, and they all planned to vote no.

"But," said the minister, "what you don't seem to know is that we haven't had a prayer meeting in six months."

Preaching

O A fine preacher was once complimented by a little boy who said, "You're not a great preacher because I could understand every word you said."

● A man wrote home that he had been to the big city to hear two great preachers, one in the morning and one at night. He said that in the morning he heard Dr. B, and at night Dr. S. "I was impressed by both. Dr. B is a great preacher, but Dr. S has a wonderful Savior."

O An older minister said to a new preacher who asked for advice, "Tell them what you know. Don't tell them what you don't know for that will take too long."

O Two Welsh preachers were on their way to a meeting. One noticed that the other had a written outline of his sermon. He remonstrated, "You can't carry fire on paper."

"True," replied his companion, "but you can use paper to start a fire."

Pride

O A salesman spotted a young couple working hard on a hot weekend afternoon on an unusually fine lawn in front of a new house. After chatting with the couple awhile, he asked for a glass of water. When the young wife jumped up to get it, the salesman followed to save her the trip, but just as they got to the door, the woman turned and said, somewhat sheepishly, "I'd ask you in, but the inside is in a terrible state. We've put all our time and all the money we had left after buying the house into the lawn, so the place would look nice on the outside.

"And what she said was true," added the salesman. "I could see through the window that there wasn't a stick of furniture in the living room. They had put everything into the lawn."

o A twelve-year-old girl became very conscious of a scar on her face when she moved to a new section of the city. One morning when it rained she carried an umbrella. Finding this the answer to her problem, she began to carry the umbrella even on sunny days to hide her face.

For several weeks she went to the dentist. One day he invited her to play with his children. She had a wonderful time playing games, the umbrella discarded. But when it came time to leave, she snatched the umbrella from the ground. The dentist took her aside. "I've heard something that shocks me. I've heard that you are the most conceited little girl in the entire city."

Taken back, the little girl answered, "How could I be?"

"Isn't it true," he continued, "that when you walk out of the house you think everyone is looking at you?"

"Oh, no, I don't think that."

"Then why do you always have that umbrella over your face?"

The little girl hung her head.

The dentist kindly said, "There's something I want you to do for me. The next time you have an appointment, leave the umbrella at home, and tell me if people looked at you."

The little girl left, leaving the umbrella at the dentist's. Walking down the street, at first she pulled her head down into her coat, but realizing no one was looking at her, she began to walk, head erect, free from the pride that had gripped her for so many weeks.

o In Great Britain every owner of a TV set must pay an annual license. Postal officers with TV detection units tour the country to ferret out owners who have not paid their fee. One officer complained that TV snobs were complicating his work. In one area he found 25 percent of homes displaying aerials that had no sets.

A lawyer who spent a fair sum of money on an elaborate aerial, but who had no set, explained that he had put it up when his neighbor erected one.

Commented the postal officer, "TV aerials without sets are an expensive form of snobbery, indulged in by social climbers."

Procrastination

o Billy Graham held a summer-long crusade in New York City, televising the Saturday-night services coast-to-coast. One day Billy Graham received a letter from a minister in North Carolina. It told of an elderly man who attended church now and again but who had never made any profession of faith in Christ. Many times the minister had talked with the elderly man but to no avail. He would make no decision for Christ. One Saturday he listened to the crusade from

Madison Square Garden. As the program went off the air, he began to sob gently. His wife asked what was wrong.

He said, "I've given my heart to Christ. I've finally given my heart to Christ."

The next morning when she awoke, he was not in his bed. She found him in the garden among his flowers. He was lying with his face against mother earth, dead of a heart attack.

O A Christian doctor called on a patient who was not a Christian, and who kept insisting he would accept Christ as his Savior later. The doctor prescribed some medicine.

The patient asked, "When do I take it?"

The doctor wrote on the bottle, "Take next month."

"Next month," exclaimed the patient, "I may be dead next month!"

"Well, then, take next week," replied the doctor.

"Next week—I may be dead next week," replied the patient.

"Well, then, take it tomorrow."

"I may be dead tomorrow."

Then the doctor showed him how foolish he was for not being willing to take the gospel medicine immediately.

O A young college student, an earnest Christian, went out to play a game of golf with a fellow student, not a Christian. During the game the question of salvation came up, but the non-Christian answered, "Well, at least we'll have this game of golf before I decide the matter."

During the game a golf ball hit him on the head, and he never regained consciousness.

Progress

O An exhibition contained a booth advertising Brink's Express Company. The attendant at the booth said, "Here is the buggy we used in 1901, when we went into the business of protecting payrolls. The man who rode in the buggy went to the bank, got the payroll, then placed it in a leather bag at his feet. Later we decided he had better carry a revolver for safety.

"But now," he said, "we have this armored motor car with thick steel plates and heavy bars and modern firearms and ammunition."

O A few decades ago when a father ordered his son, "Go to your room and stay there an hour," it was a real penalty. Now when told the same thing, in his room he's got a newspaper, a short-wave radio, a portable TV set, an intercom, a stereo, and an air conditioner.

Prophecy

O A prophetic student of the Bible went to a well-known Bible teacher and asked him who he thought the Antichrist must be.

"I wish I knew," responded the teacher, "for I have buried five of them already!"

Providence

o One night a man was speeding down a highway, when he fell asleep at the wheel. Soon his glassy stare was fixed on the center line. For a while he held the steering wheel like a robot racing through the June, moonlit night.

Suddenly a sharp pain in his chest jolted him awake. It was just in time, for looming out of the darkness were two headlights, and he was on the wrong side of the road, heading right toward them. He jerked his steering wheel to the right. He almost lost control of his car. A huge truck zoomed by, missing him by inches. He pulled off the pavement, limp.

After regaining his calm, he opened the door to get out. As he stood up, an object feel from his lap to the ground. He stooped to pick up the still form of a little bird! As he held the small brown form in his hand, he remembered the pain which had struck his chest and aroused him just in time to avoid the accident. The sparrow had somehow made a flight in the night, which sparrows seldom do, and had darted into the open window of the speeding automobile, striking him in the chest with sufficient force to awaken him. It was the split-second timing of Providence. It was God's sparrow, and the man knew it. Just then the bird fluttered into consciousness and flew into the night.

o Shortly before Christmas a jolly lady bustled through the back door of a rescue mission in Hamilton, Canada. Looking neither to the right nor the left, she headed straight into the superintendent's office and said, "Here's your goose." She had called in advance about this gift to help out for the Christmas dinner given by the mission to the less fortunate men. As she was about to leave, another lady appeared on the scene with a container. She explained, "This is goose gravy."

"So nice of you two ladies," commented the superintendent, "to get together on this, one giving the goose, and the other the goose gravy."

The two ladies looked at each other in amazement. They had never met nor spoken to each other before.

o An ancient Chinese parable tells of an old man who lived with his son in a abandoned fort. One night the only horse the man owned wandered off. His neighbors came to express their regrets about his ill fortune.

He asked, "How do you know this is ill fortune?"

A few days later the horse ambled home, followed by several wild horses. The neighbors hurried over to help him capture the horses and to congratulate him on his good fortune.

"How do you know this is good fortune?" he smiled.

A week later his son, riding one of the horses, was thrown and ended up with a crippled leg. Again the neighbors appeared to moan his bad luck.

"How do you know it's bad luck?" the man asked.

The next day along came a Chinese war lord conscripting all able-bodied men for his private war, but the boy missed the draft because of his crippled leg. Once more the neighbors came to rejoice with him in his good fortune.

Once more the old man asked, "How do you know this is good luck?" Though the story ends there, it could go on indefinitely.

Purpose

o A man heated a piece of iron in the forge, not knowing just what he was going to make out of it.

At first he thought he would make a horseshoe; then he changed his mind and thought he would make something else out of it. After he had hammered on this design for a little while, he changed his mind and started on something else.

By this time, he had so hammered the iron that it was not good for much of anything; and, holding it up with his tongs, and looking at it in disgust, the blacksmith thrust it hissing into a tub of water. "Well, at least I can make a fizzle out of it!" he exclaimed.

Quarreling

o A young married couple had a violent quarrel. In their rage they smashed all their furniture. However, a friend managed to reason them back to another try to live peaceably.

But they fell out again over the question of which one was to pick up the first stick of broken furniture.

o One morning a boy asked his father how wars started. "Well," said Dad, "suppose the USA quarreled with England and . . ."

"But," interrupted the mother, "The USA would never quarrel with England."

"I know," said the father, "but I am only taking a hypothetical instance."

"You are misleading the child," protested the mother.

"No, I am not," shouted the father.

"Never mind, Dad," put in the boy, "I think I know how wars start."

o A visitor at a zoo was surprised to see a lion and a lamb in the same cage. He asked the attendant if they got along all right.

He replied, "Most of the time, but now and again we have to put in a new lamb."

Quiet Time

o Paderewski, the great pianist, once said, "If I don't practice for one day, I notice it. If I don't practice for two days, my friends know it; and if I don't practice for three days, the whole world notices it."

o One of the English poets boasted to a Quaker lady about his study habits. He began his studies the instant he got up in the morning; while he dressed he memorized poetry; he studied his Greek vocabulary while he shaved; and so on to the end of the day.

The lady was unimpressed. "Friend," she asked reproachfully, "when doth thee think?"

o An exploring party with the help of national guides was forcing its way at fast pace through the jungles. Still far from the day's agreed-upon destination, the national guides sat down. "Are they sick?" the national leader was asked.

"No."

"Are they tired?"

"No."

"Then why are they stopping?"

The national leader explained that they had a good reason. They had traveled far and fast. Now it was time for them to stop until their souls could catch up with their bodies.

Rationalization

o A lady was walking out of church when the minister noticed she had forgotten her purse, which was lying on a seat. Calling her back to hand her her purse, the minister cautioned her, "You must remember," he said, "that there are some people in the congregation who might consider finding your purse an answer to prayer."

Readiness

o When Moody Bible Institute was putting up a new building, a stranger said to the clerk on duty at the information desk, "If this school believed in the return of Christ, it wouldn't be putting this big building up."

The clerk had a happy thought. He answered, "Jesus said, 'Occupy till I come.'"

In 1925, William Randolph Hearst, the late American publisher, saw a picture of Donat's castle in Great Britain. It struck his fancy to such an extent that he cabled his agent in London to purchase it. The price was twenty-four thousand pounds, then about one hundred thousand dollars.

He spent a million dollars on the castle—putting in an eighteen-hole-golf course, a swimming pool, and a private beach.

From 1925, the date of purchase, to 1951, the time of his death, Mr. Hearst made only a few visits to his castle. But during those twenty-six years, a staff of workers kept the estate in readiness—even to the extent of having meals ready, should he arrive.

Reaping

o A well-to-do man, caught in a crooked deal, was serving a long prison term when a friend paid him a visit one day. The well-to-do man was sitting cross-legged with an enormous needle and a ball of twine, sewing burlap bags. "Hello," said the friend, "sewing, eh?"

"No," replied the prisoner with a grim smile, "I'm reaping."

o An old legend comes down from the early Christians. It concerns the wicked Herod who slew the little babies in Bethlehem in his attempt to get rid of the infant Jesus whom he feared as a rival to his throne. Wicked Herod was so cruel and bloodthirsty that he murdered one after another of his family, including his wife and several sons. In fact it was said, "It's better to be Herod's pig than Herod's son." The legend says that he had one little grandson to whom he was devoted, the only creature on earth that he really loved. And when he sent the soldiers to Bethlehem to destroy the little children, he did not know that his grandson had been taken to Bethlehem by his nurse, and that he was among those put to death in the massacre of the infants.

Repentance

O In Kentucky a friend on his way to visit a murderer in jail carried in his pocket a letter that he had written but had not yet mailed. In this letter he had written a strong plea for pardon and release of the murderer. Visiting the prisoner, he asked, "If you were fully pardoned and turned loose, what would be the first thing you would do?"

Without hesitation the prisoner answered, "I would go and kill the judge that sentenced me here, and then the man who witnessed against me."

The friend turned sadly away, and outside the prison wall, tore the letter to shreds.

O Down in Brazil a young radio and television star, whose name was Freddie, became a Christian through the testimony of a Youth for Christ worker. The very first week he became a Christian he told a Youth for Christ leader that he wanted to show him something that had to do with his past life. Freddie took the worker to a fine apartment building in the city.

Asked if he lived there, Freddie replied that no one lived in this apartment. But like so many others in the big city, the apartment was designed, built, and used for immoral purposes. It was a very nice apartment—with indirect lighting, built-in bar, and nicely furnished. The two men knelt in the apartment and prayed together. Then they started putting gospel leaflets in the drawers, in the glasses, on the bar, and on the tables.

Freddie said that the two other men who rented this apartment with him, and the girls who came regularly, would find this gospel literature. He wanted them to be saved too! Then, as the two left the apartment, Freddie closed the door behind them, then paused for a moment—looking at the door, and said, "Good-bye. I'll never be back!"

O Several young men, enrolled in a private boarding school, tried to force their teacher to share all goods equally with them. When the teacher refused to give away school property to these students, several discontented young men stole blankets belonging to the school and left. They then tried to find work in a nearby store. The owner who knew what had happened replied, rebuffing the young students, "I would not think of hiring you as long as you have stolen property in your possession. You will have to take your blankets back to the principal of the school."

One of the young men went back to the principal and asked to be reinstated. The principal replied, "First of all, I would not consider taking you back as long as you have stolen property." The young man immediately produced the blankets he had taken and then asked to be received back into school.

Then the principal said, "Now I will consider receiving you back, but only after you have proved yourself."

The young man was angry because the principal would not take him back immediately with open arms. "Have I not repented? Will you not take me back since I have repented?" the young man asked.

"No," said the principal. "I will only consider taking you back after you have proved yourself—proved that you have really repented."

The young man was so incensed that he was not immediately allowed to reenter the school that he turned on his heels and went away—but not without first crawling back through the window into his room and again stealing the same blankets.

o A man lost his wallet. A few days later he received this letter, "Sir, I found your wallet. Remorse is bothering me, so am sending some of your money back to you. When remorse bothers me again, I will send some more money."

Reputation Differs from Character

o A young man, emerging from a certain immoral place, accidentally met his pastor.

"I'm sorry," said the young man, "I had no business being there."

The wise pastor said something that jolted the young man to his senses. "When you went in," said the pastor, "and no one saw you but God, you lost your character. When you came out and I saw you, you lost your reputation.

o A grocer was praising the new minister. "Have you heard him preach?" he was asked. The grocer admitted he hadn't.

"Then how do you know he's good?"

"Because," the grocer answered, "his members have started to pay up on their bills."

Restoration with Meekness

o A shamefaced employee was summoned to the office of the senior partner to hear his doom. The least that he could expect was a blistering dismissal; he might be sent to prison for years for what he had done. The old man asked him if he were guilty. The clerk stammered that he had no defense.

"I shall not send you to prison," said the old man. "If I take you back, can I trust you?" When the surprised and broken clerk had given assurance, and was about to leave, the senior partner continued:

"You are the second man who has fallen, and been pardoned in this business. I was the first. What you have done, I did. The mercy you have received, I received. God have mercy on both of us!"

Resurrection

o A Russian communist was lecturing to a packed audience, discrediting the resurrection of Jesus Christ. At the end an Orthodox priest asked if he might reply.

Given a maximum of five minutes, he replied, "Five seconds is all I need." Then he turned to the audience, and gave the traditional Eastern Orthodox Easter greeting. "Christ is risen," he cried.

Back with a thunderous roar came the traditional reply from the crowded auditorium, "Truly He is risen."

Reunion

O A busy physician overworked into a fatal illness. His widow, who had been deeply in love with him, bore up heroically during the funeral. People predicted she would break down when reaction set in. But to the amazement of all, her spirits continued buoyant. One day some friends, calling on her, blurted out, "What's your secret? How have you remained so calm?"

She was quiet for a moment, then answered, "Come with me to the doctor's waiting room." Leading them down the hall to his reception room, she snapped on the light, and stood in silence. Suddenly one of the friends saw a sign hanging on a doorknob of the office. Then the others saw it and understood. The widow explained, "The maid forgot to remove that sign. She put all the other rooms in order, but perhaps the Lord let her leave it here. Right after his death I spotted the hand-lettered sign, hanging a little unevenly, just as he had left it. That message gave me the courage to go on."

The sign read: GONE FOR A LITTLE WHILE. WILL BE WITH YOU SOON.

O According to a local legend, on a dark night in 1803 all the servants in the little cabins on a Virginia plantation were quiet, for the master's wife, mother of his three children, was dying. Since burials were fast in the south at that time, the young wife was laid to rest by the next afternoon in the family vault under the great house. Her husband retired to his room to sorrow in silence. Only the sister of the deceased wife was left to carry on the duties of the great plantation.

When evening came, though she knew no one would eat, she went down into the food cellar, next to the long passage which led to the burial vault. There in the dim light she suddenly stood petrified. From the burial vaults came the sound of hollow pounding. The sister screamed. In a moment heavy footsteps beat down the stairs. The husband burst into the cellar. Again came the sound, unmistakable beating of fists upon a coffin lid. The husband with one bound broke open the door to the burial vaults, rushed to the coffin, yanked off the lid. A white-clad figure sat up, reached out lily-white arms and clasped them around his neck!

Amazingly, the young wife was alive. Victim of a strange coma known as catalepsy, she had been buried alive. She regained her health to bring joy once more to the great plantation. Four years later she gave birth to a son who became a military genius, Robert E. Lee.

O A few years ago Cuban exiles made an ill-fated attack to liberate their homeland, known as the Bay of Pigs invasion. Many lost their lives; hundreds were taken prisoner. After months of incarceration in Cuban jails, attempts by a New York City lawyer to negotiate a ransom for these prisoners were successful.

Came the momentous day when a boatland of these prisoners landed in Florida, as hundreds of relatives milled around a waiting room. As the prisoners came off the boat and walked into the waiting area, relatives eagerly scanned the soldiers, straining to catch a glimpse of their loved one, hoping against hope that death had not claimed him in the invasion or during the imprisonment.

The TV cameras reporting the news were able to catch many an emotion-filled reunion. As an emaciated soldier shuffled weakly toward the waiting crowd, a mother, or a wife, or a sweetheart, would let out a cry of recognition, break through the ropes and embrace with uncontrollable tears the form of one they thought they would never see again. They clasped them as though back from the dead.

Reward

● A woman who had been well to do on earth was being conducted around heaven. She asked to see her home up there. Passing by a large place and about to enter, she was restrained.

"That's not yours," said the angel.

Shown other nice places, she asked, "Which is mine?"

"None," replied the angel, who finally took her to a one-room shack.

"Who would live here?" asked the lady.

"This is your place," said the angel.

The shocked lady asked, "Why?"

Replied the angel, "If you had sent up better materials, we could have built you a nicer home."

○ In the early years of this century a missionary, broken in health after a lifetime of faithful service to Christ, came home to America. On the same boat was Teddy Roosevelt, arriving home after a hunting safari in Africa. Big crowds gathered at the New York pier to see the famous American. Bands played. Thousands cheered. The missionary, though excited to be a part of the celebration, felt bitter loneliness because no one came to greet him.

He went alone to a little room on the east side of New York and began to complain, "Oh, Lord, I served you faithfully all those years out on the mission field, and no one met me when I came home."

Then a voice seemed to say, "You're not home yet."

○ One hot summer day in the early 1880s, a young medical student was going from house to house in a farming district in Maryland selling books to earn money for his college expenses. Near the end of the day, overheated and thirsty, he called at a farmhouse where no one was at home except a bright, happy girl in her teens. The visitor inquired of the young lady if she would care to purchase some books, to which she answered, "My mother is a widow, and we have no money to buy books." Whereupon the student asked her if she could give him a glass of cold water. Said she: "We have plenty of milk in the springhouse. Would you care for a glass of cold milk instead?"

The girl gave the young student a second glass of milk before he left. Several years went by. The young student became a doctor, a highly successful surgeon. One day he was making the rounds of the hospital, when his eyes fell on the face he well remembered. The patient was too sick to recognize anyone.

Things began to happen. Activity seemed to focus around the woman from the farm. She was moved into a private room with private nurses to wait on her. Everything known to medical science was brought to bear on her condition, and the chief surgeon himself took particular interest in her case.

After weeks of medical and surgical attention, the patient recovered and was able to sit up in her room. The nurse said to her, "You are going home tomorrow."

"Oh, I am so glad," she responded; "but the cost of all this worries me—the bill must be very great."

"I'll get it," said the nurse, and she soon placed it in the patient's hand.

As the woman looked over the items in the bill, and read the staggering cost of her operation and hospital care, it made her weep. "When will I ever get it paid!" she exclaimed, but when she read a little further down, her eyes caught sight of eight words which dried her tears.

The words were: "PAID IN FULL BY A GLASS OF MILK.—Howard A. Kelly, M.D."

The former young book agent and the great Dr. Kelly, already a surgeon of repute, were one and the same.

O A successful Christian gave the secret of his zeal. When he was about twenty-one, he heard an aged minister relate this legend: An angel was talking to an old Christian worker; the angel went into the inner vault, and came back with a crown of incomparable beauty in his hand, blazing with diamonds. "This," the angel said, "was the crown I designed for you when you were a youth, but you refused as a young man to surrender your life completely to God, and it is gone."

The angel went back into the vault and came out with another crown, still beautiful but plainer, and with far fewer jewels. "And this," the angel said, "was the crown I designed for your middle age; but you gave that middle age to a luxurious and indolent discipleship; and it is gone."

At last he went into the vault and returned with a simple, plain, gold circlet. "Here," said the angel, "is the crown for your old age; this is yours for all eternity."

O A preacher was invited to deliver a sermon at a country church on a week night. He took his little boy with him. As they entered the church they noticed a box marked FOR THE PREACHER. The minister dropped a dollar in the box.

When the sermon was over, the deacons opened the box to count the money and out rolled the dollar bill. They handed it to the preacher, whereupon, his little boy exclaimed, "Daddy, if you had put more into it, you would have gotten more out of it!"

Sacrifice

O A father tried to teach his seven-year-old girl the meaning of sacrifice. He explained that the finest gift a person can give is some cherished possession, one he values a great deal.

On his birthday he found pinned to his coat a large sheet of paper on which his daughter had laboriously printed with red crayon: "You are my faverit Daddy and I luv you heeps. My present to you is what I likes best. It is in your poket."

In his pocket he found a strawberry lollipop that he had given her a week before. It hadn't been licked once.

O Two little brothers were playing in the bathtub with a brand-new, brightly painted Noah's ark, and imagining a flood. After the bath water was let out, one brother said, "Now we ought to do what Noah did—build an altar and offer a sacrifice."

So taking some matches from the kitchen, they went outside, and found some sticks and built an altar. But they needed animals to sacrifice. Looking at the nice animals in their new ark, they felt they were too good to burn.

"I know," said the other brother, "there's an old Noah's ark in the attic." So he ran upstairs and returned with a little lamb which had two legs broken off and the tail gone. Solemnly they placed the broken, useless lamb on the altar, offering that which cost them nothing.

O During the raid on Dieppe during World War II, a British scientist was heavily guarded. Men had their guns trained on him, rather than on the enemy. It was thought that the Germans had better radar equipment than the Allies, so this expert was assigned to examine the German installation.

He landed, took a good look at it, but with guns pointed at him all the time. He was able to get back to his ship safely, but had he been chased or nearly seized by the enemy, his own soldiers had orders to shoot him.

Sanctification

O Bishop Taylor Smith was asked by a young man, "Are you saved?"

He replied, "I am in the process of being saved."

The young man, thinking that Bishop Taylor Smith was not a Christian because of this unorthodox answer, showed his surprise.

Then the bishop instructed him in the grammar of salvation, showing that in the past a transaction was completed, and in the present there is to be growth in grace, and in the future we shall be made completely in his image.

Satisfaction

O A millionaire in England in the nineteenth century, a member of Parliament, was restless in spirit. One Sunday the baron heard a preacher tell how while sitting in his garden, he had watched a caterpillar climb a painted stick that had been stuck into the ground as a decoration. The caterpillar slowly climbed to the top of the stick, then reared itself, feeling this way and that for some juicy twig or leaf on which to feed. But the caterpillar was disappointed. Groping about, it found nothing. Slowly it returned to the ground, crawled along till it reached another painted stick and did the same thing all over again. This happened several times. "There are many painted sticks in the world," said the preacher. "There are the painted sticks of pleasure, of wealth, of power, of fame. All these call to us and say, 'Climb me and you'll find the desire of your heart; climb me and you'll fulfill the purpose of your existence; climb me and find satisfaction.' But," continued the preacher, "they are only painted sticks."

The next day the preacher had a visitor. It was the wealthy baron, who said, "Sir, I heard what you said about painted sticks last night. I want to tell you I've been climbing them and today I am a weary man. Tell me, is there rest for someone like me?"

The preacher pointed the baron to the One who once said, "Come unto me, all ye that labour and are heavy laden, and I will give you rest" (Matt. 11:28).

Scars of Christ

O A workman from a tough slum area of a large city accepted Christ. His character was transformed. He began to attend church faithfully. One day, chatting with a rough pal whose face was horribly marred by scars, he told him he too ought to go to church. "I couldn't go," replied his disfigured pal. "There's no place in church for a man with scars like mine."

Came the answer, "We follow a Man who has worse scars than you."

O A small, orphaned boy lived with his grandmother. One night the house caught on fire. The grandmother, trying to rescue the little lad asleep upstairs, perished in the flames. A crowd gathered round the burning house. The boy's cries for help were heard above the crackling of the blaze. No one seemed to know what to do, for the front of the house was a mass of flames. Suddenly a stranger rushed from the crowd and circled to the back where he spotted an iron pipe that reached to the second floor. Hand over hand he climbed the hot pipe, reached an upstairs window, disappeared for a minute, then reappeared with the boy in his arms. Mid the cheers of the crowd, he climbed down the hot pipe as the boy hung round his neck.

Weeks later a public meeting was held in the town hall to determine in whose custody the boy would be placed. Each person wanting the boy was permitted to speak briefly. The first man spoke, "I have a big farm. Every boy needs the out-of-doors." The second man propounded the advantages he could give the lad. "I'm a teacher. I have a large library. He would get a good education." Others spoke. Finally the richest man in the community said, "I'm wealthy. I could give the boy everything mentioned tonight: farm, books, education, and plenty beside, including money and travel. I would like to have him live in our home."

The chairman asked, "Anyone else like to say a word?" From the rear seat rose a stranger who had slipped unnoticed into the hall. As he walked toward the front, deep suffering showed on his face. Reaching the front of the room, he stood directly in front of the little boy whose custody was being decided. Slowly the stranger removed his hands from his pockets. A gasp went up from the crowd. The little boy whose eyes had been focused on the floor till now looked up. The man's hands were scarred terribly. Suddenly the lad emitted a cry of recognition. Here was the man who had saved his life. His hands were scarred from climbing up and down the hot pipe. With a leap he threw himself around the stranger's neck and held on for life.

The farmer rose and left. The teacher, too. Then the rich man. Everyone departed, leaving the boy and his rescuer who had won him without a word. Those marred hands spoke more effectively than words.

Today many interests vie for our devotion. Young and old alike are challenged by the call of money, education, fame, pleasure, and a host of other voices. But let us never forget that down the corridors of the centuries walks one who, by merely raising his hands, reminds us of his claim upon us. Those hands are nail-pierced. They speak more eloquently than ten thousand sermons.

Scrupulosity

O A seminary student who finally had a chance to candidate for a church gave them his best sermon. They promised to let him know after a meeting the following week to discuss a call. He was the only candidate being considered.

A long week followed, but no letter from the church. A month went, then several months. A few years later, when he was preaching nearby, a woman approached him after the service. She was the clerk of the church that had considered him. Curious as to why he hadn't received a call, he asked the reason.

"Oh, they did vote to call you," she replied. "I was the church clerk, but when they instructed me to write you, I began to wonder what my husband would think of my writing to a strange man, so I never did let you know."

Second Coming

O At a gathering of a group of ministers, one of them went around the room, asking each one the same question, "Do you think the Lord Jesus is coming back to earth tonight?"

Not one said, "Yes."

Then, in solemn tones he quoted, "Therefore, be ye also ready, for in such an hour as ye think not, the Son of Man cometh."

O The night the first inflatable sphere was launched from Wallops Island, Virginia, residents in the area had no advance notice. Guesses ran wild when the bright light suddenly loomed in the sky. "It's men from Mars!" "The Russians are coming!" "It's an exploding planet!"

As the sight grew brighter one lady suggested, "Perhaps it's the coming of the Lord!"

"Oh, me," said her neighbor, known for her fastidious housekeeping, "I sure hope he doesn't come to my house first."

O A fellow in seminary worked in a factory where he handled expensive tools. Every now and again he stole one of these tools, sold it, and used the proceeds to pay his expenses for seminary.

One day a professor assigned the class a paper on the second coming of Christ. As the student wrote his paper, he came to realize that if Christ were to come soon, he would find him a thief. The next day he went to a finance company, negotiated a loan to cover the total amount of his theft, then confessed to his boss. "You know that I'm going through seminary. I've been stealing from you. Here's a check to cover the amount. I have borrowed it from a finance company and will work to pay it back. I know you have a right to call the police, but I hope you won't find it in your heart to do so."

The manager accepted the check and did not call the police.

○ A Christian doctor was trying to lead his office boy to accept Christ as his personal Savior. Late one afternoon he explained the second coming—how the doctor would be caught up while those who were unsaved would be left for judgment. The doctor said, "John, when the Lord comes, you may have my house."

The boy looked surprised.

"Yes, you may have my furniture, my car, and all my money."

The lad gasped with astonishment. "Thanks."

Then he went home and later to bed. But he couldn't sleep. He began to think, "If the doctor goes to meet Jesus, what will I do with his house, his car, his money? Where will I be?" The next morning he could hardly wait to ask the doctor how he might be ready for Christ's coming.

Self-denial

○ A pastor asked a woman to teach a class in the Sunday school. She was well qualified, not busy elsewhere, but declined, saying, "I just don't want to be tied down to anything."

Looking her in the eye, the pastor softly pointed out, "You know, we serve a Master who was willing to be tied down to things. In fact, he was willing to be nailed down to the cross."

○ A missionary was walking over the mountains into Tibet. He came across a beggar dying of cold. The beggar asked him to help him. The missionary's two companions said, "Let's go on or we'll freeze to death. If we help him we'll be lost." The two companions went on their way but the missionary lifted the beggar and carried him as best he could. The warmth of the beggar's body kept the missionary warm. After a while he came across the frozen corpses of his two friends.

○ A pastor was visiting a young couple. They had invited him for dinner and when he suggested Monday, they hesitated but then agreed. Suddenly the wife blurted out in the middle of the meal, "It seems so funny to be eating on Mondays," then realized she shouldn't have said it.

The pastor discovered that for months they had not eaten their main meal on Monday but had given the money to missions.

Self-preservation

○ A fortune-teller predicted that a good friend of King Louis XI would die on a certain day. When the prophecy came true, the superstitious king, thinking the seer had worked some kind of magic that really caused his friend's death, planned to have the fortune-teller himself killed.

When the man was brought before him the king said, "I am told you are very clever but can you tell me what your future is going to be?"

The fortune teller, suspecting the worst, answered, "Your Majesty, I shall die three days before you do."

From that day on King Louis XI took very good care of the fortune-teller.

Self-righteousness

O One man went into a rage and stormed out of a committee meeting because the chairman did not agree to his proposal. Then the man insisted on making an open apology to the entire organization at a business meeting.

Here's how he apologized. In pompous tone, he said, "In a recent committee meeting, the chairman and I disagreed. During the discussion which followed, I became emphatic. Still the chairman did not see it my way, and I became more emphatic. Before the meeting was over, I became most emphatic. At that point, I retired from the meeting. I would like to take this opportunity," he concluded, "to apologize to the chairman for becoming most emphatic."

Service as unto the Lord

● A ragged boy with a violin under his arm once roamed the streets of Europe. A famous musician hearing him play, and learning the boy had no home nor family, took him under his wing. He became a father to the lad and taught him all he knew about the violin. The boy practiced faithfully.

Came the evening of his first performance. He played so well that after each number the applause was deafening. But for some reason the boy paid no attention to the ovation. He kept his eyes turned upward and played on and on. The audience was mystified at his strange behavior.

Finally, someone remarked, "I don't understand why he's insensitive to this thunderous applause. He keeps looking up all the time. I'm going to find out what is attracting his attention!"

Moving about the concert hall the observer found the answer. There in the top-most balcony was the old music master, peering over the railing toward his young pupil, and nodding his head as if to say, "Well done, my boy. Play on." The boy played on, seemingly unconcerned whether the audience liked it or not. He was playing to please his master only.

Sin

O A boy was told by his father to hammer a nail into a post every time he did something wrong. Before long he had a post full of nails. Then his father said, "When you do something good, take a nail out." Before long, all the nails were out.

When the father congratulated him, the boy burst out crying. His father said, "You should be smiling."

The boy sobbed, "True the nails are all out, but the marks are still there."

O Cigarette smoking prevents improvement in Buerger's disease, a rather uncommon illness which is characterized by loss of circulation in hands and feet. Smoking in such instances may involve the loss of one or both legs.

A doctor, who had to perform such surgery on a patient, years later was hailed on a Chicago street by this former patient, whom he didn't recognize at first, an armless, legless beggar on a little wheeled platform.

"Hey, Doc! Remember me? Say, be a good scout. Light a cigarette for me and stick it in my mouth, will you?"

O Visitors at Niagara Falls were startled by the piercing shrieks that rose above the roar of the majestic cataract. Looking upstream they saw a floating mass rushing toward the falls. On it was a huge bird with its mighty wings outspread, rending the air with its terrifying cries. With one wild last scream it was swept over the falls and disappeared.

Days before, a large animal had drowned in the Niagara River. A soaring vulture up in the cloudless sky spotted the floating carcass, swooped down and fastening its claws deep in the hide, had begun to feast on its meal. The swirling waters kept sweeping over the carcass but the vulture went on feeding to the full. Fully satisfied, it tried to fly away but was powerless to rise. While it had been feasting ravenously, the swirling waters had frozen its talons into the hide. Held as in a vise, with terrifying cries the helpless bird had gone to its tragic fate.

Sincerity

O An older couple saved for years to make a trip back to bonnie Scotland from which they had emigrated to the United States years before. Because the depression was in full swing when they arrived, things didn't progress as well as hoped. The husband got work shoveling coal, and the wife as a seamstress. But by careful saving they were able to scrape enough for the long-dreamed-of trip.

Finally they got a booking. The day of sailing came. Wanting to be in plenty of time they arrived at the dock in the afternoon with all their luggage, and tickets in hand, which read: SAILING TIME, 12:00 M.

There was no boat in the dock. It was the right dock. When they showed their tickets to a clerk, he exclaimed, "Oh, that boat sailed this noon. It's well out on the ocean by now."

Stunned they said, "But we thought the boat left at midnight. Doesn't 12:00 M. mean midnight?"

"Oh, no," replied the clerk. "12:00 M. means 12:00 Meridian, which in steamship language means 12:00 noon."

Though these people were absolutely sincere in their belief that M. meant midnight, the boat was totally, absolutely gone. They missed the boat despite their sincerity.

O To escape the heat, one evening a couple thought they would drive through the night from their home in Iowa to Chicago. They expected to arrive about dawn. Halfway there, they pulled into a roadside restaurant for a sandwich and a cup of coffee. Then they resumed their trip.

Just about dawn, the husband said to the wife, "We should be arriving in Chicago any time now." A few minutes later the scenery looked alarmingly familiar. They were pulling into their hometown back in Iowa. Somehow at the midway mark, when they stopped for coffee, they had turned in the wrong direction, heading back home. They were sincerely wrong.

Sinfulness Should Be Admitted

O In the book *The Nuremberg Trial*, it is related that when Herman Goering, one of Hitler's close associates, was asked if he knew that he was on the list of war criminals, he replied, "No, that surprises me very much, for I cannot imagine why."

O A prince visited a prison in France. A warden, in honor of his visit, declared that the prince could release one prisoner, whomever he wished. Not wishing to select any man at random, the prince began to talk to man after man, asking each why he was there."

The first said, "I shouldn't be here, I'm innocent."

All gave the same story till he came to one fellow who moaned, "I'm here because I deserve to be. I killed a man and am getting just what is coming to me."

"Bad fellow," said the prince, "you shouldn't be here. All the others said they are good. You might have a bad influence over them. I'm going to release you."

O A preacher was invited to address a group of factory workers in their dining hall during their noon lunchhour. After the talk the preacher invited questions from the floor. One man stood and said bluntly, "We don't need religion. We have everything we want. We have plenty of money. We get good wages. The firm provides recreation. Food is served to us, and we don't even have to clear away or wash up the dishes. What need do we have of religion?"

The preacher asked the audience to turn and look at a poster displayed in a prominent place on the wall at the back. "There's my answer."

The poster read:

TWELVE HUNDRED KNIVES AND FORKS HAVE BEEN STOLEN FROM THIS DINING HALL DURING THE PAST MONTH. IN THE FUTURE, THOSE USING THIS DINING HALL MUST BRING THEIR OWN CUTLERY.

Single-mindedness

O Roger Bannister, first man in history to run a mile in less than four minutes, did so in May 1954. The next month John Landy of Australia topped his record by 1.4 seconds.

In August of that same year, at Vancouver, British Columbia, the two athletes met for a historic race.

As Bannister and Landy moved into the last lap, the other contestants were trailing far behind. Landy was ahead. It looked as though he would win.

But as Landy neared the finish line, he was haunted by the question: Where is Bannister? Finally, unable to stand the strain any longer, he looked over his shoulder. As he did, his step faltered. Bannister surged by him to break the tape.

Landy said later, "If I hadn't looked back, I would have won the race."

O A captured Indian prince was told by his captor, the rajah, "You must walk barefoot in a parade through the city, but you will also carry a bowl of milk filled almost to the top. If you spill one drop of it, you will be beheaded. Guards will be watching you every minute to see if you spill any."

The prince turned deadly pale as he heard that. As the procession began, they handed him the bowl of milk. How carefully this young prince walked! But in some way or another he managed to get through without spilling a drop.

When he was brought before the rajah, he was sternly asked: "Well, what kind of faces did the people make?"

"O sir," said the prince, "I saw no man's face; I saw only my life that I held in my hands and I knew that if I dared to look to the right or to the left, it would be forfeited."

Sorrow

O Missionaries in Calcutta, India, sent their six little children to a school in the hill country. One terrible night the monsoon rains came down in torrents. The hillside on which their cottage was situated was swept away by the onrushing floods, burying the six children amid its ruins. One little lad lived long enough to tell what had happened.

He said that the oldest sister had called the rest around her, telling them, "You mustn't be afraid. We are in God's hands. Remember what Daddy used to tell us," and then the boy added, "we were all kneeling in prayer when the hillside slipped away, and we were buried."

The tragedy seemed to the parents so pointless. Their hearts were utterly crushed. But when the first wave of grief had subsided, they said, "Our six children are gone, so we must establish now a greater family of neglected little ones." They went out into the streets of Calcutta, gathering up the abandoned children of India, and made a home for them. For more than thirty years they were like a father and mother, caring for three hundred little ones annually. When at last they made a memorial to their own six children who had perished on the hillside, this was the inscription they placed on it: THANKS BE TO GOD WHO GIVETH US THE VICTORY THROUGH OUR LORD JESUS CHRIST.

O An English preacher's wife died suddenly. In his first sermon after the funeral, he said, "I do not understand this life of ours. But still less can I comprehend how people in trouble and loss and bereavement can fling away peevishly from the Christian faith. In God's name, fling to what? Have we not lost enough without losing that too?"

O A man whose wife was dead bestowed all his affection on his little child, a little girl. When she suddenly died, the father became a bitter recluse, refusing activity of every kind that might restore him to normal life.

But one night he dreamed he was in heaven witnessing a grand parade of little children. Marching in a seemingly endless line, each carried a lighted candle, except for one little girl. Then he noted that this child was his own little girl. Rushing to her, he touched her tenderly, then asked, "Why is yours the only unlit candle?"

She replied, "Father, they often light it, but your tears always put it out."

He awoke from his dream with the lesson crystal clear. From that moment on, he left his hermit life and rejoined his former associates to live a normal life.

Sovereignty

O An unusual error in a printed program of a performance of Handel's *Messiah* made part of the "Hallelujah Chorus" to read, "The Lord God Omnipotent resigneth."

Stewardship

O A girl once said to her mother, "Who owns those lovely brass candlesticks on the mantelpiece?"

Her mother was silent a moment, then answered, "My grandmother thought she owned them, but she just possessed them for a while. She died and left them to my mother. She thought she owned them, but she too, just possessed them for a while. Then she died. I now have them, but I don't really own them. I just possess them temporarily, then some day they will pass into your hands for you to possess for a little while."

Substitute

O A newspaper carried the story of a herd of cattle in South America coming to the upper Paraguay River, which was infested by blood-eating little creatures, more bloodthirsty than the weasel. If the herd were to be led the few hundred feet across, several would be attacked and killed, blood-sucked to death.

Instead, one yearling, chosen to be sacrificed, was led into the river some distance from where the others would cross. He attracted the blood-eaters who fastened on him and did their deadly work. Water around the yearling crimsoned a sickening color, as the yearling struggled uselessly. A hissing sound was heard as blood was sucked. The herd had to be hurried across the river while the blood suckers were occupied with the yearling. If the timing were poor, the whole herd might perish. The herd went through the water, sensing something terrifying was happening, and made it safely.

Through the sacrifice of one, all were saved.

Success

O A full-page ad in a missionary magazine, shows a young man wading across a river with a large box on his back. The caption reads: JIM WAS VOTED MOST LIKELY TO SUCCEED.

Underneath are these words:

It's too bad. Jim had it made. Personality, initiative, a college degree with honors. Success and the "good life" were his for the asking. Now look at him. Back-packing across some jungle river. Giving his life to a tribe of preliterate Indians, barely out of the Stone Age. Painstakingly creating a written language from an unintelligible babble of sounds. Working night and day to translate the pages of the New Testament. Exposing the senselessness of superstition and ignorance. Relieving pain and building a bridge of love and understanding to an alienated and neglected people. And to think—Jim could have been a success.

Suffering

● A wealthy but godless man who lived in a magnificent mansion was stricken with paralysis. Unable to follow the pursuits that had kept him from spiritual matters, he turned to the things of God.

They wheeled him into church where, during testimony time, half-raising himself in his chair, he would say, "I thank God for my dear paralysis. Otherwise I might never have known the Lord Jesus Christ as my Savior!"

● In a testimony meeting a pastor asked each person to stand up and quote his favorite verse from the Bible. One man gave, "And it came to pass."

When people looked at him questioningly, he explained, "In all my trials it's been a real help to me to remember, 'And it came to pass,' How glad I am that the Bible doesn't say, 'And it came to stay.'"

Suicide

○ One summer morning a young man, twenty-six years old, climbed onto the narrow ledge of the seventeenth floor of a New York City hotel and there for eleven hours deliberated whether or not he would jump to his death, while thousands gathered in the street below to watch.

During his hours of indecision, several attempts were made to induce him back into the hotel. Firemen, policemen, psychologists, all tried but failed. The last words of the young man before he jumped were: "I'll come back if you can promise that life is worth living. I've been up here for hours trying to convince myself of a reason for living."

And he leaped to his death as flares and spotlights played on his twisting body.

○ A close associate of Ernest Hemingway wrote, "On July 2, 1961, a writer whom many critics call the greatest writer of this century—a man who had a zest for life and adventure as big as his genius—a winner of the Nobel Prize and the Pulitzer Prize—a soldier of fortune with a home in Idaho's Sawtooth Mountains, where he hunted in the winter, an apartment in New York, a specially rigged yacht to fish the Gulf Stream, an available apartment at the Ritz in Paris and the Gritti in Venice—a solid marriage, no serious physical ills, good friends everywhere—on that July day that man, the envy of other men, put a shotgun to his head and killed himself.

"Why did this come to pass? I was his close friend for fourteen years, but I cannot tell you why."

Sunday

O When the *Mayflower* reached Plymouth Harbor it was Saturday afternoon. How eager the Pilgrims must have been to set foot on solid land after exile in Holland, thirteen weeks of tossing on a rough Atlantic, homesickness, seasickness, and weariness.

Despite their longing to go ashore and make a new home, they spent Saturday afternoon in preparation for Sunday, and then all day Sunday in worship.

On Monday morning, when they disembarked, they had been forty-two hours in the harbor.

Sunday School

O A Kentucky lady who was a teacher in Sunday school for years was watching youngsters in the community swimming pool. Suddenly a twelve-year-old boy about to take his first dive ran up to her and asked, "Madam, do you go to Sunday school?"

"Why, yes, I do," she replied, somewhat surprised.

"Then," he said, "please hold my dollar bill for me while I go into the pool."

Superstition

O A stockbroker received a phone call from one of his clients late one night. "Either sell or buy one hundred shares of that stock you got me last week," the voice said.

The bewildered, stockbroker asked, "Buy, or sell—either will be all right? I don't understand."

The client explained, "I just remembered that I own thirteen hundred shares, and tomorrow morning I undergo surgery. I don't want to go under the knife with thirteen hundred shares. So either get rid of a hundred, or buy a hundred!"

Sympathy

O An American soldier on his way to see his dying son in a London hospital got lost in the thick, pea-soup fog. The doctors felt that the presence of the father might possibly rally the son. Quietly asking for someone to help him find his way, he felt a hand slip into his and guide him to the hospital.

His guide whom he couldn't see, said goodbye with these words, "Blind, sir, got it at Dunkirk."

O Two fishermen had been out in their boat all morning without getting more than a few baitstealing nibbles. The first would glumly reel in his line, bait the hook again and cast it into the water with a muttered curse. The second chuckled at every nibble, gleefully reeled in and said, "Great! Great!" as he examined the bare hook.

Finally, the first fisherman couldn't take any more and he exploded: "Will you tell me what's so hilarious about losing a fish?" I don't see anything funny about it!"

"That," said the first, "is because you think of fishing only from your own end of the line. I think of it from the fish's end, too. It's twice as much fun my way."

Television

O A speaker was giving a dramatic description of what is currently seen and heard on many TV plays. He told of programs depicting violence, murder, and blood. "What can we do about it?" he asked with a despairing gesture.

"I'll tell you," came a voice from the audience. "We can turn the thing off!"

Temptation

O A man went forward at every consecration invitation. He always prayed the same way, "Take the cobwebs out of my life."

The preacher, tired of hearing the same petition, knelt down beside him at the altar one night, and prayed, "Lord, kill the spider!"

Ten Commandments

O An English preacher called on a shoemaker who declared he would not come to church to hear the Ten Commandments read for said he, "The Ten Commandments were long ago abolished."

The preacher said, "Oh, I am very glad the eighth commandment is abolished for I need a pair of shoes, and I think these are my size." Whereupon he picked up a pair, and hurried out of the shop with the boots under his arm.

The shoemaker ran after him, and after that never raised objections to the reading of the commandments.

O A prisoner was breaking up rocks in the prisonyard, when a visitor stopped by. The prisoner remarked, "Those stones are just like the Ten Commandments. You can go on breaking them, but you can never get rid of them. You can't break them as much as they break you."

O A minister was driving along a country road with one of his young parishioners who liked to argue about religion. The wise old minister listened to him without much comment as he expressed his views, then commented, "So you object to the Ten Commandments?"

"N-no," stammered the young man, but a fellow hates to have a *shall* and *shan't* flung in his face every minute! They sound so contrary."

The old minister turned down another highway. A few minutes later the boy caught his arm suddenly.

"You've taken the wrong turn. That sign said: THIS WAY TO DOVER.'"

"Oh, did I?" returned the other carelessly. "Well, maybe it might be a better road, but I hate to be told to go this way and that by an arbitrary signpost!"

An embarrassed laugh from his red-faced companion told the minister that his shot had struck home. They were soon facing the other way and following the directions of the "arbitrary" signpost.

Thankfulness

O Dale Carnegie, once in a deep depression which he couldn't shake, did a strange thing. Assuming that he had lost everything, he listed his losses on a sheet of paper:

Broken in health.

My wife has deserted me.

I'm fired from my job.

My money is gone.

My children are all in jail.

O After building up this horrible picture he looked at the paper and said, "There isn't a word of truth in it." Then he tore the paper to pieces. Dramatizing the blessings that he did have helped him to realize how well off he really was.

O A little boy in the darkest hour of World War II, when the British army was being evacuated from the beaches of Dunkirk, came many days to a church to pray. After the minister had seen him several times, he said to the boy one day, "I see you make it a habit of coming here, my son."

The boy answered, "Yes, I have been here five times in the last five days."

The minister said, "I suppose you have one of your family in the thick of it, across the channel."

"My father, sir," said the boy, and then added, "but he got home yesterday, so I came to say my 'thank you' to God."

O The phone rang late one evening in a home in California. "Mrs. Otto," a voice asked, "did you give a pint of blood to the Red Cross last December fourteenth?" Hesitating a moment, Mrs. Otto recalled the occasion. The speaker identified himself as a public-relations officer of a nearby military hospital. "I'm sorry to call so late, but a patient has just arrived who wants to meet you." Mrs. Otto learned that her pint of blood, flown as whole blood to an island in the Pacific, had saved this soldier's life. Said the voice, "He wants to thank you, but he leaves early in the morning for the East Coast."

A stunned Mrs. Otto made her way to the hospital. She learned that rarely did a soldier ever meet the person whose blood saved his life on the battlefield. Most blood donations were mixed plasma, but her particular pint of blood had gone into an individual container labeled with the donor's name.

Just before the bottle of her blood had reached the island, the sergeant had been fighting for his life against terrific odds. He was covering the withdrawal of his group when fifteen slugs hit him in the left leg. Medical corpsmen carried him to a makeshift field hospital where the leg was amputated. When he regained consciousness a doctor handed him the tag from a blood container, "It was this woman's blood which saved your life, sergeant!" Clutching the tag, the soldier muttered through clenched teeth, "Maybe—someday—I can thank her—for saving my life!"

As he told her the story he wept unashamedly. Mrs. Otto wept too.

Thoughts

O A few years ago a well-known author, as a spoof, announced his intention to publish a bibliography of passionate pages in legitimately published novels. He said he was going to call the book, facetiously, *Show Me the Good Parts.* He had devoted five years of research which involved combing nineteen hundred novels in search of six hundred "titillating passages." He claimed his volume would "save people a lot of eye strain. A great many modern authors put sex into their novels like so much salt and pepper. You don't have to read anything before or after. And this is what people buy the books for," he said.

To prove his point that people read mainly the juicy parts, he explained how finding these parts was easy. He noted, "Most of the novels I read I got through the public library. And often, if I looked at the edge of the book, I'd see a dark strip where the book had been read and reread. And it would be a sexy part.

"Or sometimes I'd just put the book down on a table and let it fall open. Again, a juicy section. It always fell open to what I was looking for.

"Or I'd get a book with pages ripped out. That was almost a sure sign. And when I got another copy, it would be those pages that were the sexy ones.

"My book will help librarians, you see. They'll know where to look to find mutilations of the books."

O During a Billy Graham London Crusade a medical doctor gave his heart to Christ. Prior to his conversion he lived a life of unchastity. His library was full of obscene and lewd literature and photographs. But after he was converted, he promptly tore up all his salacious literature, carried it to a London bridge, and threw it in the Thames River. Yielding himself to a new Master, he became an active Christian layman in the city of London, respected by all.

Time

O A Norwegian businessman spent his eightieth birthday concentrating on how he had used his time through the decades. He figured out he had spent nearly five years waiting for people, three months scolding children, and half-a-year ordering dogs to lie down and be quiet.

O One day a woman asked Mr. Wesley, "Suppose you knew that you were to die tomorrow night at midnight, how would you spend the time until then?"

Wesley replied, "Why, just as I intend to spend it. I should preach this evening at Gloucester, and again at five tomorrow morning. After that, I should ride to Tewkesbury, preach in the afternoon, and meet the Society in the evening. I should then repair to the home of my friends who expect to entertain me, converse and pray with the family as usual, retire to my room at ten o'clock, commend myself to my heavenly Father, lie down to rest, and wake up in glory."

O A man in his midfifties was dying of cancer. To his pastor, at his bedside, he said, "Pastor, ten years ago the church asked me to teach a class of teenage boys in

Sunday school. I told them I was too busy. And I was—with all the heavy demands on my time and energy. I was in the prime of my life, and rapidly rising in my business firm. And now, ten years later, here I am, dying, with the greatest regret of my life ebbing that I did not accept that responsibility. I know that when I die I shall go to be with the Lord, for I have accepted him as my Savior, but if ten years ago I had taken time to teach that class of ten boys, and each year a new class would have been given me, by now one hundred boys would have passed through my class. I would have invested my life in the lives of one hundred boys, and many of them would be scattered throughout the world, perhaps becoming Christians partly through my teaching, and growing in service and usefulness as Christian young men. I would have an investment for eternity through them."

Then he sighed. "I can't take any of my money, or my stocks, or my bonds, with me. What a fool I have been."

Tithing

O Dr. Russell Conwell, founder of Temple University in Philadelphia, once asked for testimonies in prayer meeting of those who had tithed for several years. Six gave glowing witness to blessings received. The seventh to speak, a frail woman of seventy, reluctantly said, "I wish I could bear such testimony but I cannot. I have skimped and saved and denied myself through the years to keep a vow made many years ago that I would tithe my income. But now I am old, am losing my job, and have no means of support. I don't know what I shall do." When she sat down, the meeting was closed in a depressing chill.

The next day Dr. Conwell was lunching with John Wanamaker, founder of Wanamaker Department Store. The latter said, "Dr. Conwell, I think you will be interested to know that our store is about to inaugurate a pension system for our employees. We have thought about it for years. Finally the plan has been worked out. We are about to issue our first life pension today to a woman who has served our firm for twenty-five years." Then he mentioned the name of the woman. It was she who had given the pessimistic testimony in prayer meeting the night before.

Transformation

O An unbeliever said to a converted alcoholic, "Surely you don't believe those Bible miracles such as Christ changing water into wine?"

"No difficulty in believing that kind," he replied. "You come to my house and I'll show you how Christ changed beer into carpets, chairs, and a piano!"

O One dark night two brothers stole two sheep from a neighbor's fold. They were captured, tried, and convicted. It was a custom in those days to brand guilty men with the sign of their crime. "ST," which meant "Sheep Thief," was branded on their foreheads. It would serve as a constant reminder of their guilt.

One brother could not stand to face the shame, so he left home to live in another place. But the people were curious and asked questions about the strange letters on his forehead. When he gave evasive answers, they found out the truth about him. He left for another area, where the same thing happened. He kept moving from one place to another all his life, never having any peace. Finally he died a bitter, old man.

His brother chose to stay at home. He found an honest trade. He helped the poor and afflicted. His life was a light to all in the community. Soon people forgot the mark on his forehead.

Years later a visitor to the town noticed the letters "ST" on his forehead. He asked one of the natives what the letters stood for.

The man replied, "It was such a long time ago, I have forgotten exactly what happened. But I think the letters stand for *Saint*."

The famous sculptor, Michelangelo, once lingered before a rough block of marble so long that his friend complained.

Said the sculptor in reply, and with great enthusiasm, "There's an angel in that block, and I'm going to liberate him!"

The National Episcopal Cathedral in Washington, D.C., has many stained-glass windows. One of those windows portrays the loving, tender face of the Good Shepherd. Lawrence Saint, the stained-glass artist who painted that kind face, used for his model the face of a man who had been an alcoholic derelict in Philadelphia.

For years this man lived on the streets and in the saloons of Germantown, a Philadelphia suburb. Many a night he would sleep in alleys with a brick for a pillow. In wintertime he would often have to pull his frozen beard away from the brick. One day he staggered through the swinging doors of what he thought was a saloon but which turned out to be a rescue mission. He was converted to Christ. He was reunited with his family, and later became superintendent of that mission where he had been converted. When the stained-glass artist was looking for a face from which to paint the Good Shepherd's face in the window of Washington's National Episcopal Cathedral, he chose this man as the model.

Once a derelict—with face frozen to the ground or to a brick in alcoholic stupor. Now his face portrays the Good Shepherd!

Transitoriness

O At an alumni gathering an old professor said, "I have a good position, a fine wife, a happy home. In fact, I have everything the way I want it. There is only one thing that bothers me. It cannot last."

O A bishop delivered a sermon on the truth that we do not own things, but merely possess them for a little while, then leave them behind. A wealthy man took the bishop home, showed him his assets, bank balances, bonds, bluechip stocks, then asked, "Bishop, do you really mean I don't own these things?"

Quietly the bishop answered, "Ask me the same question one hundred years from now."

Treasure in Heaven

O A rich man showed a preacher around his estate. Pointing to the north, the man said, "As far as you can see, I own." Then pointing to the east, then the south, then the west, he repeated, "As far as you can see, I own."

It was the preacher's turn. Pointing skyward, he asked, "How much do you own up there?"

o In a vision a couple were seen nearing the end of life's journey. They were lugging a lot of baggage, money, stocks, bonds, finery, jewels, and furs. Just outside the gate of the New Jerusalem was a junk pile. "Throw all your things in that heap," the angel ordered. Slowly, most reluctantly, the man and woman parted with their earthly treasures, which they held so dear, but which were worthless up above.

Another couple approached. Carrying very little baggage, they looked expectantly toward the gate, which swung outward as songs of praises rang within. A group of people were awaiting them whom they had never met. The angel explained, "These are they who have been won to Christ in distant lands through the money you gave to missions." Then the converted heathens thanked the newcomers, saying, "We were in darkness. One day missionaries came and told us of the Lord. That's why we're here. The great Savior looked over his records and told us it was money you gave that sent the messengers out." Then together all praised the Lord Jesus Christ.

Unity

● At a college summer retreat out in the mountains of California soon after World War II, among those present were a young man who had flown in Hitler's Luftwaffe, another who had flown with the Japanese, and a third who had been in the USA Air Force and had bombed the cities of Germany. None of these knew that the others were present at the retreat, nor did they know each other, and none was a Christian.

At the final meeting, the traditional fagot service, when any person deciding to accept Christ and give his life to serve the Savior tossed a fagot or stick of wood on a bonfire symbolizing his life would now be given to burn for Christ, the German stood to accept Christ, walked to the fire and threw a fagot in; a few moments later, the Japanese; then following him, the American pilot, all receiving the Lord Jesus Christ.

Then the three ex-war pilots, with their arms around each other and tears streaming down their faces, sang with all those present,

>Blessed be the tie that binds
>Our hearts in Christian love.

o Some survivors from the march on Bataan were herded into a troop transport bound for Japan, then jammed into small, filthy holds, unable even to lie down.

A Japanese naval lieutenant, moved with sympathy, secretly kicked ajar the closed hatch cover to admit fresh air. He told the imprisoned men that he was a Christian, converted through some American missionaries.

Later an American torpedo ripped into the transport. The enemy crew battened down the hatch cover and swarmed into lifeboats. The Americans thought they were goners. Suddenly the hatch opened to reveal the face of the young

Japanese lieutenant. The next moment a spray of bullets sent the Japanese crumbling to the deck. There he died, while some Americans escaped.

Values

o A noted artist arrived at a European art gallery to look at a painting he had sent on ahead. When he gazed on it, he was furious. By mistake they had failed to hang his great work of art but had hung the wrapping paper (in which it came) on which he had a little dabbling.

o A huge crowd had gathered in the street outside a hotel in Glasgow, Scotland. They were giving an uproarious welcome to the local football team, which was returning victorious from a game in England. A quiet little man slipped into the hotel, unnoticed. He didn't amount to much in that big crowd. He was just the man who discovered penicillin!

Vindication

o Down in Brazil, Maria, a girl who had recently become a Christian, stepped carefully down the well-worn path of the river bank. She had come to get water. Usually she found other women at the water's edge, but this day she was alone. As she stooped to dip the pot into the stream, she happened to glance to one side—and froze with horror. From the bush on the bank not fifty feet away, a large crocodile emerged, stalking to attack. There was no time to run away or jump into the river—what should she do? "Lord, save me!" she cried. Instantly as the crocodile dashed at her she found herself heaving her water pot with all her might into its open mouth. Distracted, it let her escape.

Seeing her rushing home almost out of breath, Maria's relatives quickly gathered around her to find out what was the matter. Her enthusiasm knew no bounds as she told of her miraculous escape until she noticed that no one seemed to believe her. She was a new Christian, and if her relatives didn't believe her, certainly the townsfolk wouldn't, and they would not think much of a Christianity whose followers told such lies. Maria at first was heartbroken, but she committed the matter to the Lord.

Ten days later she was walking back to the spot where she had nearly lost her life. But this time a big crowd had gathered. They were listening to a couple of fishermen who had a story to tell. She arrived in time to hear one of them say, "Yes, we found a big dead crocodile decaying on the sand down the river. And we found a water pot in its throat. It had choked to death."

Watchcare

o A new road was being built. Trees had to be torn down to make way. The superintendent on the job noted that one tree had a nest of birds that couldn't yet fly, so ordered that tree be left standing for the present, and then be cut down late at the end of the tree-cutting operation.

A few weeks later the superintendent came back to the tree. The birds were gone. The tree was felled. The nest fell out, and several pieces of materials which the birds had used to build the nest were scattered in a heap. One such piece fluttered near the feet of the superintendent. He picked it up. It was a piece of paper that had been torn from a Sunday school paper.

On it were these words: HE CARETH FOR YOU.

o "Do you suppose," said little Jimmy to his smaller sister, "that God cares about such little things like us? He's probably too busy taking care of the big folks to notice us much."

Little sister shook her head and pointed to mother. "Do you think that Mama is so busy with the big folks that she forgets the baby? She thinks of the baby first 'cause he's so little. Surely God knows how to love just as much as mothers do."

o At a busy intersection in New York City, a thirty-gallon can fell from a passing truck, spilling milk all over the street. The policeman halted traffic while the driver retrieved the can. The policeman was about to blow his whistle for the GO signal, when a small white cat crept out on the road and started lapping up the milk. The whistle remained unblown, traffic stood still, and the light changed to green three times. Only after the cat had drunk its fill and returned to the sidewalk did the patrolman give the signal for traffic to proceed.

o David Brainerd, missionary to the Indians, on one of his many journeys to visit a tribe was overtaken by a severe storm. He looked for a place of shelter and eventually found one in a hollow log of a very large tree. While there, he prayed for the Indians and also that the Lord would take care of him and his needs.

When mealtime came, he was hungry, but there was nothing to eat. He noticed a squirrel approaching the tree. The squirrel chattered a while. When the little animal disappeared, Brainerd noticed that he had left a few nuts behind. The missionary ate those nuts.

Three days the storm continued, and for three days, Brainerd remained in the log. Each day the squirrel came to deposit some nuts at the entrance. David Brainerd knew that the Lord had sent that squirrel.

Wealth

o A young couple of meager circumstances was discussing their financial problems one evening when the wife wistfully sighed, "I wish we could be rich and not have to juggle our funds this way!"

Her husband with a smile placed his hands over hers, and said, "Honey, we have the Lord; we have each other; our health is good; and our home is happy. We are rich. And maybe some day we will even have money!"

Weights

o Before a young athlete left to represent his country in the Olympics, some businessmen held a banquet in his honor at which occasion they presented him with a silk running suit. Down the seams was a little gold braid. "What's this for?" the athlete asked.

"That's gold. Gold means tops. Since you're a top runner, we had these golden stripes put on there."

The athlete asked, "Does it hold the thing together?"

"No, it's just a decoration."

"Then take it off," requested the athlete. "Because, when you're running a mile race and half-way through your heart is pumping like fury and your feet feel like lead and a fellow is breathing down your back, you don't want to carry any more weight than you have to!"

Widow's Mite

O A church treasurer was giving his annual report. "Mr. *A*. has given five hundred dollars." There was a round of applause.

"Mr. *B*. has given one thousand!" Louder applause.

"Mr. *C*. has given fifteen hundred." Tumultuous applause.

"Widow *D*. has given fifty dollars." There was silence.

In the hush the chairman said, "I think I hear the clapping of pierced hands."

O A prosperous merchant was asked for a contribution to a charitable cause. "Yes, I'll give my mite," he replied.

"Do you mean the widow's mite?" asked the collector.

Receiving an affirmative answer, the collector exclaimed, "I shall be satisfied with your mite. How much are you worth?"

The merchant did some quick arithmetic. "Around seventy thousand dollars."

"Then," said the collector, "give me your check for thirty-five thousand. The widow had only two mites, so her 'mite' was half of all she had."

Witnessing

O A woman at a banquet was asked by an elderly man seated next to her, "Do you love the Lord Jesus?"

When she related this to her husband he asked, "Why didn't you tell him it was none of his business?"

She replied, "If you had seen the expression on his face, and heard the earnestness in his voice, you would have thought it *was* his business."

O When Dr. Ralph Keiper was a new Christian and a student at Lafayette College, he witnessed to his philosophy teacher. "The blood of Jesus Christ can cleanse from every sin," he zealously affirmed.

"There is one sin it can't cover," retorted the professor.

After a few more rounds of affirmation by Keiper and denial by the professor, Keiper thought to ask, "Which sin can't the blood of Jesus cover?"

Replied the prof, "A late philosophy paper."

O A man didn't know what to buy his wife for her birthday. Setting out to shop for something "different," he found the solution to his problem in a pet show. Here was a very rare, and very expensive, talking bird—the Mexican "wordy-

bird." He ordered it crated up and sent to his home with the note: HAPPY BIRTH-
DAY, DARLING.

A few hours later he called his wife to find out whether his present had arrived
and how she liked it.

"Just fine," came the reply, "it's in the oven right now."

The husband was appalled and astonished. "But that was a smart and very rare
talking Mexican wordybird," he exploded.

"If it was such a smart bird," she said sweetly, "then why didn't it speak up
and say something?"

A man said to a friend, "Come and have a round of golf on Sunday morning."

"Oh no. I have to attend service at church."

"Well," replied the friend, "I do not know what your religion is, but you sure
keep it to yourself. I have asked you to play golf half-a-dozen times, but you have
never once invited me to go to church with you."

Words

O A couple living in New Jersey agreed to serve as guinea pigs in an experiment
sponsored by the Civilian Defense. The purpose of the project was to study
survival techniques after nuclear explosion. So husband and wife, along with
their three children, ages five, three and two, climbed down into a "nuclear
fallout" shelter on the Princeton University campus, and stayed for approximately two weeks. What they didn't know was that every sound they made was
being recorded on tape.

They said, "Of course we would have lived much differently if we had known
we were being recorded. We would have been much more self-conscious."

The family was confined to a small size shelter, 9 feet long, 8 feet wide and 8
feet high, not even the area of a 9 x 12 rug. They passed their time with the aid of
tranquilizer pills for the children and many books. They were delighted to be
back in their own home, a seven-room renovated farmhouse on an acre of ground.

The wife said she had been tempted only once to press the panic button in the
shelter, which they could have used any time to win immediate release from the
chamber. "My husband and I had a quarrel just from the frustration of being
locked up all that time. I got very angry and wanted to storm out," she recalled.
And with a sigh of relief she added, "The tapes are not going to be released!"

Work

O A father who had climbed the ladder of success by dint of hard work told the
dean of a college where he hoped to send his son to school, that he wanted to
spare his son from such hardship, and that he intended to give him all the money
he wanted.

Whereupon the dean suggested he send the boy to another college. "Our
college already has enough students on that road to perdition."

A girl said to an accomplished soloist, "I'd give the world to be able to sing like
that."

Back came the answer, "Would you give two hours a day?"

O When it came time to move books to a new library at Wheaton College, the president announced to students in chapel that on the following Saturday there would be employment for all who wished to help move the books. He stated clearly that they would be paid in proportion to their work, that is, so much for each trip with books from the old library to the new—and not on an hourly basis.

On Saturday morning a visitor on campus asked why the students were running across campus.

Looking out the window, the president explained, "You will notice that the students carrying books to the new library walk so that the books will arrive in proper order, but when they return for another load of books they are on their own, and those who want to earn more hurry back to the library. None loiter to chatter on company time, or stop at the water fountain."

Works Prove Faith

One noon the opera singer Enrico Caruso entered a bank near the Metropolitan Opera Company in New York City to cash a check. When the alert, young teller saw the famous name on the check he became suspicious. The more Caruso tried to convince the distracted teller that he *was* Caruso, the more convinced the latter became that he was a fraud.

Then Caruso had an inspiration. Stepping back a few paces from the teller's window (so that he would not blow the money around), he placed one hand on his breast and began to sing an aria. Long before he finished, the teller began to count the money out.

When he came to the end, Caruso bowed and took his money, while the customers and clerks cheered.

Worldly Outlook Disregards Divine Connection

O A Danish allegory tells of a spider who lived high up on the beams of an old barn. One day he let himself down by his silk rope to a lower rafter. There he found the flies so fat and so numerous that he scarcely had to work for his lunch. He soon forgot all about the place of his birth on the upper beam, from which he had spun himself down and which supported his life.

After a long time, he noticed the rope that went up into the darkness above. Once he got entangled in it. He decided to break it. When he did, his whole house came tumbling down, collapsing over him, for it all depended on that one strand.

Yieldedness

O A tramp, on reaching a crossroads, threw a twig three times into the air.
A bystander asked, "Why did you throw the twig into the air like that?"
The tramp replied, "To give me guidance as to which way I should go."
"But why three times?"
"Because the first two times it didn't come down the way I wanted it to go."

Youth

O In a testimony meeting a man rose and said, "I have spent twenty years in prison for murder, but God has saved me.

Another said, "I have been an alcoholic for twenty years, and God saved me."

Another said, "I've been a printer of counterfeit money for a long time and the Lord has saved me."

Then another arose, "Men, listen, God has done wonders for you, but don't forget he did more for me than for all of you put together. He saved me as a boy before I got in prison, or became an alcoholic, or a counterfeiter.

Zeal

● An old washerwoman noted for her soul-winning zeal was partially blind. One day she stepped in front of what she thought was an Indian on the street and began to tell him the gospel.

"Sophie, don't you know that's a wooden Indian you're talking to?" said a bystander to her.

Sophie replied, "Well, I'd rather be a living Christian talking to a dead Indian, than a dead Christian talking to no one!"